FISHING THE BIG D
James S. McKay

(Delaware)

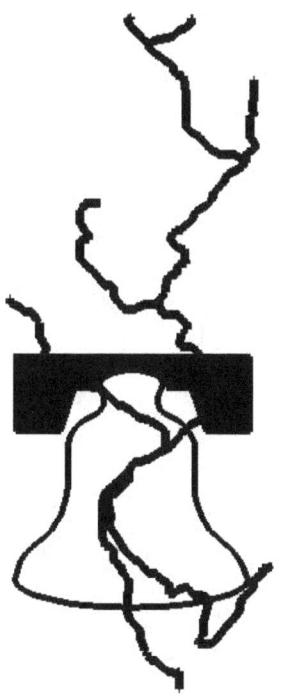

Condensed from Fishing the Free and Open Waters of the Delaware and the web site
"Fishing the Big D"
www.fishingthebigd.com
Formerly Fishing the Wihittuck
Revised 2015

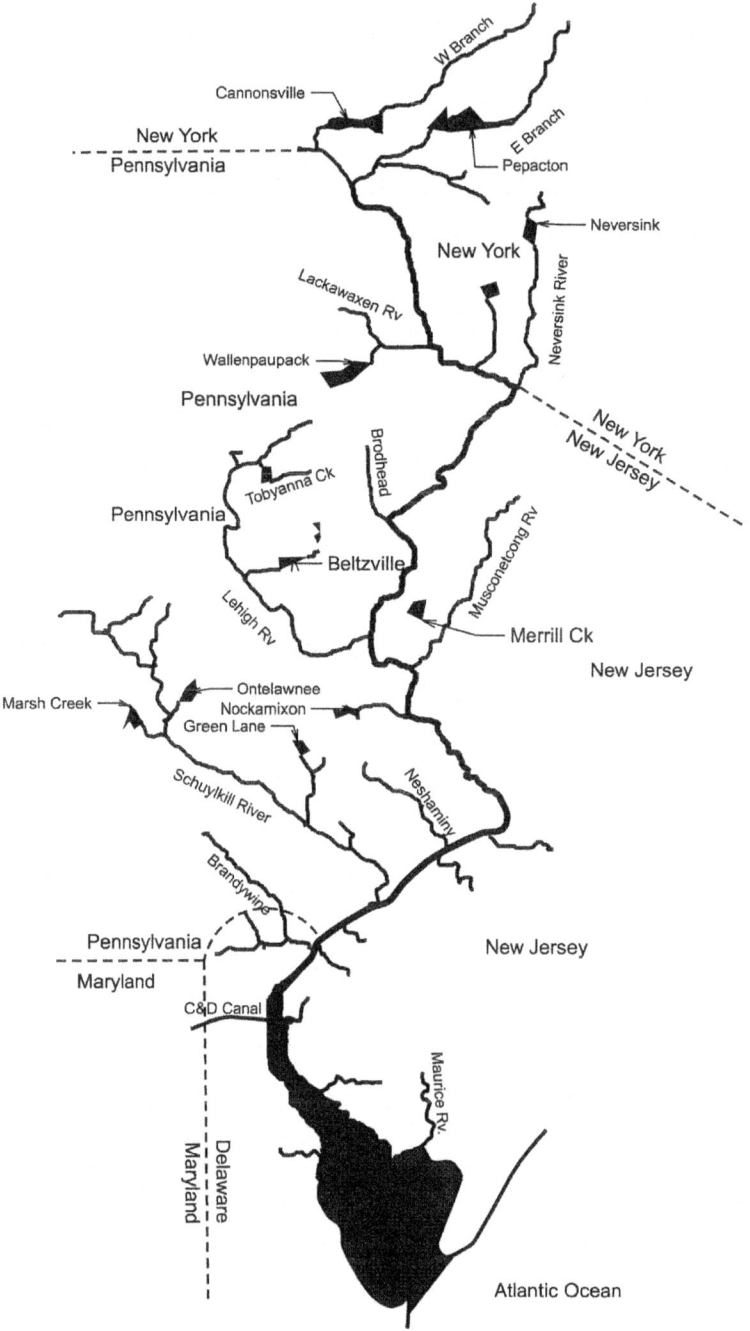

The Delaware Watershed

The Lenape Indian's Wihittuck

I would like to dedicate this book to my growing family. They were the ones who accompanied me on the river, edited my work, and put up with me in general on this project.

All Rights Reserved
James S. McKay

Copyright 2012
All maps, graphic pictures, photographs, and charts, by author.
Revised 2015
ISBN 9780615692319

Chapters

I History	1
II Upper Delaware	11
Trout	24
Eels	33
River Herring & Shad	39
Pickerel & Pike	51
III Middle Delaware	53
Walleyes & Yellow Perch	54
Lehigh River	60
Black Bass	67
IV Tidal or Urban Delaware	84
Catfish	94
Schuylkill River	100
Freshwater Mussels	104
Lung Fish	111
Saltwater	113
Striped Bass	114
Sturgeons	122
V Delaware Bay	125
Croakers	142
Flat Fish	149
Sea Bass	153
Blue Fish	155
Sharks & Rays	157
Surf Fishing	161
GPS Hot Spots	164
VI Delaware Salmon	174
Bibliography	176

Credits
I would like to give credit and thanks to the follow people and organizations:

Army Corp of Engineers

The Corp still say, the river needs a dam, but they did build many of the lakes we enjoy today

Delaware River Basin Commission

Let hope they can control and protect the river from special interest groups

The State Game Agencies of Delaware, New Jersey, New York, and Pennsylvania

They protect us from our own greed

Members of the Eastern Pennsylvania Fish Report

Special thanks to follow member Tom McDuffie

"It is hereby declared to be the policy of the United States that certain selected rivers of the nation which, with their immediate environments, posses outstandingly remarkable scenic, recreational, geologic, fish and wildlife, historic, cultural or other similar values, shall be preserved in fee-flowing condition, and that they and their immediate environments shall be protected for the benefit and enjoyment of present and future generations."

Today, approximately seventy-five percent of the Delaware River is on the Wild and Scenic list.

Wild and Scenic River Act of October 2, 1968.

The policy states that: [78] the mission of the nation scenic river system is not to "lock up it ", "but to preserve its character" and to work with the community to enhance that character [78]. To get on the list, the candidate river section must be carefully surveyed, evaluated and fall into the following categories of scenic, wild or recreational. All rivers must be free flowing, relatively clean, un-developed, with some unique cultural, scenic, recreational, geologic and wildlife attributes. The Act prohibits dams and other activities along the river that are detrimental to the rivers character. The Act encourages all recreational activities as permitted by local state law, which includes hunting and fishing. No portion of the Delaware is considered wild, but it has more than it shares of scenic, diverse cultural history and recreational categories.

The Delaware is noted to be the longest un-dammed river in the East Coast.

Free flowing is the potential of river to be a good fishery, it is not much different from our potential to be productive and reach our greatest potential in our own lives. To reach the optimum fishing qualities, waterways must be free flowing. Free flowing rivers provide a variety of water environments to meet the many different type of wildlife. By inhibiting the freedom of the river like us, the foundations of both, become filled with lazy soft mud and silt, not hard stone and gravel. The channels must be permitted to meander in the valleys on their accord so to form deep secret holes to hid walleyes and shallow exposed ripples for small mouth bass. Its power to slowly weave these curves provides a different view to the angler's eye and a tug from a different fish at every turn and bend. A watershed is a family where each stream has its own character, strengths, and weakness. When one is stricken, it can affect the whole family. The valley that was created by the river belongs to the river and provides life to all who live there. When it escapes its banks, the river is merely inserting its rights and we must adapt to it

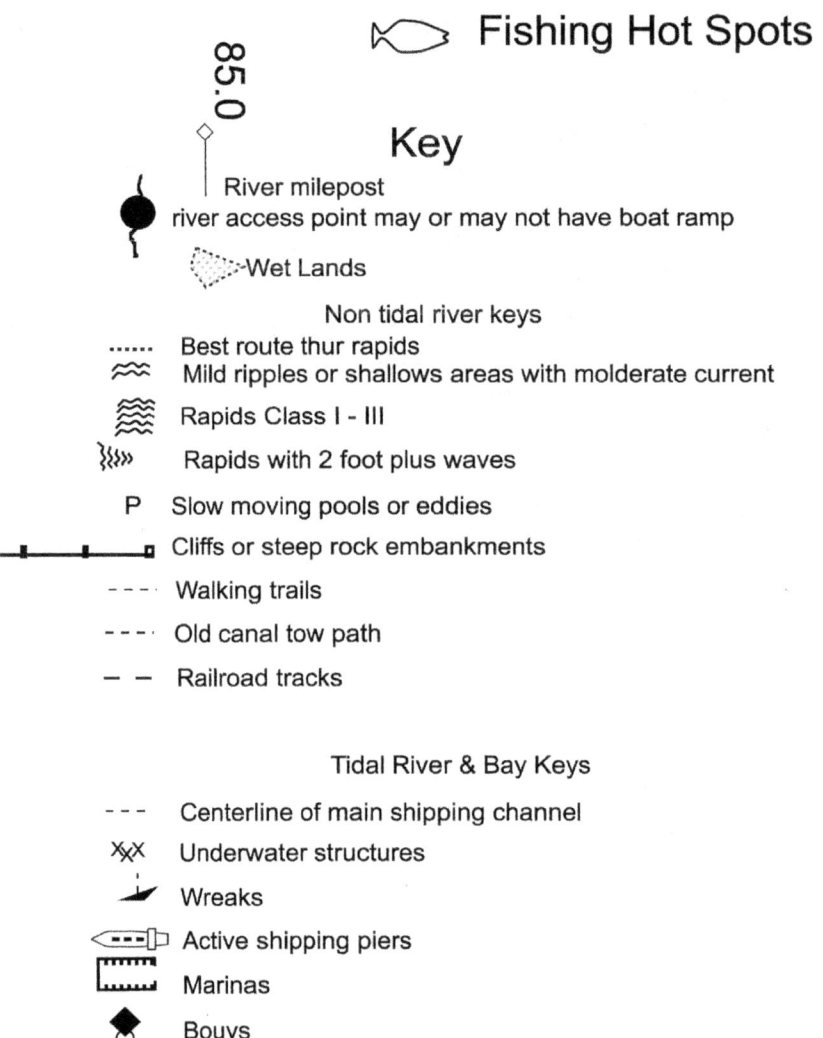

Fishing Hot Spots

Key

- 85.0 River milepost
- river access point may or may not have boat ramp
- Wet Lands

Non tidal river keys

- ······ Best route thur rapids
- ～～ Mild ripples or shallows areas with molderate current
- ≋ Rapids Class I - III
- ⁾⁾⁾ Rapids with 2 foot plus waves
- P Slow moving pools or eddies
- ▬▬▬ Cliffs or steep rock embankments
- - - - Walking trails
- - - - Old canal tow path
- — — Railroad tracks

Tidal River & Bay Keys

- - - - Centerline of main shipping channel
- ✕✕ Underwater structures
- ⇃ Wreaks
- Active shipping piers
- Marinas
- Bouys

Water levels based on low tides and average summer flow levels
Sources: USCG Navigation charts, DRBC Maps, Federal Fish and Wildlife maps, Delorme maps, Google Earth, Saltwater Directions Recon maps, Author's visit.

Fishing The Big D

Chapter I
History

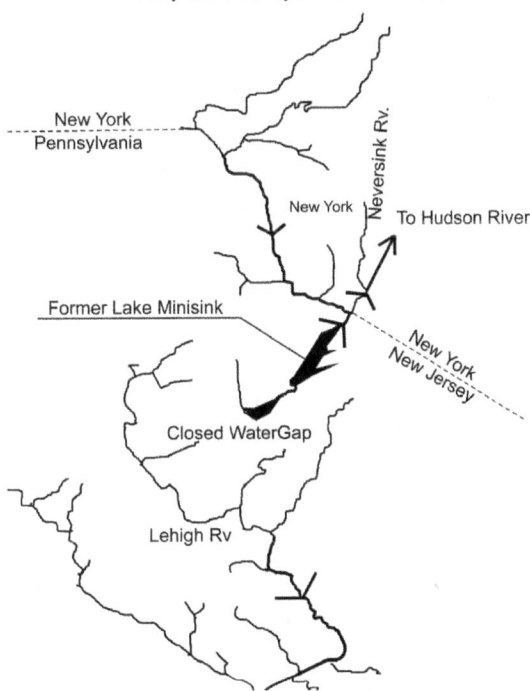

Early Two River System of the Delaware

The Delaware's age, as rivers go might be considered young. The formation of the Upper Delaware Valley began 420 million years ago when the first Appalachian mountain chain appeared just east of its present location. The early mountain ridge eroded away to form what geologists called the Shawangunk formation and would become the bedrock of the second and third final folded mountain chain that we see today. Portions of the latest mountain chain that contained limestone and shale eroded away to form the present gaps and valleys we see today. Only a few million years ago the Delaware was two rivers separated by the Kittatinny Mountain. In this early time frame, portions of the valley north of what is today's Water Gap was a large lake and drainage was north and than eastward, emptying into Hudson watershed by means of the Neversink and the Roundout Rivers. When the Water Gap opened up only a few million years ago, the upper river's Minisink Valley reversed flow and transformed itself into a new single independent watershed of the Delaware Valley. The alluvial sediment from the prehistoric lake would play an import role in the Big D's future.

    The formation of the Bay began 35 million years earlier from outer space. Due to the fact the moon was closer than it is today the State of Delaware and lower New Jersey, was partially under water caused by massive daily tidal flows. Geologist estimate about that time we were hit with a shot gun blast from outer space. The existence of these

The History of the Delaware

strikes only came to light recently when geologists noticed a lack of fresh water aquifers in a 100 mile diameter circle in eastern Virginia just north of the mouth of the Chesapeake Bay. The biggest meteor of the group created a blast zone with a diameter of 96 miles and a crater 3,000 feet deep at Cape Charles Virginia. Soil sample indicated that the tidal wave created by the blast went as far as the mountains of North Carolina. A collection of smaller meteors, most likely a break off the bigger one, landed 100 miles east of Atlantic City in Tom's Canyon. Scientist that study nuclear blast estimate the Cape Charles Virginia strike was from a three mile size rock, only half the size of the one that hit eastern Mexico, which may have killed off the dinosaurs [155]. Even though these meteorites landed in water and the carters are invisible today from the surface many geologists believe they played an important role in the location of rivers and bays of the region. On today's maps of the Chesapeake Bay, all of the rivers, including the Susquehanna, and the flow from the southern rivers like the James all point to the center of the impacted zone. The deep crater created by the Cape Charles, or Chesapeake Meteorite, may have altered the flow of the Susquehanna from what would become the Delaware Bay to the Chesapeake Bay. The rime of the crater may have generated the formation of the State of Delaware.

Later when the great ice shield covered New York State the now complete Delaware Valley provided a direct drainage channel to the Sea. When these giant earthmoving machines melted, the flash floods crossed over existing watersheds. Looking at the topography maps of southeastern New York, the Delaware River could have easily remove melt water and gravel from the Hudson, Susquehanna and as far north as the Finger Lakes of New York. The Delaware's West Branch at Deposit NY is only separated from the Susquehanna by a ten miles valley full of glacial deposits. The original channel of the Upper Delaware could have gathered overflow from the Hudson. Basically the Big D Valley would act as a funnel for glacial flooding from three separate watersheds. Such flooding today would dwarf anything we have ever seen. Today, the river bottom is littered with different rocks types. The gravel and sand from the floods build much of the land we see in South Jersey and northern Delaware. The deposits from the Hudson also built Long Island and large deposit of rocks on the ocean floor. These rock beds and the position of Long Island control migratory fish movement today.

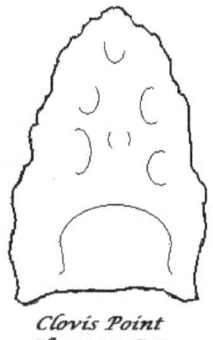

Clovis Point Shawnee PA

These ice shields move more than gravel and water, they moved aquatic life from one watershed to the next and forced early man to migrate from one continent to another.

No one can say when man the first global invasive species appeared in the

Fishing The Big D

Lenape's Wihittuck (Lenape's name for the Delaware). But the oldest Paleo-Indian site at Shawnee at the mouth of the Brodhead, produced a 9,700 year old Clovis point arrowhead. When the Paleo-Indians lived in North American at the end of the Ice Age, it was a cooler dryer climate than what it is today. Portions of the Catskills and Pocono were ice covered. When man first appeared on the middle river, the land was a dry grassy savanna environment. In what is now Delmarva the wind carried dry sand that blanketed the soil. When the earth's axis shifted to its presented location, North America got warmer, the rainfall increased, the grasslands gave way to hard wood forest, land ice disappeared, river flows became more consistent and the wind stop carrying sand. The appearances of forests were a lot different then what we see today. It's not clear if it was man himself, the changing climate or another calamity from outer space but the larger mammals disappeared from North America and a cultural change in people happen at the same time. Due to the yearly burning of the forest by the natives people, the floors of the forests is believed to have had less underbrush with larger trees than what we see today. Judging from the many Indian named rivers in North American, the people must have lived exclusively along the waters. The waterways were a source for food and travel. Many Big D favorite fishing hole may have had an Indian village on its banks at one time. They used thorns and the claws of prey birds like eagles for fishing hook, but most were caught in traps made of sticks, much in the same manner as minnows are trapped today. The Lenape Indians that lived by the bay and ocean called themselves the Unalachtigo (people from the Ocean). In the river to the north, they called themselves the Unami (the up river people). The Lenape Indians that lived on the upper section of the Lenape Wihittuck wanted to be known as Minsi (people from the stone country) [114]. Our maps today carry many of these names from these early people. What can be said about the early history of the Lenape's Wihittuck can be said about any of the eastern rivers. In the late 1500's when Western Europeans sailors visited the rivers in North American in search of the passage to Asia, they found a land rich with wildlife and other humans beings living along the banks and marshes. The Asian route was never exploited, but the land of the Lenape's Wihittuck was.

So rich was the fish life in the bay that as early as 1620, English and Swedes whalers conducted the first documented commercial fishing enterprise. Reports that one could walk on the back of fish were common on all of the eastern rivers during this age. Captain John Smith commented that his landing in the Potomac River was delayed because of the amount of fish in the water. Henry Hudson was the first to document a visit (1609) in the Bay and was quickly followed by Dutch and Swedish explorers (1614). The Swedish and Dutch settlements sprung up first along the lower and upper rivers. The English came next and would have to compete with the earlier Swedish, Dutch, and Indians for good land along the river and bay. After the English established control, all the native people, rivers and bay would then be known by the name printed on the English navigation charts "De La Warr" (name of the 1610 Governor of Virginia) [114]. By 1680, a small collection of Swedish and Dutch settlements at the mouth of Schuylkill

The History of the Delaware

would become the center of the region under a new concept called urban planning by its new British owner and recently converted Quaker, William Penn.

This was not a discovery of a new world but a merging of two old worlds into one new world order.

What was in our waters at this time may always be a mystery. Few painting of fish type from this period can be found. The different languages of the time would make identifying fish types confusing. Even English names for lower River and Bay fish like Troutes, Oldwives and Plaice leave the reader confused and guessing what was in the water at that time. The early freshwater fish populations of the Atlantic coastal rivers were very different than the central rivers of North America. In the Salmonidas family only the small purple colored brook trout was hiding in our streams. Not until the invention of the

Arrowhead

railcar would its cousins, the brown, and the rainbow would take control of the upper rivers creeks. In the Exocidae family (pikes), only the chain and redfin pickerel would be flashed by glacial flooding into our watershed. Of the Cyprinidae (Carp) family, which made up the minnow population called shiners, but here the largest native carp were creek chubs and fall fish. The big carp or common carp would later come from Europe. In the Ictaluridae family (Catfish), the only native cats in the river were white catfish, yellow and brown bullhead with the madtoms. The channel cat it's believed followed the canal boats to our river. In the darter family only the yellow perch found its way here, it's bigger brother the walleye would have to wait. Within the Centrarchidae (Black Bass) family, the most prized native North American game fishes, the small & large mouth bass would not be on the native list of Delaware River Fish. Like the channel cats it's believed they first moved in by canals before conventional stocking methods existed. In the Black Bass family the river did have a good population of sunfish, but most of them were the dark colored mud, blackbanded, and banded sunfish. Today, the banded sunfish is on the endangered list. Long nose gars once patrolled the lower river but not today, instead snakeheads are the new invasive species of air breathing fish. Today, what we call trash fish such as Eels, suckers, shad, river herring, sturgeons, bullheads, perch, fall fish and pan fish was the main food fish caught by settlers and Indians. Red fin, chain pickerel and striped bass may have been the only game fish in the waters of the Delaware at that time. Today the Pennsylvania game commission states that 160 species of fresh water fish with 24 fish families live in the commonwealth [1]. It is not known the exact number of fish types in the Delaware during this early time. We may never know, but it is believed that our presence has actually increased the number of fish species in local waters, but with fewer quantities of individual fish.

Fishing The Big D

The movement of new ideas, food, animals and humans was not a one way street on the Atlantic Ocean. The European agricultural practices, which included domesticated animals, honey bees and steel axles, would alter the appearance of woods in the valley. The introduction of diseases such as small pox, yellow fever, malaria along with steel muskets would alter the human diversity of the land as well. The discovery of tobacco and potatoes would forever change the economics of Europe and the rest of the world.

In the 1600 and 1700's, fishing was done for food and commercial values rather then recreation. On the bay and ocean side, communities would construct towers to observe surface fish activity like schools of blue fish, skip-jack and whales. One assumes the towers were manned in a particular seasons to look for certain fish. The fish would be salted or smoked and stored in barrels for shipment and storage. Shellfish were most lightly consumed locally because of spoilage. Before eating, salted fish had to be soaked in water to remove the salt. Fish that could not be locally consumed or salted were used for fertilizer. The Indian name for menhaden or commonly called bunker today meant fertilizer. Some fish were used to feed livestock. Hogchockers was a name given to a small flounder because the hogs chocked on them while eating the fish. Codfish was a particular important fish at the time because it could be preserved in salt and stored longer than other fish.

No other type of fishing would have such a profound impact as whaling on the early nation. At first, dead whales were scavenged off the beaches of New Jersey and Delaware. It became custom here for people to owned beached whale salvage rights. The person that had the whaling rights on that beach could lay claim to the dead whale, and have it boil down. As the demand for wax's, lamp oil, creams and other oil based products grew people would have to go to sea to capture live whales. The larger baleen whales such as humpbacks, finback, and blue whales were more prized than the smaller toothed whales like pilots, harbor porpoise and orcas. Ironically, the most prized whale, the largest of the toothed whales family, the sperm whale, which had a large cavity it it's skull that stored a milky white high quality oil.

The need for the oil to lubricate the machinery of the industrial revolution would propel the colonies and the new nation into a maritime world super player, searching for whales across every ocean. Even though the industry was centered in New England, Philadelphia would produced many of the ships, barrels, refined and consumed much of the oil of the enterprise. The early whaling industry did more than create local ship building skill but it was the start of the petrol chemical industry here. The ugly side of the industry surfaced in 1820 when the whaling ship Essex was sunk in the Pacific by a sperm whale. The surviving Essex crew members were found three months later, along with their half eat shipmates' bodies. The event inspired Herman Melville's novel, Moby Dick. Ironically it was the invention of petroleum drilling rigs first used and made in Pennsylvania that would save these magnificent animals.

In 1822, [64] the Fairmount Dam was constructed on the Schuylkill River for drinking water. In 1828, the Lackswaxen Dam with the Lehigh River dam, all combined to close off eighty percent of eel and shad's normal spanning grounds. Even though the canal dams block the movement of migratory fish the canals them self provided an avenue to move fish from one watershed to the next bring in more fish type (possibility small mouth bass and catfish). The impact of lower fish catches were noted in the fishing records of Howell family fisher at Woodbury. In the years leading to 1825, their average catches were 130,000 per year and began to decrease to a quarter of that by the 1870's [6]. Still the demand was so big that people still continued fishing the migration runs with even more vigor with a peak catch of 1,500,000 pounds peak in 1837 [6]. By the mid 1860's, the freshwater migration fin-fishing industry was near collapsing with records indicating that only hand-full of shad were being caught in the tidal sections of the river and the many fishermen reported the fish were half the size of what used to be caught. This was not the only river to experience this drop in migratory fish and people started to noticed it across the nation.

The population of the Philadelphia region by the start of the American Civil War was now over half as million people [115]. We think that the destruction done during the American Civil War was in The South, but an additional cost of the war was the devastation of the upper basin to produce the needed munitions for the war. Early pictures of Manch Chunk and Lackswaxen showed a tree-less mountain landscape behind the towns. The wildlife situation became so bad that the State of New Jersey banned deer hunting in 1862-1867 and both Pennsylvania and New Jersey banned Sunday hunting and fishing,[93][91]. Fishing became no better. A private citizen in 1870 ordered 450 bass from the Potomac River at Harpers Ferry so to release them in the Delaware at Easton [91]. After the winds of war had stopped, a new attitude must have developed or did the States have more money to spend. The Pennsylvania legislature finally put money to regulate the trapping and taking of fish in 1866 [91]. The first fish commissioner, James Worrell, duty's was to restore the shad runs of the Commonwealth's rivers. To do this, he pushed laws requiring fish channels to be built to permit fish to travel the waterways (1866), forbade the use of fish baskets and weirs (1871) [91] but most importantly he was able to get funding for these projects. The concept of fish ladders was investigated, with the first one in Pennsylvania constructed on the Susquehanna River. Fish hatcheries were constructed. The first hatchery in the area was on the Little Lehigh to help populate the waterways with trout and other fish in 1883[91]. New York and New Jersey (1870) [93] followed the same courses of action in establishing a separate and independent agency. The federal government in 1871 established the United States Fish Commission to study the decline in the nations fishery and make recommendations[6] [95]. One of the first things this new organization did was a shad-restocking program at the Federal level. It tried to establish a shad fishery in the Pacific by shipping shad in specially built railroad cars sent to the Sacramento River in California in 1870's, (this later proved to be successful in the 1880's)[6]. Shad and striped bass were transplanted to other inland waterways to see if they could inhabit without the migration patterns [6]. The Federal Fish commission also introduced carp

Fishing The Big D

[91]. It don't take long before paid game warrens paroled the waterways and were authorized to destroy unlawful weirs and fish traps. Efforts were made in the 1870-1890's, to stock salmon in the river system with limited success [95]. Because of these late 19th century transplants, and experiments our waterways today have a larger variety of fish than before the Europeans came. Railroad cars with tanks would soon change the aquatic life of our waterways. These early bucket biology programs would alter the aquatic life in the Atlantic coastal rivers into a cookie cutter of fish type, where every channel cat and small mouth bass would look the same.

The first and only dam built across the entire width of the main stem Delaware River was at Lackswaxen for the D&H Canal in 1829. By the end of the Nineteenth Century the dam was removed making the Delaware River the longest un-dam River on the east coast. The reason for the river remaining dam free through the Twentieth Century had little to do with the 1796 agreement between Pennsylvania and New Jersey, restricting dams on the Delaware River. The Agreement could have easily been revoke by both states by the end of the nineteenth Century since there were no more Durham crafts, coal barges, log raft and small steam boats moving up and down the non tidal river sandwich between the two States. By the beginning of the Twentieth Century with the thirst for electric power and clean water both Philadelphia and New York City would turn the Delaware River into a battle ground for dam construction. The Electric Companies bought large tracks of low land along the river including the islands for possible flooding. The water authorities of both cities proposed massive water distribution system using tunnels and old canals. Every major rapid and chock point on the river was mapped and study for a possible dam site. By the 1930's there were plans to place half a dozen hydroelectric power plants churning out cheap electricity on the Delaware River. These projects were on the same scale as the Tennessee River Valley and other massive western dam projects of the time. One such plan even called for a sea level canal crossing Central New Jersey connecting the Hudson the Delaware and Chesapeake. The biggest impediment to these grandiose projects of the time was the cost, the Valley by this time was mostly urban and flooding eastern urban areas was more costly then flooding rural western land. The independent reports of the Army Corp of Engineers, Philadelphia Water Authority, New York City Water Authority and the Interstate Commission of the Delaware River (INCODEL) were all faced with the same dilemmas on how to control flooding, provide portable drinking water, harness electric power and at the same time justify the cost of such projects to tax payers and users.

Before the end of the Twentieth Century, New York City would get its Catskill reservoirs, a lock free canal would be built from the Delaware River to the Chesapeake, Philadelphia would get its water using a diverse systems of underground aquifers with surfaced water, the Federal government would offer, then withdraw funds to dam the Delaware River.

The History of the Delaware

Questions for the future

- The introduction of invasive species in the river only promises to bring change, for better or worse?

In 2011, the Pennsylvania Game Commission surveyed the river and determined that is was infected with Year of the Youth (YOY), a disease that affects small mouth bass. This disease has seriously impacted the small mouth fishery in the lower Susquehanna and now threatens the Delaware. Will the decreasing numbers of small mouth bass be replaced by snakeheads and flathead? The invasive algae, Didymo (rock snot) has now progress through out most of the river carpeting the bottom and rocks with brown stringy fiber where it will foul hooks, lures and turn the blue water brown.

- Since the mid twentieth century has the river flow rates become more eradicate?

Between 1913 and 1960 there was only two years where the average flow exceeded 15000 cu feet per second while after 1960 there was 8 years that flow rate exceeded 15,000 cu feet per sec. at Trenton. Prior to 1960 there was were 11 years with flow rates less than 10,000 while after 1960 there was 15 years where flows was less than 10,000.

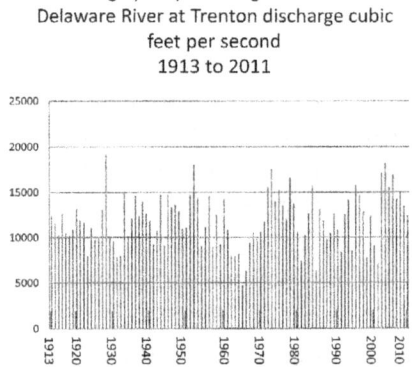

- Will these eradicate yearly flow rates and the need to break from fossil fuels drive political pressure to build a dam?
- How will these increases in drought and floods affect the fishery?
- Can Pennsylvania, where global petroleum production and fracking begin, be counted on to protect our waterways in the new natural gas boom?

Fishing The Big D

DELAWARE TIME LINE

Dated Event
- -420,000,000 Formation of the first Appalachians Mountains
- -290,000,000 Formation of the second Appalachians Mountains
- -35,000,000 The Chesapeake Meteor strikes forming a depression that becomes the Chesapeake Bay
- -2,000,000 The Delaware Water Gap opened, river reversed flow in Minisink Valley
- -15,000 Melting of last Ice Age which shaped the current drainage
- -10,000 Possible first human habitations begins
- 1609 Henry Hudson visits the Bay
- 1610 Thomas West name Bay after Lord De La Warr, title of First Governor of Virginia
- 1614 Dutch and British explorers map and chart the bay and river
- 1614 Dutch Traders in upper Delaware River
- 1620 English whalers start harvesting the Bay for Whales
- 1682 William Penn lays the groundwork for Philadelphia
- 1683 First fishing restriction - Rake fishing outlawed in Pennsylvania, other Colonies follow
- 1769 Survey and boarders of upper-river
- 1791 Coal discovered in Panther Valley in 1791
- 1796 No Dam agreement Pennsylvania and New Jersey "no dams on the Delaware River"
- 1808 Gill net restrictions enacted in NJ and PA for shad
- 1822 Fairmount dam and water works is completed
- 1827 Schuylkill Canal was completed
- 1828 Completion of the Delaware and Hudson Canal & Lackswaxen Dam on the river
- 1829 Lehigh Canal was completed
- 1832 Delaware division lower canal completed
- 1837 1,500,000 pounds of shad catches peaks, decrease catches begin until the late 1800s
- 1841 Flooding on the Delaware, five bridges are destroyed
- 1860 Shad catches reported dropped to near zero on Delaware River
- 1865 End of the American Civil War & Pennsylvania Fish Commission is commission
- 1870 NJ Board of Fish Commissioners is created
- 1870 450 bass come from the Potomac River at Harpers Ferry and released on the Delaware
- 1885 Dredging operations in the Delaware lower river begins
- 1891 Philadelphia had two cholera outbreaks with 2nd 1899
- 1900 The world begins the industrial build up for the First World War
- 1900 Philadelphia population at 1,200,000 people
- 1900 Peak record of sixteen million pounds of shad were landed in the bay and lower river
- 1903 All time record flood, recorded at Montague at 35.50 feet, seven bridges destroyed
- 1906 The mosquito control program starts
- 1910 Bluefish and weak fish catches peak and decrease afterwards
- 1916 Shad catches decrease back to less than one million pounds
- 1923 First of three planned Philadelphia sanitary water treatment plants is built
- 1926 Lake Wallenpaupack is built by PP&L
- 1927 Chesapeake and the Delaware Canal becomes lock-less
- 1930 DDT is used widespread on wetlands for Federal Mosquito Control Program
- 1931 US Supreme Court ruled in favor of New York City to draw water from the Delaware
- 1936 Interstate Commission of the Delaware Rive (INCODEL) was formed
- 1945 World War II ends & State approved $ for a sanitary sewer system for Philadelphia
- 1948 Federal Pollution Control Act brings federal money for sewer systems
- 1950 Rondout Reservoir is places into services to store water from the Del watershed

The History of the Delaware

- 1954 US supreme court decree that NY could withdraw a maximum of 800 million
- 1954 Neversink reservoirs is completed
- 1955 Three sanitary sewer plants in Philadelphia are finally completed
- 1955 Flooding from hurricanes Connie and Diane floods valley, kills 99 people
- 1955 Pepacton Reservoir is placed into services
- 1959 Dyberry or Edgar Jadwin dry dam on the Lackawaxen River
- 1960 Prompton Dam on the Lackawaxen River
- 1961 DRBC (Delaware River Basin Commission) formation
- 1961 Francis E. Walter Dam or Bear Creek on the Lehigh River is completed
- 1961 New Jersey Wildlife, Management Areas get funding by Green Acres Bonds
- 1962 Toaks Island Dam project has funding
- 1964 Cannonsville Reservoir is placed into service
- 1971 Beltzville Dam is built in the Lehigh Basin
- 1972 Clean Water Act, brings in more money and control of wastewater
- 1975 Corinthos dumps a million gallons of crude oil at Marcus Hook
- 1976 The Teton Dam in Idaho collapses triggering the end of Tocks Island
- 1978 The two upper sections of the river join the list of Wild and Scenic Rivers
- 1979 Blue Marsh Lake is built in the Schuylkill Basin
- 1985 435,000 gallons of Nigerian Crude leaked from the Grand Eagle at Marcus Hook
- 1989 The Rivera pores 306,000 gallons of industrial grade oil #2 at Marcus Hook
- 1992 Congress cancel Tocks Island dam funding
- 1993 Maurice River joins the list of Wild and Scenic Rivers
- 1999 Flooding from Hurricane Floyd floods the lower River
- 2000 White Clay Creek joints the list of Wild and Scenic Rivers
- 2000 Delaware River between the Gap to New Hope join the list of Wild and Scenic
- 2001 Floods from Tropical Storm Allison, kills seven people in PA (lower section)
- 2002 DRBC reported that 76% reduction in BOD discharge in the estuary
- 2003 Floods from Hurricane Isabel floods entire river system
- 2004 Flooding in July, August and September (TS Charley), (TS Ivan, Frances) entire system
- 2004 Athos-I leaked 265,000 gal of heavy Venezuelan Crude
- 2006 Flood crest at Montague NJ at 32.16 third highest recorded
- 2006 Musconetcong River joins the list of Wild and Scenic Rivers
- 2007 Upper River - top on the list to lose the Wild and Scenic title (parallel power line)
- 2010 Dredging depth is increase from 40 feet to 45 feet and the process begins
- 2010 Natural Gas drilling begins in Wayne Co PA by the rock fracking process.
- 2011 Small Bass have YOY disease as per Pennsylvania Game Commission

Fishing The Big D

Chapter II
THE UPPER DELAWARE

By an act of Congress and Former President Jimmy Carter, in 1978, the valley of the upper Delaware, Hancock to Milrift, and from Port Jervis to the Water Gap, joined the list of Natural Wild and Scenic Rivers [78]. Today, each of the three states that share this basin and the Federal Government has bought a total of 200,000 acres of land encompassing the streams and rivers that feed and surround the upper Delaware [73].

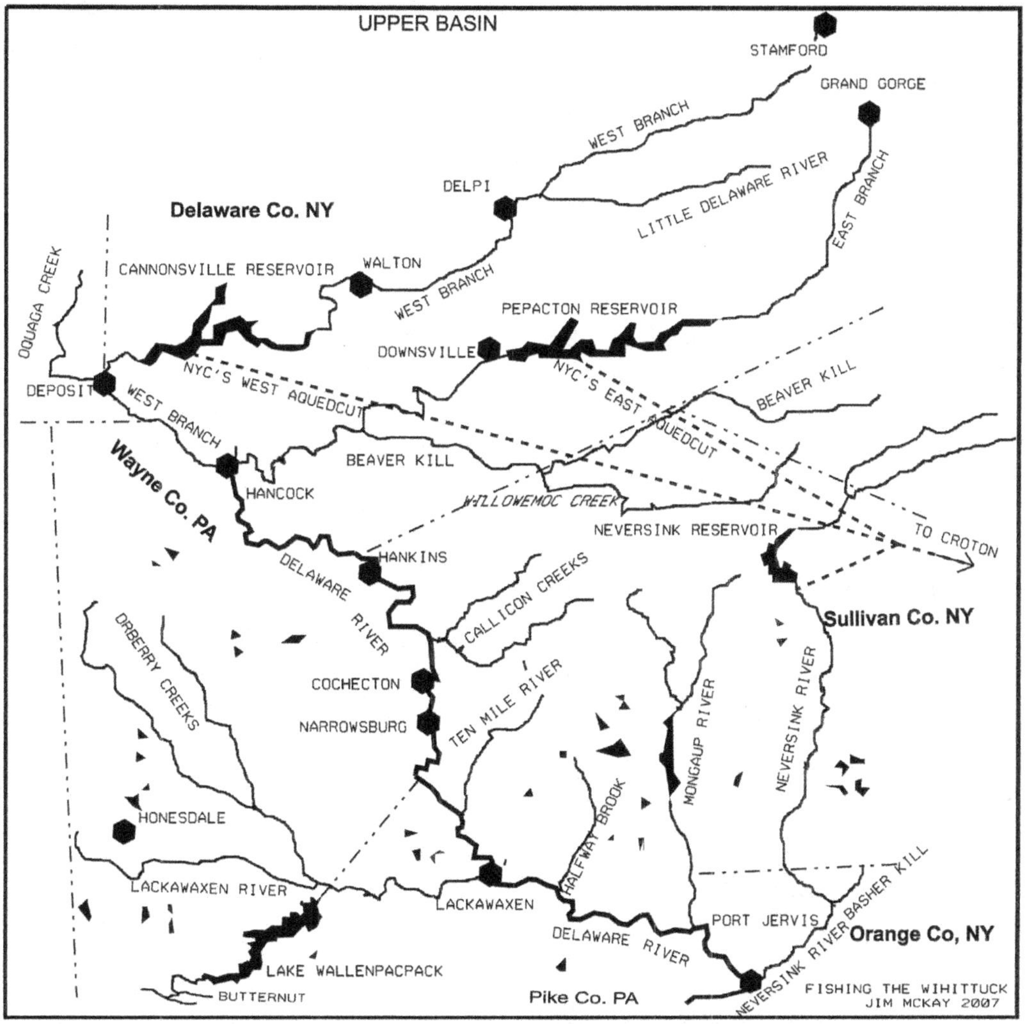

The Upper Delaware

The Upper Delaware Basin's economy has always been base upon the exploitation of its natural resources. The early removal of its massive coal, timber and stone reserves may have unwittingly enhanced its present, and most important economy today - recreation. Even the latest resource extracted from the region, water, has enhanced the basin's fishery and recreation attraction. The abandoned Delaware & Hudson Canal completed in 1828, [33] and the smaller abandoned rail lines that transported coal from the anthracite fields of Pennsylvania now permit limited public access to some of the best trout and small month bass waters in North America. The active railroads that snaked through the river valleys halted private development of countless miles of river shoreline. Through the 18th and 19th century, the logging industry, requiring free river access to the southern markets, prevented dam construction. The beauty of the region has been well recognized in the last 150 years. Owners of large property tracts capitalized on the location and beauty by restricting their property for hunting and fishing for the industrialists, politicians, and other influential people of the second half of the nineteenth century. They built their own small private hatcheries and imported fish from Europe for their clients on the Neversink River, Willowemoc Creek and others. The H.L. Leonard Rod Company perfected and manufactured the first early bamboo fly rod here in the 1860's.

Look at any map of the Upper Delaware in the Lower Catskill and Upper Pocono Mountains and the major feature that stands out is the numerous water bodies. Most of these water pockets were magnified by our desire to control the basin for our power, water, and recreational needs. The drainage is typical of glacial deposition and scoring, which produced the many ponds, marshes and pronounced river valley that we see today. The shallow, always visible bedrock holds the water on the surface making it ideal for surface water reservoirs. The Upper Delaware is made up of four large sub-basins and in each of these basins are lakes, both large and small, with a purpose. Most are the shallow more natural ponds that people tend to overlook but produce our native pickerel in great quantities. The region also has the man-made coldwater mega-lakes for a richer variety of introduced coldwater fish. The variety of these lakes should fit everyone's needs, from high performance boats to small isolated ponds for canoes and kayaks.

The Upper Delaware River has always been under litigation concerning withdraw of water for New York City. New York City is surrounded by saltwater and exhausted its underground aquifer in the early 1830's. The Hudson River salt front can extend as far north as West Point on the Hudson River. As the City grew, so did its needs and in 1905 it began to draw its water from the Catskills. When plans were drawn to provide water from the Delaware tributaries near the proposed Rondout Reservoir (which is in both watersheds) New Jersey objected and filed suit. In 1931, the US Supreme Court ruled in favor of New York City and held that the city could draw 400 millions gallons a

Fishing The Big D

day from the Delaware headwater [94]. After years of further problems with withdrawals and discharge rates, in 1954 the US Supreme Court decreed that NY could withdraw a maximum of 800 million gallons of water per day (that was twice what it was in 1931), and prescribed that a minimum flow be required at Montague NJ. Today the Delaware supplies half of the water that New York City uses [94].

In 1937, New York City started construction of the Delaware water system and a series of reservoirs connected by tunnels into the Delaware watershed. The first two lakes, were completed in the mid 1950's. The Pepacton Reservoir also known as Downsville had a population of 974 people before it was flooded [46]. The former farming village of Cannonsville had a population of approximately 900 who had to be moved [54]. Each one of these reservoirs met resistance from relocated residences, sportsman, and downstream government agencies that draw their water from the River. At the bottom of the Neversink Lake were the former private trout hatchery of Mr. Hewitt and the fishing grounds of Theodore Gordon of the quill Gordon fly. Both of these men's writings and research contributed this region as the birthplace of American Fly fishing. Now some of these excellent trout streams are channels under lakes.

In 2004, it was agreed to permit a minimum flow rate for fish in the upper limits of the basins [96]. Local trout fishermen have never liked New York City's water withdraw policy. In the summer the flow can be too low on the East and West Branch for fishing. The city claims that improvements in water release technology and data information has helped make water release management program a feasible practice for fishing. The discharge today is not just based on local rainfall amounts, but on a river/basin management program controlled by the Delaware River Basin Commission [108]. The program looks at and considers the impacts from the amount of water that New York City and other communities need, the salt front line in the lower river, time of year, demand for electric power, and threats of floods and drought. The litigations over the discharge rates will resurface every time a major flood, drought or a new governor is elected, with the DRBC in the middle. It might be best to let the balance act be managed by the experts in river management not special interest groups.

The River's most northern limits come from three Catskills New York City reservoirs, Cannonsville, Neversink, and the Perpacton. The lakes can be fished, but permits for boat operation and access are highly regulated. No motors of any kind are permitted on these lakes, so most people will rent several slips to store row and sail boats at different locations. Once a year, the city will announce an auction for any unregistered boats that fail to be renewed. The land around the lake is open to the public but because of Nine-Eleven, special permits are required to visit it. At the far northwestern part of the basin in the West Branch sub-basin is the Cannonsville reservoir, just east of Deposit, New York. The lake is 17 miles long and averages one-half mile in width with a maxim depth of 140 feet with an average depth of 60 feet. The reservoir's water, like the other NYC reservoirs is partially diverted to New York City

The Upper Delaware
via the West Delaware Tunnel [54]. The Pepacton reservoir is a 5,700-acre lake, which is located in the East Branch sub-basin of the Delaware. The Pepacton water quality is cleaner due to its mountain sources than its western sister's (West Branch) agricultural sources. The Pepacton bottom topography is a long, deep, narrow valley that runs the length of fifteen miles. This makes it an excellent lake to deep troll for brown trout in the summer time. The Neversink Reservoir is the smallest of the three major New York City Catskill western reservoirs. This lake rests in the middle the southern Catskill Mountains. Like the others, it advertises excellent fly-fishing at head and tail waters of the Neversink River. In these large manmade coldwater lakes, you can expect to catch large collection of cold and warm water fish such as brown trout, small and large mouth bass, brown bullheads (catfish), rock bass, yellow perch, white suckers, and carp. Pictures of ten to twenty pound brown trout caught in these lakes cover web pages of local sporting good stores advertising the fishing potential. In fall, large browns move into the upper ends of the tributaries during spawning. Fishing rumors have it that lake trout can be caught in these lakes.

Lake Wallenpaupack is in the Lackawaxen River sub-basin. At the time of construction, the Electric Company paid an average of $20.00 per acre [97]. With a length of 13.5 miles, 60 feet depth and 52 miles of shoreline it is the largest lake in Pennsylvania and is an excellent place for anglers who like to fish shore lines, shallow inlets and near islands in high performance boats. It has many marinas and permits most any kind of boat in its waters. Because of its unrestricted boat class, it's a favorite site for fishing tournaments [66]. Due to the high boat usage, the lake can be very noisy on the summer weekends. Numerous other water bodies reside to the north of the lake. The lake has the usual fish found in all of these lakes: bass, yellow perch, large brown trout, plus stocked hybrid stripers, pickerel and walleye. In spring, the walleye are netted and milked for the eggs, and later in the fall, the fry are released back into the lake.

Most of the smaller lakes and ponds in the Pocono and Catskill area have been modified for water management. Still, these small lakes had their beginning from the glaciers that once came through here. Today, these small lakes and ponds have the typical clear brown-stain water with a slightly lower acid PH level. In geological time, lakes and ponds have a very short life span. These small shallow water bodies surrounded by woodland swamps are ideal pickerel and pike hideouts. So good is the pike fishing here that the County of Pike in Pennsylvania should have been named for the fish, instead of General Zebulon Pike [75]. Many fishermen who visit the upland waters want to go for trout and drift fish the upper river's beauty. If the crowds are too deep on the river, one should be able to find one of the 700 plus ponds or lakes without the weekend summer madness. Many of these are on state parks with boat access. The better ones are access by a trail with a kayak in tow. The larger man-made mega water bodies that drive our turbines, feed our cities with water and provide a playground for

Fishing The Big D

fast boats are clearly unnatural here. The majority of fish that live in large lakes are not in the natural environment that they evolved from. The native fish in our watersheds are more at home in rivers, streams, and small lily pad ponds and swamps. They may reproduce better in the small water bodies and are easier to locate and catch. So if you are experience problems catching fish in these super lakes, you might not be alone, try the smaller pond, streams and river for achieving tight lines and a good time.

The introduced fish with the biggest impacted in the Upper Delaware, beside the small mouth bass, would be the European brown trout. These fish once placed in our water would quickly move into every stream and connected pond in the upper watershed and become self-sustaining. Today the biggest attraction to the upper river is fly fishing for these magnificent fish. Besides browns the west coast rainbow and the native brook, has done well in the upper basin. When the older browns lose their golden color and begin to take on a salmon appearance exhibiting a lighter color, teeth and a hook jaw they become a prized catch for any angler. The variety of license plats on cars in the west branch parking lots is a testimony to the draw that trout fishing brings to the regions. The success of the trout fishery is more then just cool clean water but the discipline of anglers to return what they catch.

The West Branch of the Delaware starts above the Town of Stamford and travels 45 miles to the Cannonsville Reservoir. On its route to the Cannonsville Reservoir, it follows a valley of diverse agriculture uses. Route 10 and an abandoned rail line follow much of its length providing some pocket of access to the stream. The West Branch after the Cannonsville Reservior, is shallow with lots of islands. The bottom is littered with small round river rocks making it an easy river to wad between the reservoir and Hancock. Because of public game lands on the Pennsylvania side of the river, and many New York public parking spots, access for wading is an efficient way of fishing the West Branch. According to the New York DEC studies, this section south of Deposit, within the no kill zone has the highest concentration of trout per mile [2].

The East Branch of the Delaware begins at Grand Gorge and travels southward along Route 30 which mirrors the rivers contour closely and provides many trout stocking points throughout the entire upper length. The section above the reservoir is a small fast flowing stream with numerous small tributaries. Some of these come from state parks, making it an excellent waterway to visit hidden out of the way tributaries for possible small native brook trout or holdovers. In the fall, you can still expect to find large browns heading upstream for spawning from the reservoir. The slower moving stream of the East Branch, below the dam, becomes warm quickly but still provides good fishing early in the season or fall. Due to the diverse character of the landscape surrounding the stream, the lower east branch has an excellent multiple insect environments. The insect hatches can be intense and common here, making this stream

The Upper Delaware

a popular place for the fly angler. Some popular holes are at Pea' Eddy and between the Town of East Branch and Bolton's Eddy [16]. The East branch also has two other famous tributaries, the Beaver Kill and Willowemoc. The lower East Branch has a completely different character than the lower West Branch. The lower East Brach has no or limited access from the shore line. It has deeper slow moving pools with fewer islands than the West Branch. The lower East Branch is a river which is best fished from a draft boat while the West Branch is a wading river.

The most noted trout stream on the Pennsylvania side is the Lackawaxen River, which is the tail water of the Lake Wallenpapack. The river is stocked below the Wallenpapack to the mouth at Lackawaxen and locals say that it supports hungry trout year around. The Lackawaxen River has good access at many locations, but because of its steep grade, it might be better as a white water river for rafting than a trout fishing stream. The tourist broachers say that Lackawaxen means "fast moving water", in the original Indian language. Zane Grey in this story, The Lord of Lackawaxen Creek 1908, thought it meant ", the brown water that turns and whispers and tumbles"-. The signs warning of rapid water fluctuations should be taken seriously for this is the tail-waters of Lake Wallenpapack. During times of peak energy demands, hot days on an afternoon the flow will increase by several feet in a very short span of time.

Hancock to Port Jervis

Map 1:

At Junction pool, the start of the river, every kind of fish can be caught, striped bass and shad will start to appear as early as May, and large browns, rainbow walleyes and smallmouth bass are common all year long. Wading along the islands and meandering channels provide river access from the NY parking lots down stream for a mile.

The Main Branch of the Delaware River begins at Hancock, New York at the junction of the East and West Branch. At river milepost 330.7 in Hancock, set by Delaware River Basin Commission, the river begins its count down to milepost zero at the end in the lower bay [31]. It is also at Milepost 330.7 that the small mouth bass or as some call them "smallies" starts to become the king of the waterway. At Long Eddy, the current begins to pick up and the waterway takes on a more river like appearance. Normal flow here is still too shallow for motor boats. Shallow strong rapids will restrict travel with outboard motors. Because of the summer's shallow water depth, this section is best fished from drift boats, canoes or kayaks. You will experience a regular repeating series of rapids followed by mile long pools of slack water. The river's bank from Hancock to Port Jervis is mostly privately owned, and access to the river from the bank is limited to along highways and a few pockets of public ground. The most

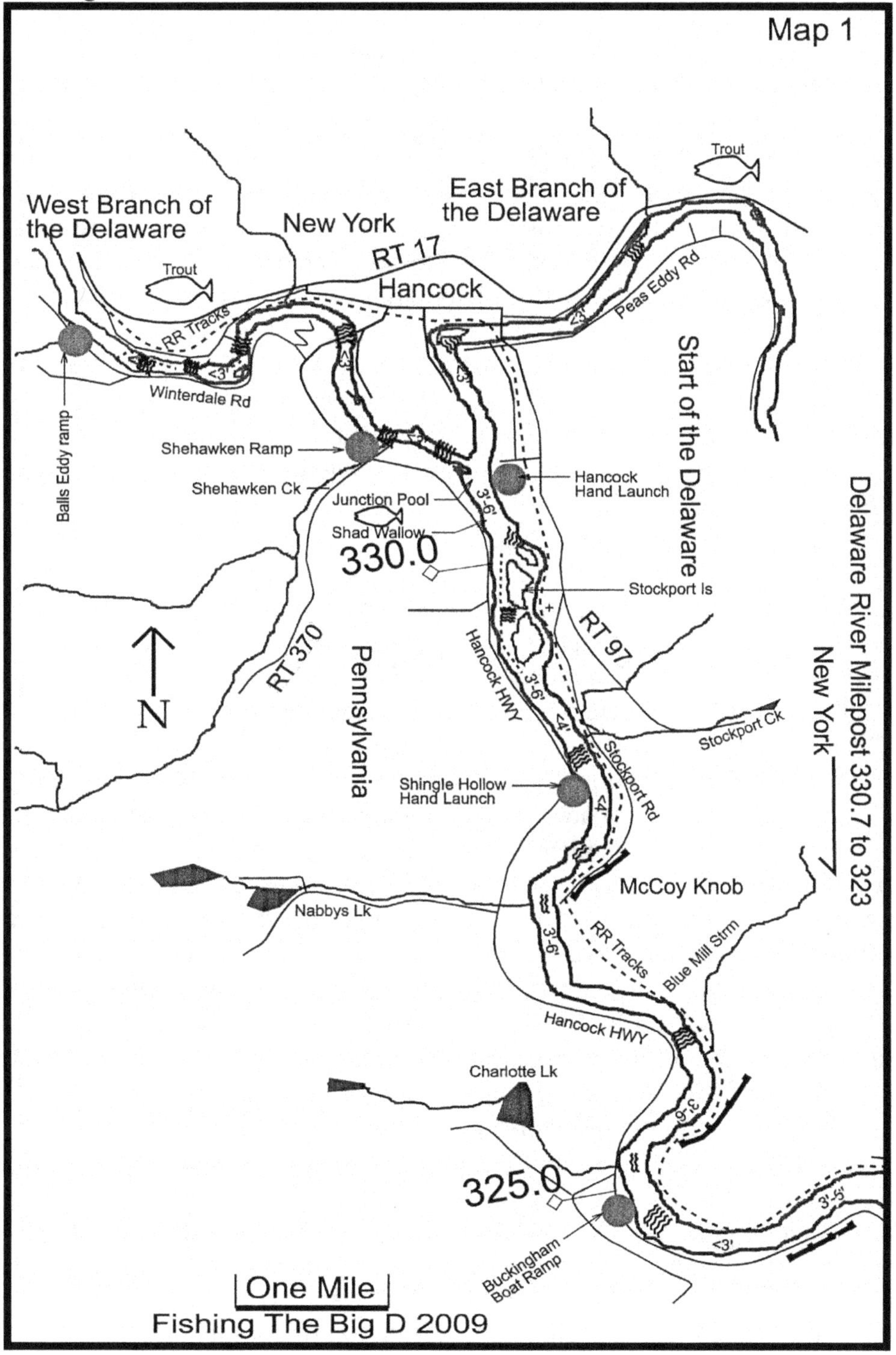
Map 1
West Branch of the Delaware
New York
East Branch of the Delaware
Trout
RT 17
Hancock
Peas Eddy Rd
RR Tracks
Winterdale Rd
Balls Eddy ramp
Start of the Delaware
Shehawken Ramp
Shehawken Ck
Hancock Hand Launch
Junction Pool
Shad Wallow
330.0
Stockport Is
RT 97
RT 370
Pennsylvania
Hancock HWY
N
Delaware River Milepost 330.7 to 323
New York
Stockport Ck
Stockport Rd
Shingle Hollow Hand Launch
McCoy Knob
Nabbys Lk
RR Tracks
Blue Mill Strm
Hancock HWY
Charlotte Lk
325.0
Buckingham Boat Ramp
One Mile
Fishing The Big D 2009

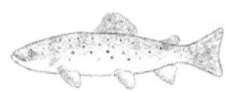

The Upper Delaware

precarious part in this section begins at Skinners Falls, north of Narrowsburg. At Skinner Falls, the river's quick drop can be hazardous. The pools in this section during summer flows vary from 6 to 10 feet deep with a few at 20 feet. One pool at Narrowsburg measured 113 feet deep, the deepest hole in the fresh water river, and was caused by a whirlpool action of suspended sediments. The gorge south of Narrowsburg is marked with natural high rock formations. At the tops of these high rock formations, large eagle nests command the best view of the river below. Class II rapids begin to appear as the river picks up flow from tributaries and its descending grade increases at Woodman's rift. South of Lackawaxen, manmade stone walls for the railroad and canal start to replace the natural stone walls of the river. As one proceeds southward toward Port Jervis the rapids tend to get stronger. The height of this ride is through Hawk Nest Valley section near the Mongaup River. Still, most of the rapids are class one, and can easily be navigated by canoes. Once you have floated this section of the river, you will understand the popularity of it.

Map 2;

The variable depths of the River at Lordville can provide good locations for walleyes. The addition of strong rapids down stream of Lordville and Long Eddy should produce small mouth bass. River access for wading can be found at Kellams Bridge. River access by the Railroad is illegal and park service agents will enforce it here. It is best to get in the river by kayaks and canoes. Peak Shad Run June

Recently a new invasive alga called didymo or AKA "rock snot" has appeared in the Delaware River. Didymo originated in cold water rivers of Northern Europe-Asia and than spread to Alaska and Canada. Today, the alga has been showing up in popular trout streams across the US. It's believed that it started in the East and West Branch but has now spread down the River as far as Easton. The bloom accurse in late winter as a brown carpet which covers the gravels and rocks and in strong current it grows what appears as brown dread-locks or snot clinging to rocks. The algae's growth is accelerated at high flow locations on rapids. Didymo will remain on the rocks until spring floods and warmer water flush it down stream in a current of brown stained water. Didymo is carried from one watershed to the next by man caring contaminated water in felt waders, cloths, sneakers, boats and boat trailers. Ironically it's the people who spread the alga that are most affected by it when the brown fibrous material fouls fishing lines and lures on every cast. Once in the river it's here to stay and waiting to travel into the next river. With all interconnecting pumps and canals such as Point Pleasant and the Chesapeake and Delaware Canal it will not take long before it to spread to other watersheds without the help of fishermen. The book is not out yet on how it affects the aquatic life of the river but dipping flies, nymphs and lures into the cold water soupy mess leads to frustration. Hopefully it's cleared out by summer when the warmer water crowds appeared on the weekends.

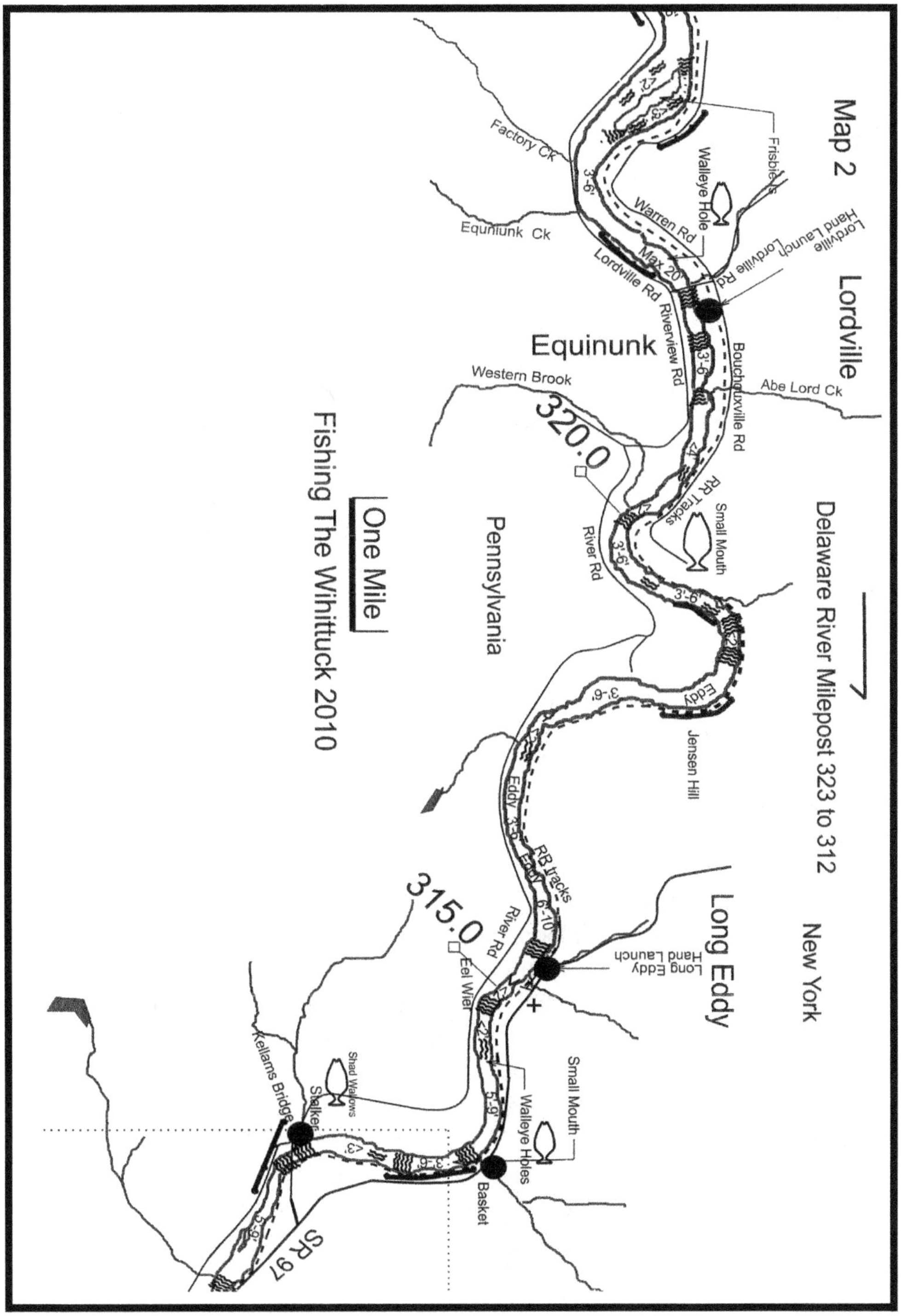
Map 2
Delaware River Milepost 323 to 312
Fishing The Whittuck 2010
One Mile
Pennsylvania
New York
Lordville
Equinunk
Long Eddy
320.0
315.0
Frisbie's
Walleye Hole
Lordville Hand Launch
Lordville Rd
Warren Rd
Max 20'
Factory Ck
Equinunk Ck
Riverview Rd
Bouchouxville Rd
Abe Lord Ck
Western Brook
RR Tracks
Small Mouth
River Rd
Eddy
Jensen Hill
RR tracks
Long Eddy Hand Launch
Eel Wier
Small Mouth
Walleye Holes
Basket
Shad Wallows
Stalker
Kellams Bridge
SR 97

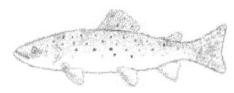

The Upper Delaware

Outfitters dot the shoreline of the river here, more than any section of the river. The canoeing action on summer weekends starts in assault-like waves around 9:00 AM ending about 4:00 PM. If you go out on a weekend between Memorial Day and several weekends after Labor Day, you must get started before the morning fog burns from the water and is replaced by the noise and never-ending tubers and canoeist. Start your fishing before the assault begins, then go out again in the evening when the traffic slows down and the fish begins to feed and provide action.

Between Hancock and Port Jervis most of the land along the bank is private and fishing from the bank on private property without permission is illegal and the officers on the water will stop you. Railroad property is also private and in most cases the railroad owns to the river's edge and you be order to leave if caught.

Because the water temperature starts to increase south of Hancock, the warm water fish begin to replace cold-water fish as you proceed southward. Trout can be still caught but the excepted southern limit is Callacoon. Any trout caught in the main branch will most likely be a holdover from another tributary because there is no stocking of trout in the Main Branch. Still the Delaware Main Branch, north of Port Jervis to Hancock, will produce the richest variety of fish in any fresh water section of the Delaware. Good fishing holes in the upper main branch are too numerous to mention by name. Instead, look for river features that will produce certain fish. Good population of walleye and pike are prevalent in deep slow moving holes that are separated by swift rapids every mile or so. In pockets of rapids and inside channels with large rocks, expect to catch small mouth bass.

This area also gets visited by striped bass, eels and other anadromous and cartadromous fish. One odd fish that is caught on a regular basis on lures and flies in the upper river is the Delaware fall fish. Fall fish have the appearance of a sucker but with a large forward facing mouth and can get very large at times. This section of the Upper Delaware between, Port Jervis to Hancock is the primary spawning area of shad, as well. This is the ideal location to fish for these creatures. The period from May through June is the season for shad in the upper river and the boat ramps will be busy with fisherman rushing to get their boats in and out of the water. In the lower sections of the River, since the water temperature has not raised enough to get them active shad move through quickly and can be hard to catch. Once in spawning grounds of the upper river, they tend to slow down and start their ritual in the shallow edges of pools in the evening. In the upper reaches of the waterway the fish starts to spread out increasing your odds of catching some.

Map 3: *Wading near the mouth Callacoon Creek is a favorite spot for locals. In periods of low flow one may have to walk the canoe or boat around the island up river of Callacoon and at the eel weir near Milepost 300. Peak shad run is in early June.*

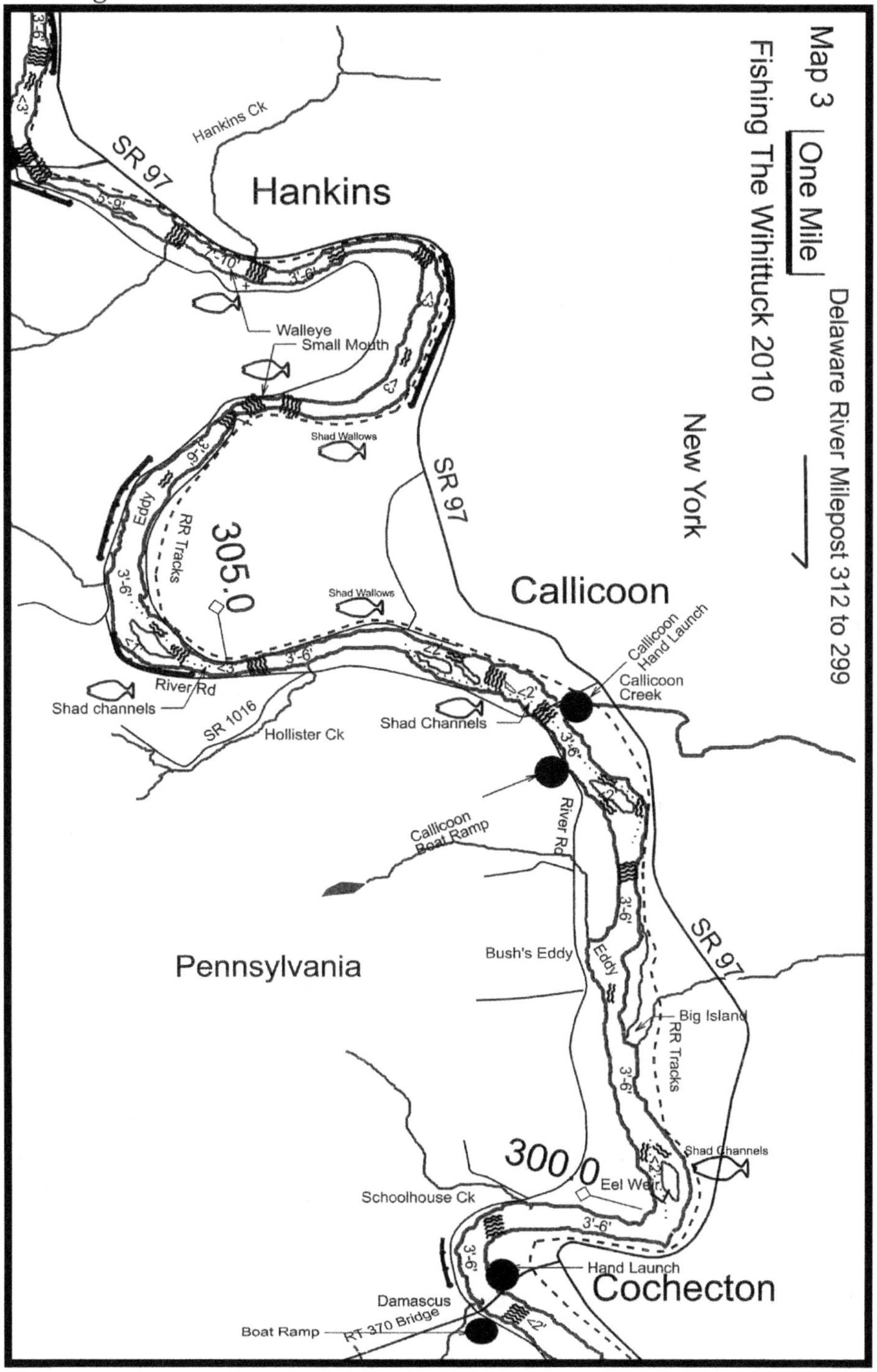

Fishing The Big D

Map 3 — One Mile
Fishing The Wihittuck 2010
Delaware River Milepost 312 to 299

The Upper Delaware

The river town of Lackawaxen, an early transportation center of canal, train and rafting traffic, has its stories of violent Indian wars and fatal train accidents, but its claim to fishing, has two noteworthy landmarks. The infamous Lackawaxen dam, built in 1828 to supply water to the D&H canal and assist with the crossing of canal boats to reach the Lackawaxen River. It was the first and only dam to completely cross the Delaware River. Commercial shad catch records correspond very well with the construction and removal of this low barrier in the early nineteenth and twentieth century [6]. The dam is not visible today but it rested just upstream of the Roebling bridge. In order for the canal company to adhere to the free navigation of the river, the dam employed a "dam keeper" that would direct and help with getting log rafts over the weir of the structure. The second important fishing fact is that this was also the home of ten world recorder holders of fishing, early western writer and movie producer, Zane Grey. His home sits at the mouth of the Lackawaxen within sight of the Roebling Bridge and at an excellent fishing hole for spring shad. His first publication was not Riders on the Purple Sage, but a short story titled "A Day on The Delaware"-1902. He wrote several short stories about fishing with his brothers in the local waters of the area. His rich colorful prose painted a rustic mountain backdrop for a simple fishing story that by today standards, seem dated. His written descriptions, which were full of color, sound and smells, which describe the valley better than any of his black and white films. He was a dentist by trade, but his passion for the outdoors and writing about it pulled him away. It was said that during his career as a writer and film director, he spent 300 days out of the year fishing [76]. On many of his later world fishing trips he brought film crews to document the events; thus making him not just a pioneer in western moving making and books but in fishing videos. He held ten world records for fish caught by rod and reel. The largest was a 1,040-pound blue marlin caught in 1930 at Tahiti. His favorite fish was the native black bass, not the recently introduced European trout. His favorite baits were shiners, hellgrammites and stonecats over flies and wooden lures. After reading his story "Fighting Qualities of Black Bass-1907" One might think he would rolled over in his grave if he heard the nickname used by locals "smallies". His early writing career did a lot to promote the area and draw anglers from New York City. The town has a museum, his former home, dedicated to him. .

Map 4; *Skinners Fall may have the steepest grade drop in the river, about 10 to 15 feet in less than quarter mile. A sign on the highway bridge just above the rapids give warning and advising people to stay to the right of center toward the Pennsylvania side. If one goes straight down the center of this channel with minor adjustments they should get through without incident. Fortunately at the base of the main channel there are no high rock lines to collect trees and there are plenty of places on both banks to de-water the craft if one becomes swamped. Access is just above the rift and several miles south. These falls may be more treacherous in low flow periods. Because this is a popular place for visitors, this rift has a high collection of drowning victims. Peak shad run is in early June.*

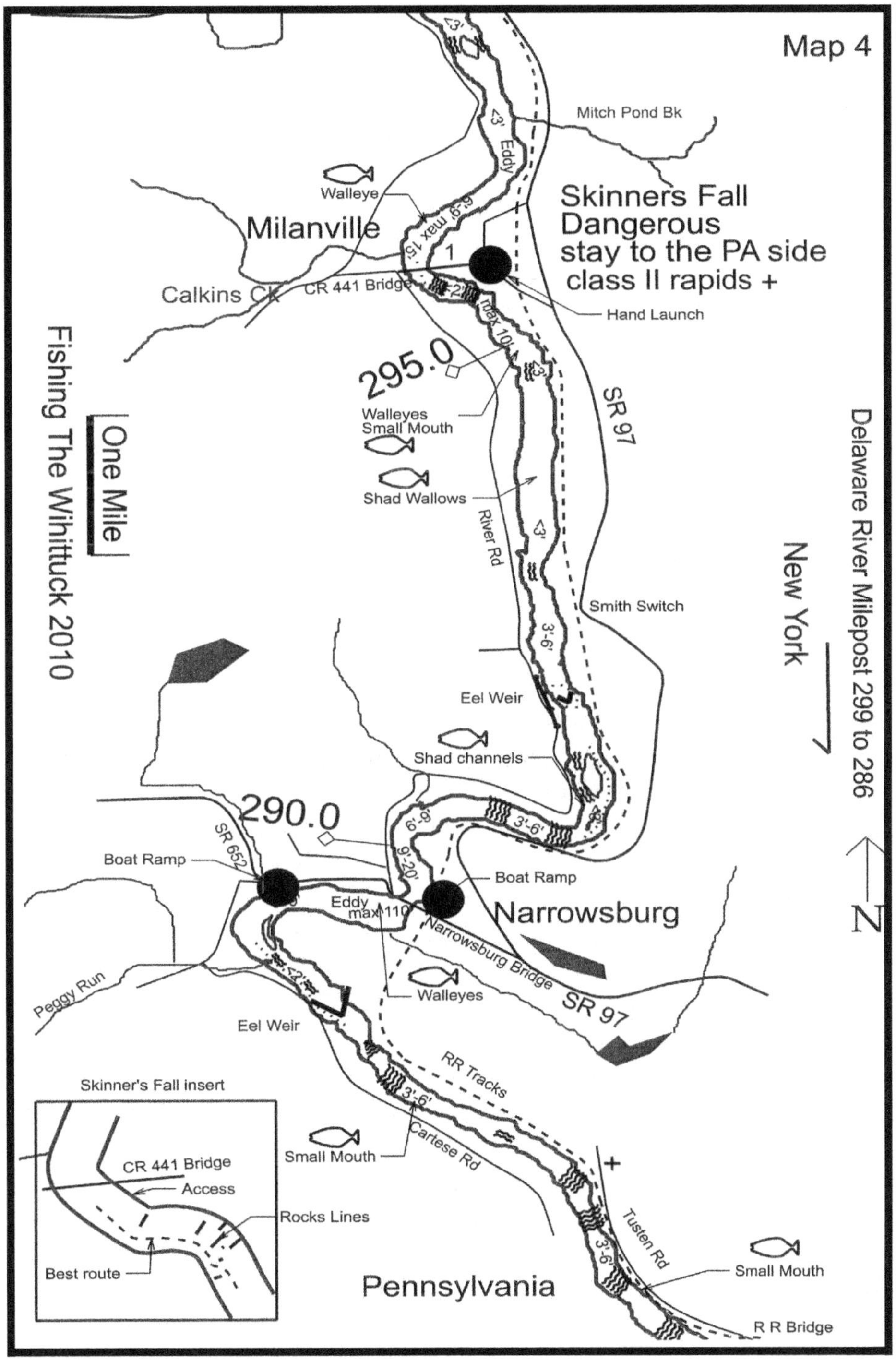
Map 4
Mitch Pond Bk
Walleye
Milanville
Skinners Fall
Dangerous
stay to the PA side
class II rapids +
Calkins Ck
CR 441 Bridge
Hand Launch
295.0
Walleyes
Small Mouth
Shad Wallows
River Rd
SR 97
Smith Switch
One Mile
Fishing The Whittuck 2010
Delaware River Milepost 299 to 286
New York
Eel Weir
Shad channels
290.0
SR 652
Boat Ramp
Boat Ramp
Eddy
Narrowsburg
N
Narrowsburg Bridge
SR 97
Peggy Run
Walleyes
Eel Weir
RR Tracks
Skinner's Fall insert
CR 441 Bridge
Access
Rocks Lines
Best route
Small Mouth
Cartese Rd
Tusten Rd
Small Mouth
Pennsylvania
R R Bridge

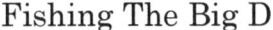

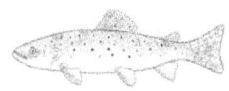

The Upper Delaware

The Trout Stream Environment

Map 5: *Three Class II Rapids make up this six mile section of River. The first starts just below a railroad bridge, five miles south of Narrowsburg New York. The rift starting at the railroad bridge is best navigated from the center of the river. The second and third Class II's rapids begin about five miles downriver and end just before entering the Lackawaxen Eddy. These rifts are made up of large boulders that create winding channels down a steep grade. During low flow these riffs are shallow and grounding is common. This section also has old stone eel weir or fish traps. Navigate outside of the V. Use Narrowsburg and Lackawaxen to enter and leave the river. This is not motor boat friendly water. Peak shad run is in early June late May*

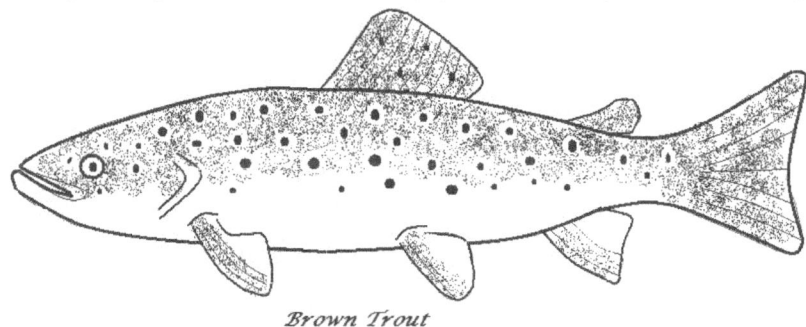

Brown Trout

The best and easiest indicator of a healthy stream is to look under rocks within the stream channel. Are there many small insect larvae clinging to the bottom of the rocks? If so, you have found a healthy water system. Insects are just as sensitive, or more so, than trout to pollution. The bottom must be stone or gravel, as a soft muddy bottom will not hold the insect population that trout require. Trout, in general, have a thermal limit of 25 degrees C (77 to 80 F) with brown trout at the high end and brooks much lower [77]. Before the water temperature even comes close to these limits, the trout will become stressed and stop feeding. Trout are active under ice and through out the winter when the eyes on one's rod freeze shut. Dissolved oxygen is very important and will decrease as water temperature increase causes stress on trout. The elements that add oxygen to water are, for the most part the same factors that keep the temperature down. Movement of water over dams, rocks, and wind action of waves increase dissolved oxygen contents and remove heat by evaporation. Thus, streams under cover of trees, with numerous waterfalls, will retain the cooler temperature. If you have underground springs inside a deep gorge, this will add a cooling effect also. Slow moving, meandering, sunny open waterways with shallow ponds will absorb heat much quicker than a fast moving mountain stream and deep lakes. The PH of the water for the best fish environment is

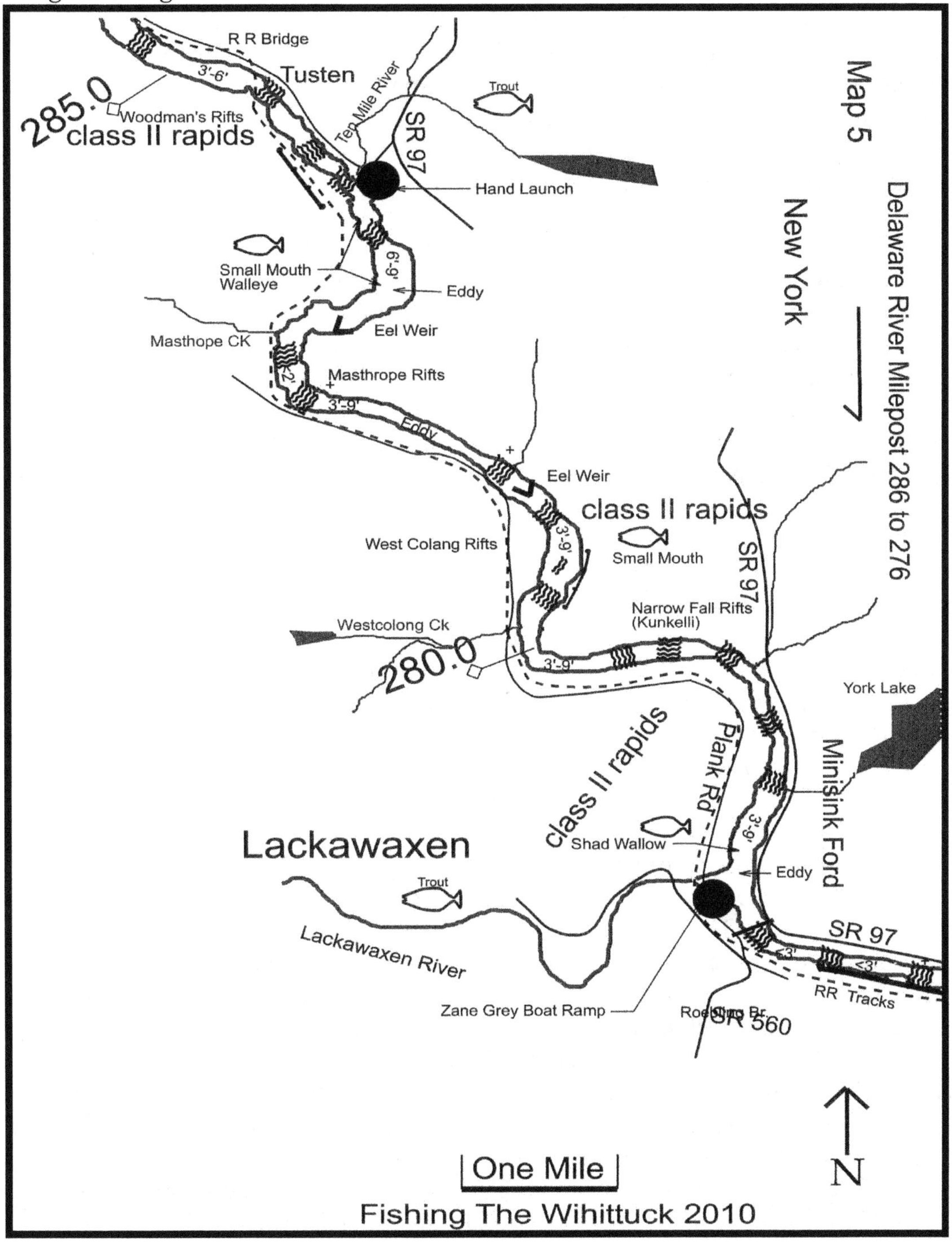

Fishing The Big D

Map 5 — Delaware River Milepost 286 to 276

Fishing The Wihittuck 2010

The Upper Delaware

between seven and six, but there are reports of trout handling a wider range although their survival will depend upon other limiting elements. Another important factor is a consistent water flow to maintain a steady population. You will hear the term in fishing circles of limestone and freestone creeks. The Upper Delaware has freestone creeks. The piedmont regions of the Delaware basin have limestone creeks. These mountains, freestone creeks have clear water with high oxygen contents. The main drawback with freestone creeks is the fluctuating water flow and temperature ranges. Hot summertime droughts or spring floods affect the fishery greatly in freestone creeks. The water temperature and flow from limestone creek is more consistent and does not fluctuate as much because of the underground sources. Limestone creeks will have high calcium carbonate, which enriches the plankton production, and is good for any fish. The water in limestone creeks is not as clear as the freestone creeks and because they flow through mostly agricultural farmland they have problems with farm runoff and blooms. You can tell a limestone creek by the bright green layer of water crest that will grow on the water surface and along it banks. Long-term consistent water flow is common for limestone creeks.

Map 6: *Several miles south of Lackawaxen is Cedar Rapid which begins at some campgrounds, this short, but brutal, rift has no set channel, just lots of rocks. Four miles south, just pass the Highway 473 bridge, at Berryville New York is the Shohola Creek rifts. This one is longer with a defined channel on the right side of the river. From Lackawaxen to Pond Eddy is a good mixture of slow moving eddies, fast moving channels, eel weir, and fantastic mountain views. With the many rafting companies and youth campgrounds here, this section of the river has heavy traffic on summer weekend. Peak shad run is in early June late May.*

Brook Trout

Only the brook trout is native to this region, all other trout were introduced in the late 1800s. . State stocking of brooks trout have dropped in recent years due to the short life span of the stocked brook and the threat of problems with genetically alternating of the native fish [121]. The native brooks were smaller, darker with highly bright orange bottoms compared to the stocked fished. Today it's a treat to pull one of these beautiful fish from a stream and as such it must be returned. These small, dark, olive colored fish are sometimes called speckled trout for their white, tan and red spots on the fish's flank. The fish also has bright red fins separated by black band and white tipped fins. Most native brooks will not meet the state's minimum size requirement anyway. Brooks need cool and clean water such as what one would expect to find at the upper limits of a stream. Good wild native brook streams are small, shallow creeks, not heavy fished, usually because of lack of access by the general public. They spawn in the fall in the lower section of the stream in pools with small gravel beds where the eggs cling to the rocks. After the eggs are fertilized, the adult brooks will remain in the lower deep sections of the creeks to sit out the winter.

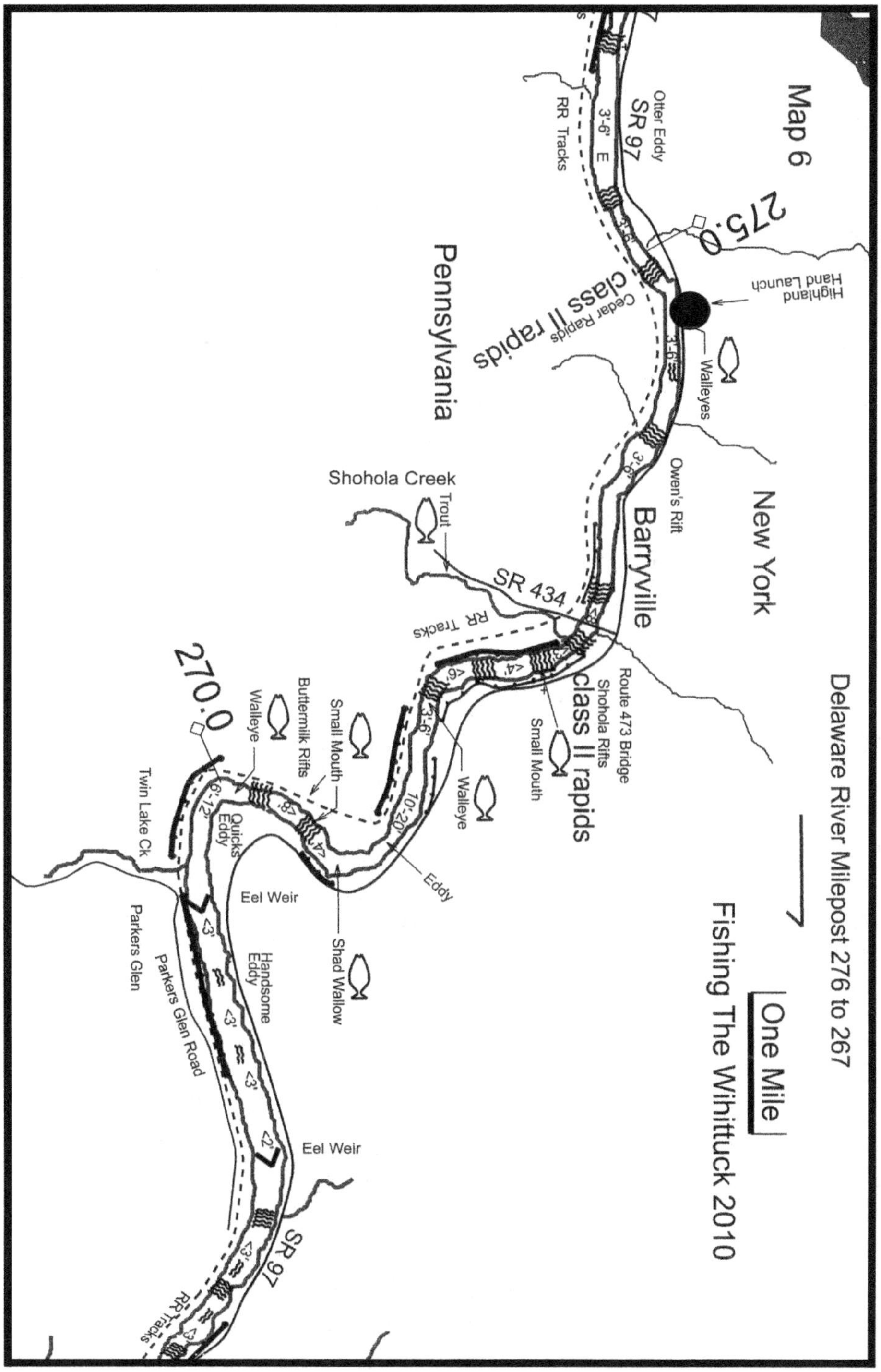
Map 6
Delaware River Milepost 276 to 267
Fishing The Wihittuck 2010
One Mile
New York
Pennsylvania
275.0
270.0
Otter Eddy
SR 97
RR Tracks
Highland Hand Launch
Cedar Rapids
class II rapids
Walleyes
Owen's Rift
Barryville
Shohola Creek
Trout
SR 434
RR Tracks
Route 473 Bridge
Shohola Rifts
class II rapids
Small Mouth
Walleye
Small Mouth
Buttermilk Rifts
Walleye
Eddy
Quicks Eddy
Twin Lake Ck
Eel Weir
Shad Wallow
Handsome Eddy
Parkers Glen Road
Parkers Glen
Eel Weir
SR 97
RR Tracks

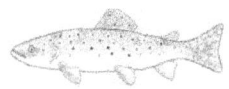

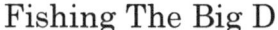

The Upper Delaware

In the spring, the fish move back upstream. They love streams with lots of overhanging brush that provide shade, along with its source of insects and cover. These brushy streams may require an angler to travel on his knees to transverse its length. The most distinguished give away of the brooks present in such a stream is the quick darting action of a shadow as they head for cover or hit your lure.

Rainbow trout

These colorful fish are native to the Western Pacific North America basins. The pink and red bands on their light colored sides can easily identify them. They can grow slightly larger and can tolerate warmer water than brooks can. These trout are noted to be better dancers when hooked. Rainbows can live in lakes as well as streams and will grow to 15-20 pounds or more in large lakes. In the Great Lake basin rainbows that live in the lakes are called steel heads. The Pennsylvania State Record for a rainbow came from the Jordan Creek off the Lehigh River in 1986 at 15 pounds 6.25 oz [1]. While brooks and browns spawn in the fall, rainbows spawn in the spring and, like brooks and browns, will move into shallow gravel bottom streams to lay their eggs in prepared nests, called redds. Once the eggs are laid, the fish leave the nest. The hatching time of the eggs is dependent on the water temperature, not the time of year so all trout eggs brook, brown, and rainbows will hatch at the sometime [121]. Rainbow that migrate to large lakes open to the sea or live in saltwater are called steelheads

Map 7: *A good collection of rapids begin downstream of Pond Eddy, New York and end at a Railroad bridge near Sparrowbush, New York in a gorge called Hawks Nest. This six mile run is by far the most enjoyable ride on the entire Delaware River. It has few eddies to slow the trip making it one of the fastest flowing parts of the river. Many of the rifts in this section have names. The most dangerous is just past the mouth of the Mongaup River. This section is heavily used by rafting companies so on summer weekends this is a busy place, which can lead to injuries. One can easily do all of the rifts between Lackawaxen and Port Jervis in a day. Peak shad run is in May.*

Brown Trout

These are the bread and butter fish of the state-stocking inventory. They can tolerate warmer water, grow faster, live longer, and get larger than other stream stock trout. For that reason, they are the most prevalent trout stocked. Despite local protest, these fish were brought over from Western Europe in the second half of the 1800's. Since then, they have done very well in our streams and lakes. In streams, the truly large ones will max out at two pounds but still tend to be slightly larger than the other trout. In lakes, they can grow larger than rainbows with the New York State Record at 33 pounds 2 oz taken in at Lake Ontario. In the fall, the large lake fish will travel up stream and spawn, providing an exciting experience for a lone cold fly-fisherman.

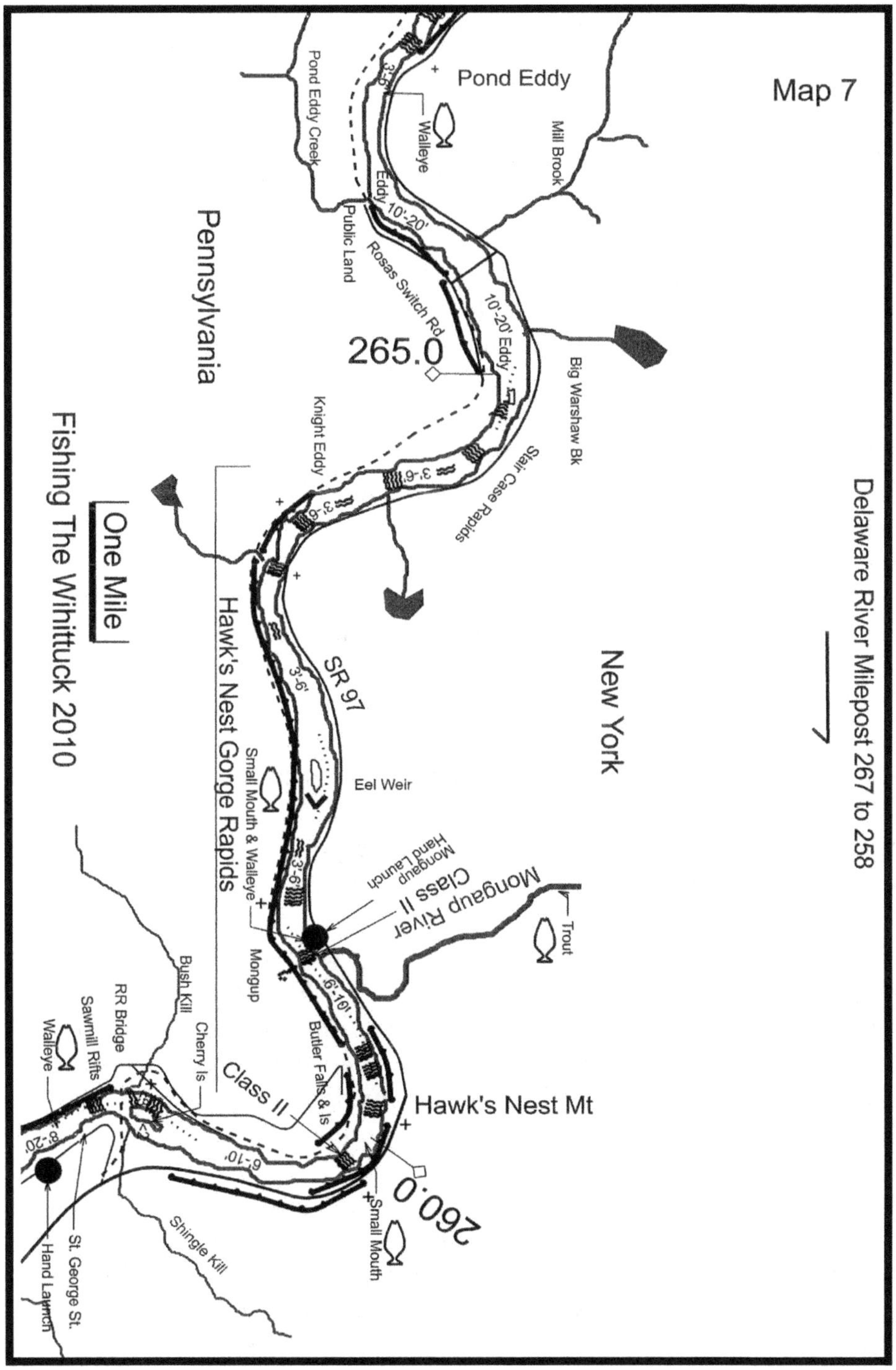

Fishing The Big D

Map 7 — Delaware River Milepost 267 to 258

Fishing The Wihittuck 2010

The Upper Delaware

These fish are selective eaters and can tolerate stronger fishing pressure than brooks and rainbows. Whereas brooks tend to inhabit the upper sections of creeks, browns tend to do well in the lower sections [121]. Like Steelhead there is a Sea Brown trout that can live in saltwater.

Lake Trout

Although these fish are native to North America, they are not to the Delaware Valley. The Merrill Creek Reservoir in northern New Jersey and the New York City Reservoir are rumored to have these fish. As the name implies, these fish, live in deep clean lakes. They can be easily identified from other trout by their fork tail fin. They can grow up to 15 pounds with a New Jersey record of 32 pounds 8 oz taken in Round Valley Reservoir [3]. Unlike other trout that can live only a few years, these fish can live up to 20 years. Lake trout spawn in the spring near shorelines on gravel without making nest. After ice-out, they can be caught near the surface or shoreline but as the lake warms, they go deep. The preferred method of catching these fish is by deep trolling with downriggers or heavy weighted lines [121].

When we say that the upper Delaware is the birthplace of American Fly Fishing, you must understand the relationship with the development of the fly rod, which took place here. The early development and manufacturing of rods by several local firms began in this valley. The most notable and still in production, H. L. Leonard Rod Company which started around the 1860's, was one of several local companies that capitalized on the sport. The early rods were made of strips of bamboo glued together to form a hexagonal blank. The cost, maintenance, and care of these rods restricted its use to the rich or the most dedicated angler. Bamboo rods can still be ordered but the cost is still restrictive to the most dedicated and purest of fly-fisherman. With the development of fiberglass rod in the 1950's, the sport became popular. The rods today are mostly graphite, which are lighter and faster over the fiberglass.

Map 8: After *leaving the gorge one should take a jump into the river at Elephant feet cliff. Here the River slow down and enters the Minisink Valley. The channel makes a sharp turn southward and flows into the bank of an old, but scenic, cemetery. A stop under the highway bridge I-84 is a nice place to view the scenic river's turn, tri point rock and an impressive collection of cemetery monuments. At the end of Mashipacong island begins the Delaware National park. Peak shad run is in May.*

To understand fly-fishing for any fish, you must understand the bait you are imitating. Flies are classified in into three types. The first is the traditional dry fly, made from feathers and hair that have natural floating capabilities. The object of this is to imitate the natural aerial hatch cycle of the wing stage of aquatic insects. The second type of fly is the wet fly, non-floating, nymph stage of the aquatic insects. The wet fly

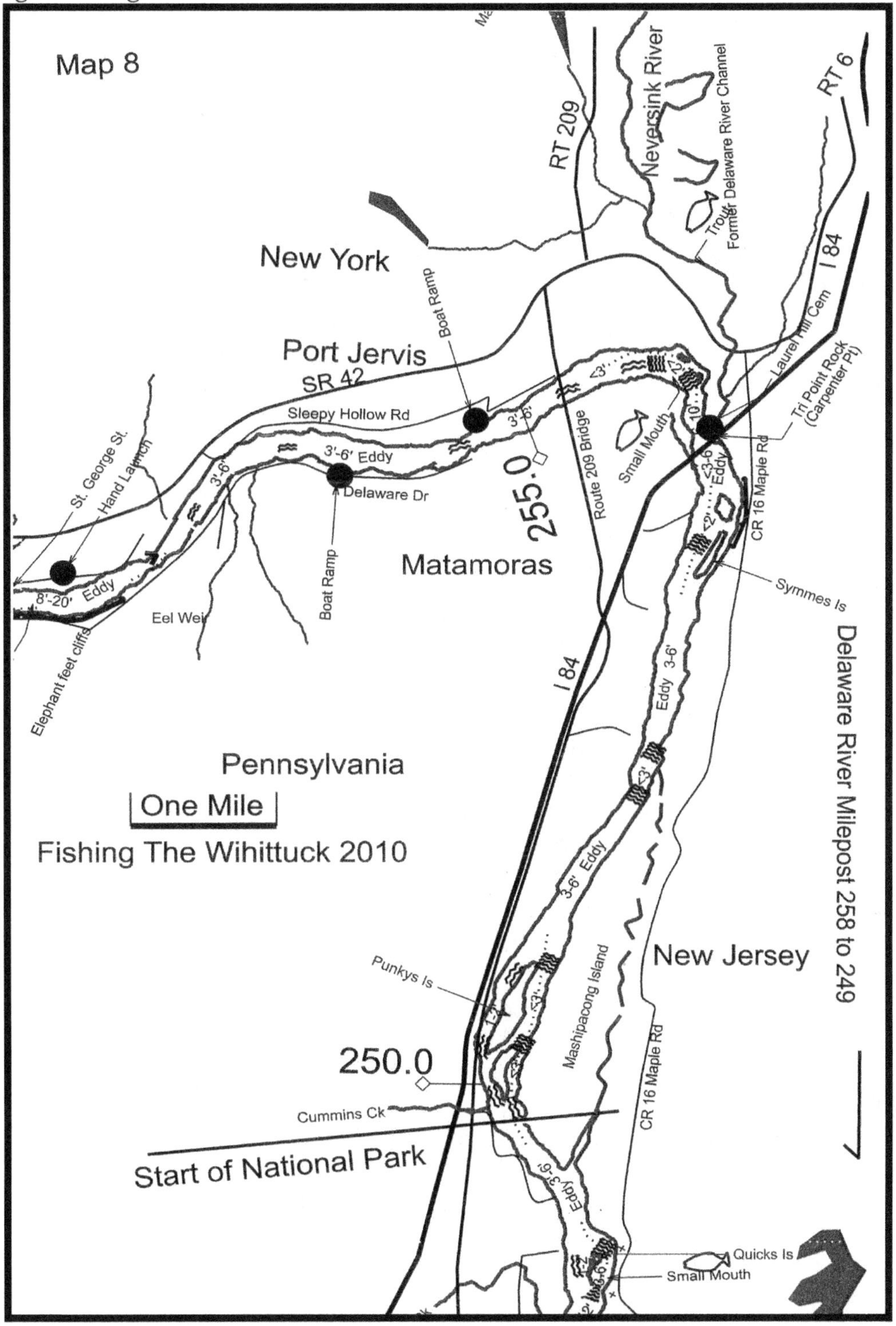
Map 8
New York
Port Jervis
SR 42
Sleepy Hollow Rd
Boat Ramp
RT 209
Neversink River
Former Delaware River Channel
Trout
RT 6
I 84
Laurel Hill Cem
Tri Point Rock (Carpenter Pt)
St. George St.
Hand Launch
8'-20' Eddy
Elephant feet cliffs
Eel Weir
3'-6' Eddy
Delaware Dr
Boat Ramp
255.0
Route 209 Bridge
Small Mouth
CR 16 Maple Rd
Matamoras
Symmes Is
Delaware River Milepost 258 to 249
I 84
Eddy 3-6'
Pennsylvania
One Mile
Fishing The Wihittuck 2010
3-6' Eddy
New Jersey
Punkys Is
Mashipacong Island
250.0
Cummins Ck
CR 16 Maple Rd
Start of National Park
Eddy
Quicks Is
Small Mouth

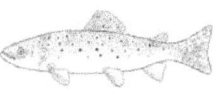

The Upper Delaware
is best used when the flying hatch is not in process. Using nymph fly, may be the bread and butter technique for catching trout for this is the longest stage in the insect's life. As in aerial hatches, you can also have under water hatches as well and trout can be just as selective with that. The third type is called the non-aquatic insect imitations. These would be flies presented as minnow, crayfish, grasshopper, and ants, and are presented completely different. Always remember this, that during a heavy insect hatch, aerial or underwater, trout and bass will be very selective and the only object they go for is a fly that mimics the present hatch. When the fish are feeding the surface, they are not jumping into the air but rather swimming just near the surface.

It's not the scope of this book to cover the all the aspect of fly fishing. One doesn't need a PHD in aquatic insect growth to understand hatches, fly types and casting skills. But a basic understand and instructions in the sport will save hours of frustrations. A typical cheap fly rod combo set with green floating line bought at the local department store will do find for the beginner who should start out dipping nymphs and stripping streamers. For the more advance levels of laying dry flies on the surface, weight forward floating line, a faster rod and instructions are needed. Good fly fishermen learn to observes, they will spend more time watching for rising fish and what they are eating than the act of casting for them. For using dry flies on the surface an aquatic insect hatch must be in progress. There are names for these hatches that correspond to the name of fly that should be used such as Trico, Henderson, Sulfur and Olivers. The most import thing to learn is to match the hatch. Look for small gulp on the surface of water indicating a rising trout, not the big splash of a small mouth bass or a carp. Look for the rise and gulp to repeat and noticing what it's going for each time. Once a patterned has established than it's a matter of skill to lay the selected fly several feet up stream of the hungry trout and at the same time not spook it with a bad cast or sloppy movement. A dry fly cast is a long cast to a small target where the primary object is to lay the tippet or leader straight on the water, not in a ball. If one spooks the fish with a bad cast be patience and don't move, it may forget you're there and start feeding again. Most of the time you will not see flies floating down the creek in large numbers with raising trout. In times like that one needs to learn to cast nymphs or streamers. Casting nymphs is not really a cast but a short dip and retrieve process where one is on top of the fish

	March	April	May	June	July	August	September	October	November
Quill Gordin		●	●						
Blue Gordin			●	●					
Blue Quill		●							
Hendrickson		●	●						
Tan Caddis		●	●	●	●	●			
March Brown			●						
Sulfur Color May Files			●	●					
Light Cahill			●	●					
Streamer Flies		●	●	●	●	●	●		
Gray Fox			●	●					
Green Drake			●						
Winged Olivers				●					

Fishing The Big D

and waits for the trout to suck up the down stream floating nymph. The require skill here is not casting but to detect a hit before the fish spits out the hook. Many use indicators or small bobbers and keep the cast short to feels the hit. To determine the type of nymph to use a small hand net is used to sample the bottom aquatic life. The most productive nymphs are the flies with a gold ball at the eye of the hook. Striping streamers, like nymph is used when there is no surface hatch going on. All game fish like to chase bait and here the fly is thrown out and retrieved by hand in order to get a strike. The serious fly streaming angler will use weight forward sinking line with a small hip bucket to store the line.

The American Eel

Anuilla *rostrata*

The American eel may not be the most desirable game fish to be caught in the Delaware River but its secretive life and impact on the valley is an amazing story that needs to be told. The world record American Eel (9lbs 4oz) was caught off Cape May on November 9, 1995 by Jeff Pennick. Much is written about the important of river herring in our early history but it was eels and catfish that fed people all year long. In the procurement of this fin-fish, early man may have modified the landscape and channels of the river more than one might think.

Truly, we don't understand these fish and the water environment they live in. This fish has broken all of the rules, or at least the rules that we make. Eels were an important food source in early American and still are today but on a much smaller scale Eels are netted in the open ocean, trapped in the bay with wire baskets, or caught in fish weirs on the upper river where they are sold overseas or used for bait. Eels, having an economic value, should make it easy to measure, record and track the population but, like the secretive life of the eel themselves, catches are not always recorded. In Maryland and Virginia the heights of catches in 1981 was 700,000 pounds but it has been decreasing every since. It has not been determined if the reduction was a reflection in the population or a drop in demanded from Europe and Asia. Every year the US Fishing and Wildlife Service consider placing these fish on the Endangered Species List [14]. Putting the American eel on the endangered species list would create a major hurdle for any new hydroelectric power plans.

The Upper Delaware

Eels are classified as Caradromous, which means a fish born in the ocean, matures in freshwater and then returns back to saltwater. Amazingly the New Jersey State record size eel weighed in at six pounds thirteen ounces and caught at Round Valley Reservoir in 2005 [3]. In the spring small 6-inch eels have been observed slithering over and around the dams, explaining how they get into isolated water bodies. The American eel begins its life in the windless stagnate weed full Sargasso Sea. This warm body of water lies in the middle of the Atlantic Ocean where it received the name " horse's latitude". The name "horse's latitude", came from mariners who sailed ships got stranded, and had to rely on rowing sailors and swimming horses to help them move through it. This windless sea is where the eggs of eels hatch and begin the slow drift in the anticyclone circulation of the Atlantic Ocean. Today the Sargasso Sea is a cesspool of our technology in plastic material that does not degrade like normal trash. The sea is full of floating plastics and what it brings to the future of eels is anyone guess. The larvae are transparent and will slowly take the shape of their parents as they move from the Sargasso Sea. At this early transparent stage, they are called grass eels. Already at this age, a strong Asian demand supports commercial netting. Within a year in this slow clockwise drift halfway across the Atlantic, they begin to develop a yellow green pigment. After several months they are ready to swim on their own and will soon find themselves in the bays of the Northeastern United States as "elvers" or juveniles eels. The yellow "elvers" will begin their slow growth to maturity in both brackish and fresh water. Some, mostly females, will begin their journey up the freshwater rivers while others, mostly males will remain in the estuaries. The color of the eel will signify its maturity. Fully mature eels will be bronze to black on the top with silver undersides. The length of time to reach maturity can be as much as 40 years for fresh water females, and three years for the brackish water males. In the fall, large sexually mature female eels and the smaller male eels will start their journey back to the ocean. These females can reach the length of five feet at the fully mature stage while the males may average two feet. As some anadromous fish do, eels refrain from eating during spawning runs. The American eel is believed to do the same. The route back to the Sargasso Sea is longer for the eels for now have to fight the current. The route could be a direct route, which would mean it would have to fight the current to the Mid Atlantic Ocean or a slow and longer route that would permit the eel to drift to the Eastern Atlantic Ocean and then back to the Mid Atlantic Ocean by following the Atlantic Gulf Stream.

Because the American Eel is mostly a long fin it is lousily classified as a member of a group of fish called fin-fish which are made up of ling. Eels are basically nocturnal feeders that live on a variety of food including insects, mollusks, worms and minnows. They prefer to hide during the day under cover and come out looking for food at night. A strong light shone into the water at night can attract the smaller ones in great number. The eel has a relatively small jaw but can tear food from a larger source by spinning their bodies at a rate of six to 14 spins per second. They also have a mucous layer

Fishing The Big D

covering their entire body which makes them impossible to hold with the bare hand. This mucous layer also permits them to slide across ground and can move with ease across grassy surface. The term "slippery as an eel" is well defined when trying to handle one with your bare hands. The eel's ability to twist it body rapidly will enable it to wrap itself around your arm and generally make a complete mess of your boat, equipment and nerves when trying to remove the hook from its boney mouth. The mouth of an eel is such that getting a hook out of it is almost impossible. Its best to just cut the hook with wire cutters and remove it that way or cut the line and leave the hook in place to rust out at a later date. Most eels are caught during night by fisherman going for catfish. The process is simple: just throw a baited line out in a deep hole and wait. These fish normally don't hit lures but prefer stink-bait like chicken liver, dead minnow, and worms. Hooks for these fish tend to be on the small size of # 6-8. Because of the eels, appearance and behavior when caught, most fisherman want nothing to do with them.

On the none-tidal river, eels were traditional trapped in reversed V-shaped rock dam called an eel weir. A weir is the part of the dam where water flows over the top. I believe many of the islands and present wing-dams we see on the river today had their foundation laid from such structures. These dams have always been controversial because they infringe on the movement of other migratory fish as well as navigation. Today a small group of individuals still operate these facilities from the New York side of the upper river, since such practices and structures are illegal in Pennsylvania and New Jersey. Even though these traps are a hazard to recreational traffic I suspect that the State of New York still permits them out of a concern to keep alive a traditional fishing method. Today as yesterday, they acted as choke point for drifting boats, where they funneled river traffic to a wooden box. At the base of the V an upward angled wooden trough is built with several open slots for the fish to fall into. A wood box is placed beside the trough where the fish are collected. The box is move up and down the trough based on the water level. At the end of the trough a net might be placed to catch more fish. At the heights of the fall eel migration, the amount of trap eels can be so great that people have to stay all night in order to empty the box and protect their catch. It is labor-intensive and dangerous work to maintain the structures. Every spring the box and trough has to be rebuilt because winter ice will destroy it. Every few years the rocks elevation might have to be increased because of the collection of upstream gravel.

Eels are sold to local ethnic demand and are one of the seven fish that Catholics must eat on Christmas Eve. It can't be the money that drives people to operate these weirs but the excitement of a good haul and the love of the river

The Upper Delaware

Port Jervis to the Gap

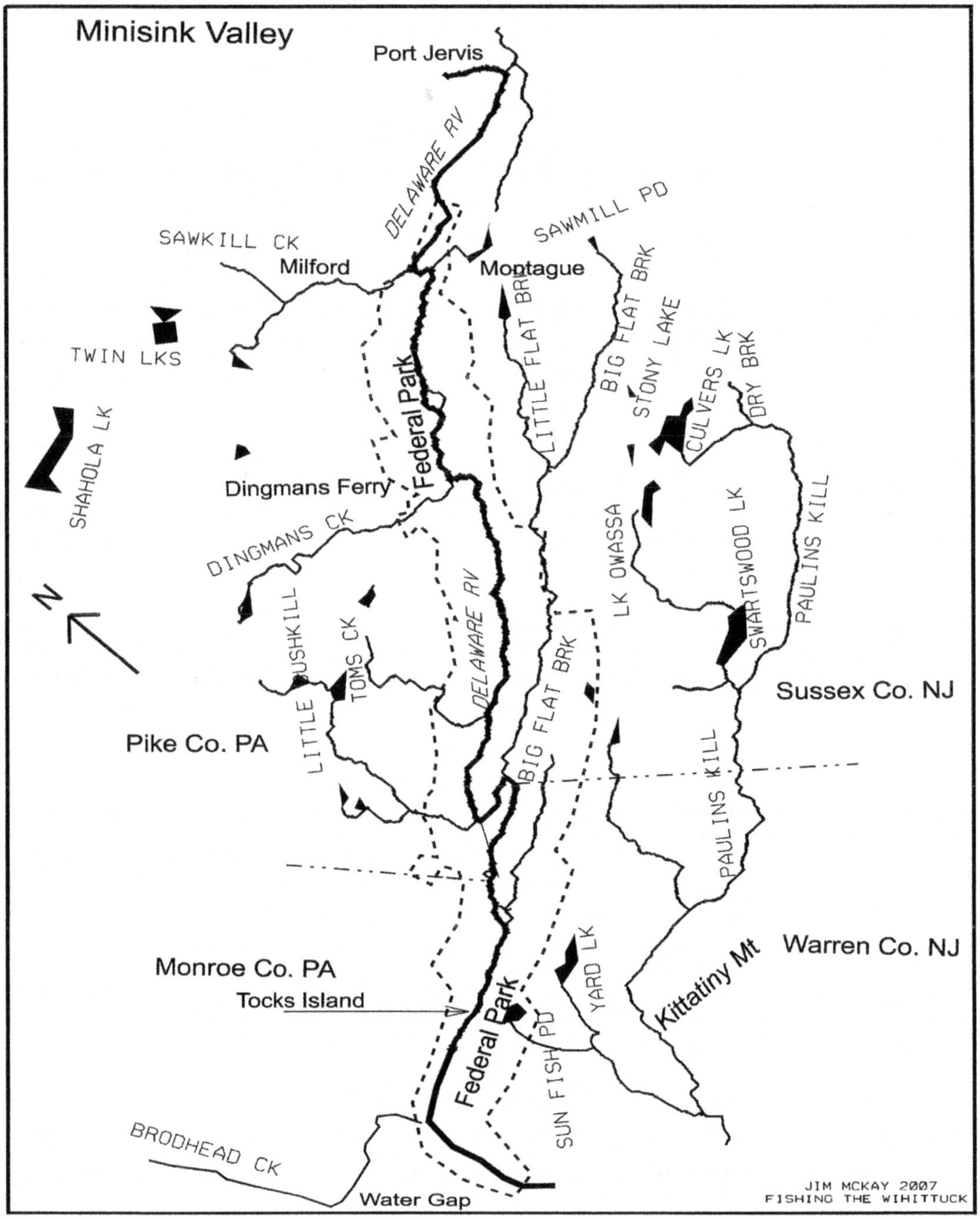

Fishing The Big D

When the river reaches Port Jervis, it enters a new phase. It is here that the river makes a permanent change in direct from its eastward flow to a southward flow and into a new valley with different characteristics. The geology of this valley speaks perfectly of a waterway that is different than it is today. Based on the depth of the soil bank in the fields above the river, at one time, before the Gap opened, the flow was slow and possibly northward resulting in a long north-south lake. When the ice melted 15,000 years ago, with the southern gap open, this river valley must have been a raceway of flash floods from glacial melting. The profile of the Valley as it winds its way southward take the shape of a U-type valley. The bottom portion of the valley has a flat grade in the center containing rich flat farmland, low hills and the river. While on the edges of the valley, the grade and land turns sharply upwards revealing a continuous vertical rock wall just below the crest of the ridges. Occasional tributaries that drop from the surrounding mountains break this U-shape valley scene. Within the merging tributaries ravines one can always discover a trail leading to a waterfall hidden deep inside the forest.

Here the pools or eddies are long, slow and deep separated by islands with mild rapids. As such expect the bass to be fewer but bigger. This section is ideal for canoeist and kayakers who like a lazy journey through a quite beautiful river valley in search of a camp site along the river's banks. When the valley funnels wind from the south padding downstream can become work. At one time a steam boat even operated here. As can be expected, this section of the river through the Federal Park provides an enjoyable journey around the many islands that abound here. At the beginning and end of each island, where the water converges or separates, one can find shallow rapids with down stream holes. The average speed of drift through here is about 1.5 miles per hour, much slower than the section upstream from Port Jervis. This part of the river is a better choice to boat or drift for fish in low summer time water flows. One can get caught walking the boat or canoe over short stretches of shallow water and rocks if taken the wrong channel around an island. Most of the main channels are on the west side of the islands. The bottom is mostly gravel with a uniform pool depth of six-ten feet, with some pockets of exposed bedrock, mostly on the New Jersey side of the river. Unlike the section between Narrowsburg and Port Jervis, river access is everywhere here, with plenty of parking and walking trails along the banks. Most of the boat access ramps are spaced about five miles apart. Primitive camping on the park is permitted in selected areas without

```
WELCOME TO.........
TAX ISLAND DAM
DOLLAR-WEAR NAT'L
WEAK AREA
   • YOU PAY
   • NATURE STAGGERS
   • INDUSTRY
     PROFITS
```

The Upper Delaware

reservations. On the Pennsylvania side, miles of flat farm fields, owned and leased out by the federal government, line the valley floor, and in the fall provide an ideal place to walk with a shotgun in search for pheasant and woodland grouse. On the New Jersey side, the bank runs up to the toe of the mountain slopes through most of the valley. With the many channels that flow through the riverbank it's hard to determine what state you are in. The state line follows the main channel of the river, thus making most of the island in New Jersey.

In 1960, [4] the Tocks Island Dam Project was started which meant that this Valley would be flooded. This was not a new idea, or a knee-jerk reaction to the 1955 flood that killed a 100 people but a dream started as far back as the 1930's to dam the Delaware River. This was the biggest Army Corp of Engineers job east of the Mississippi at the time. In fact, once done, the lake would be 37 miles long and visible from outer space. At first only 12,000 acres was purchased, but as projects go, so did the budget. In the end, the Government bought 70,000 acres. Plans called that the lake would draw 700 million visitors a year. The dam was never built and the 700 million visitors per year never came.

The organized protest that killed the dam was started by fish but not the migratory shad and striped bass that traveled the river but the local black bass, pickerel and pan fish that lived in a pond just above Tocks Island. Large tracts of land including Tocks Island and a small glacial lake called sunfish pond were owned by the Walton family. This was the same family that the New Jersey State Park would be named for. Sunfish pond lacked the collection of cheap summer cottages along its bank. Beside its scenic qualities, it was an ideal place for the power companies to build a peak power reservoir. During peak power demands, the lake would be drain quickly to drive emergency generators and be refilled later. The State bought the pond in 1960 and sold it to the power companies a year later. Before selling the lake the New Jersey game commission, not knowing it was to be sold, poison the pond to make room for none native brown trout. The Lenni-Lenape League group claimed 1,000 pounds of native fish were killed by the State. Feeling akin to the concept of removing native life for non-native life the local people join the Indians League in protesting the process. Every year during the propose dam building years the Lenni-Lenape League organized a protest march to the lake. On several of these marches retired Supreme Court Justice Holmes joined in the march to "Pox the Tocks". Sunfish pond was the start of the act to dump the project.

"The River is more than an amenity, it is a treasure. It offers a necessity of life that must be rationed among those who have power over it."
Supreme Court Justice Oliver Weddell Holmes ruling on New Jersey vs New York
1931

Fishing The Big D

It is not the scope of this book to go into detail about the failed Tocks Island dam project. It may have been a bad ideal to begin with. Most of the deaths of the 1955 flood happen on the Brodhead Creek at a church camp site, which was caused by small private dam failures which were use to hold trout and private swimming holes. The water quality of the proposed Minisink Lake was question along with the dam's foundation and cost benefits. Granted, a new super lake on the river would have brought more recreation fishing hours but it would have destroyed the unique fishery of the last free flowing river on the Northeast. By the mid 70's most of the proposed water control projects were completed or near completion on the tributaries of the Delaware. The only project missing from the grand 50 year plan to dam and harness the Delaware River was Tocks Island.

Credit for the dam's failure to be built should be given to the thousands of protester, increasing environmental laws and irresponsible government spending. In 1975, a vote by all states involved turned down the dam projected by a single vote. But Pennsylvania continued to promote the dam's construction. The final death bell for the dam rang on June 5, 1976 when the earthen Teton Dam in Idaho, collapsed while being filled. Both dams had problems with sub-base material: the Teton had volcanic ash and the Delaware had alluvia soil and glacial till. The major difference between the two was the Teton was a rural river and the Delaware was an urban river. The failure of the Teton caused the death of 11 people and 13,000 head of cattle. The Teton dam failure marked the end of the Federal government dam building programs like Tocks Island.

To make judgment on the failure to flood the valley and develop it into a mega tourist vacation spot one needs to compare a weekend journey thru the congest urban strip malls of Marshall Creek's RT 209 and then float the isolated river.

River Herring

Some use the term river herring to apply to five basic herring's type fish, blue back, alewife, hickory shad, gizzard shad and the larger American Shad. There are over 200 species of herring. Common saltwater herring are anchovies, sardines, and menhaden. Many members of this large herring family can survive in both fresh and salt water. They are generally fish that live in schools. The common attributes of herring are uniform scales, long flat bodies, bony, silver in color with some spots, soft dorsal fin, fork tail, large eyes, upward protruding lower jaw with no clearly defined lateral line. They reproduce rapidly and have a short life span thus making them a perfect bait fish. Because of this generic description of a herring, classify these fish is confusing and many commonly used names are incorrect or misleading. Before man harness the rivers for power to move canal boats up river, cut wood and grind flower the rivers was full of herring in the spring and early summer. These fish were a diet stable for early Americans in the spring. Many a life was saved from spring starvation by these fish.

The Upper Delaware

Blue back and alewives herring are small 3 to 4 inch fish that were commonly used as bait for striped bass but today it is illegal. They follow the main run of the larger American shad up the river. A marine biologist with a knife can distinguish the different between the two. The blue back has a darker color interior lining than the alewives. Alewives also can live in fresh water their entire life and because of that are stocked in fresh water as bait fish. Both spawn in the spring on firm bottom when the water temperature gets in the 60 degree reach and eggs hatch at 70 degrees. On good runs the fish were so thick at wing dams that one can net them. The presents of these fish are an indication that other bigger fish might be present. The most common way to catch them seems to be with a string of small golden color hooks. Because they school in such dense formation snagging seem to be the most efficient means of hooking.

The fighting spirit of the Hickory shad marks it as a game fish. The Pennsylvania game commission has the fish on the endangered list. The most common place to caught hickory shad is not the Delaware but the Susquehanna River. The hickory is a migratory herring that travels from salt to fresh water to spawn. They range in size from 12 to 15 inches. They can be distinguished by the wedged shape cross section of the fish. Hickory shad hit small darts and once hooked they will dance on the water like fresh water bass.

Map 9: This is in the Federal Park and river access is every where. As such procession of fishing Licenses and rules are aggressively enforced. This is an excellent place to launch a canoe full of camping gear and not worry over losing it in rapids. Many primitive camp sites can be found in this section of the River. Peak shad run is in May.

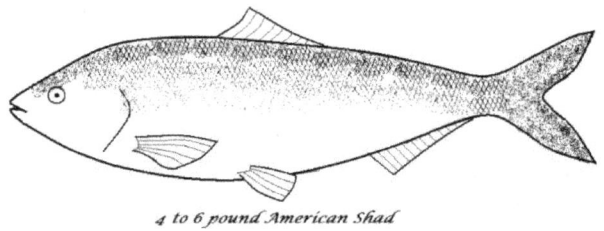

4 to 6 pound American Shad

The American Shad
No other fish's history comes closer to our heritage than the American Shad.

The Lower Delaware has an excellent gradual salinity mixing zone which permits the herring to adjust to the change. The lower non-tidal river is still open with deep well defined channels for the fish to travel in. The upper river has lots of shallow pools for the fish to spawn and deep slow moving pools along the way for the fish to rest at night.

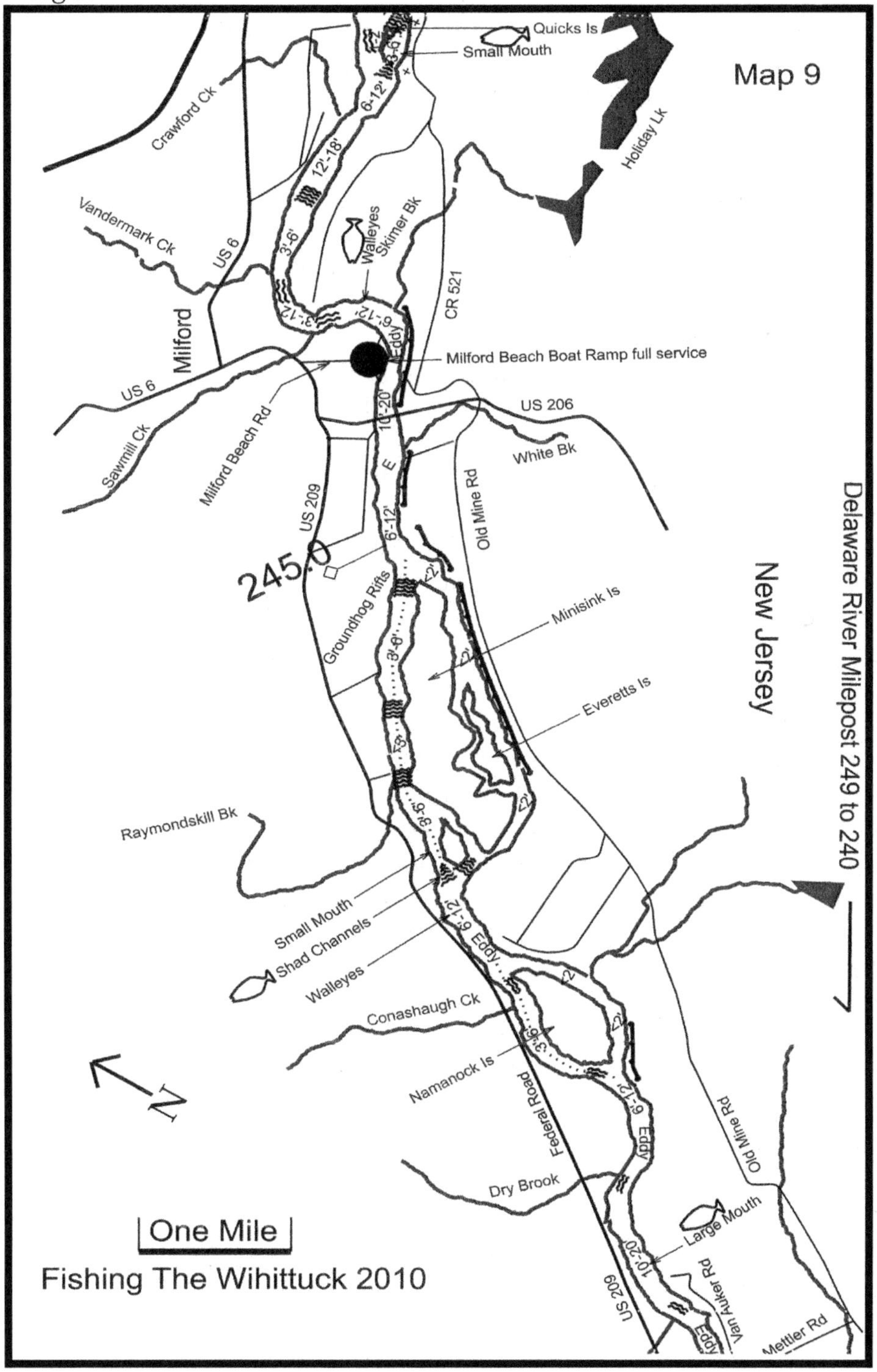
Map 9
Quicks Is
Small Mouth
Holiday Lk
Crawford Ck
Vandermark Ck
US 6
Walleyes
Skimer Bk
CR 521
Milford
Milford Beach Boat Ramp full service
US 6
US 206
Sawmill Ck
Milford Beach Rd
White Bk
US 209
Old Mine Rd
245.0
Groundhog Rifts
Minisink Is
Everetts Is
New Jersey
Delaware River Milepost 249 to 240
Raymondskill Bk
Small Mouth
Shad Channels
Walleyes
Conashaugh Ck
Namanock Is
Federal Road
Dry Brook
Large Mouth
Old Mine Rd
Van Auker Rd
Mettler Rd
US 209
One Mile
Fishing The Wihittuck 2010

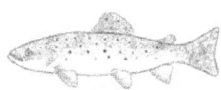

The Upper Delaware

Map 10: *In the month of May this is a prime location to land shad along the bank in the evening in shallow slow moving pools. They congregate in great numbers on this section of the River. The slow deep pools make this section an easy place to seek shad by small 12' motor boats.*

One can research shad and find stories of how the fish changed our history, but nothing attracted more attention and belief than a story that appeared in 1938 by a Harry Emerson Wildes. He described an Army near starvation at Valley Forge in the early winter months of 1778, which might be the only part of the story that could be true. In the story, the army suddenly found thousand of shad in the shallow cold waters of the Schuylkill River that ran by the encampment in February. He described in detail how the fish were cornered by the cavalry and corralled into nets which enabled the men to feast for weeks on the bounty that was sent to them. This appealing story of how the American shad saved the Army and won the war reappeared in several versions over the following centuries but no references were revealed for the sources of this fish story. Joseph Lee Boyle a historian for the Valley Forge Park researched this legend and found no documentation in any journals or letters of the time to support it. In fact, the British had blocked the river with nets hung from a floating bridge on the Schuylkill River to prevent such an event, and the cavalry units were not at the site at that time. General Washington was also returning empty wood barrels for more fish. In the letters and journals, it became apparent that salted fish was an important food for the soldiers. Today as in the pass shad are netted with gill nets in the Bay alone the shore line in February in large numbers. Salted or smoke shad, cod and herring were shipped and stored in wood barrel. In the articles, found and translated by Boyle, shad was the most common fish fed to the men, with the cod being the most preferred, while the troops sometimes threw out the salted herring. In Washington's letters, there were more problems with securing the barrels, salt to preserve the fish, and transporting the barrels past the British troops back to the camps than the act of catching the fish. If salt could not be located, Washington recommended that the fish be smoked. Records failed to show were most of the fish brought to the encampment that year come from. Today, it matters little whether the Wildes fish story is fact or faction. Boyle research clearly showed how important these migratory fish were to the nation and the army at this time in history [8]. Those who want to believe the legend that the American Shad fought their way by the British nets to feed the starving American Army at Valley Forge take heart. Would General Washington, a Potomac River shad fisherman, have commented in his endless correspondences for food and supplies admitted that his men were now fat and happy with fresh caught shad from the Schuylkill River?

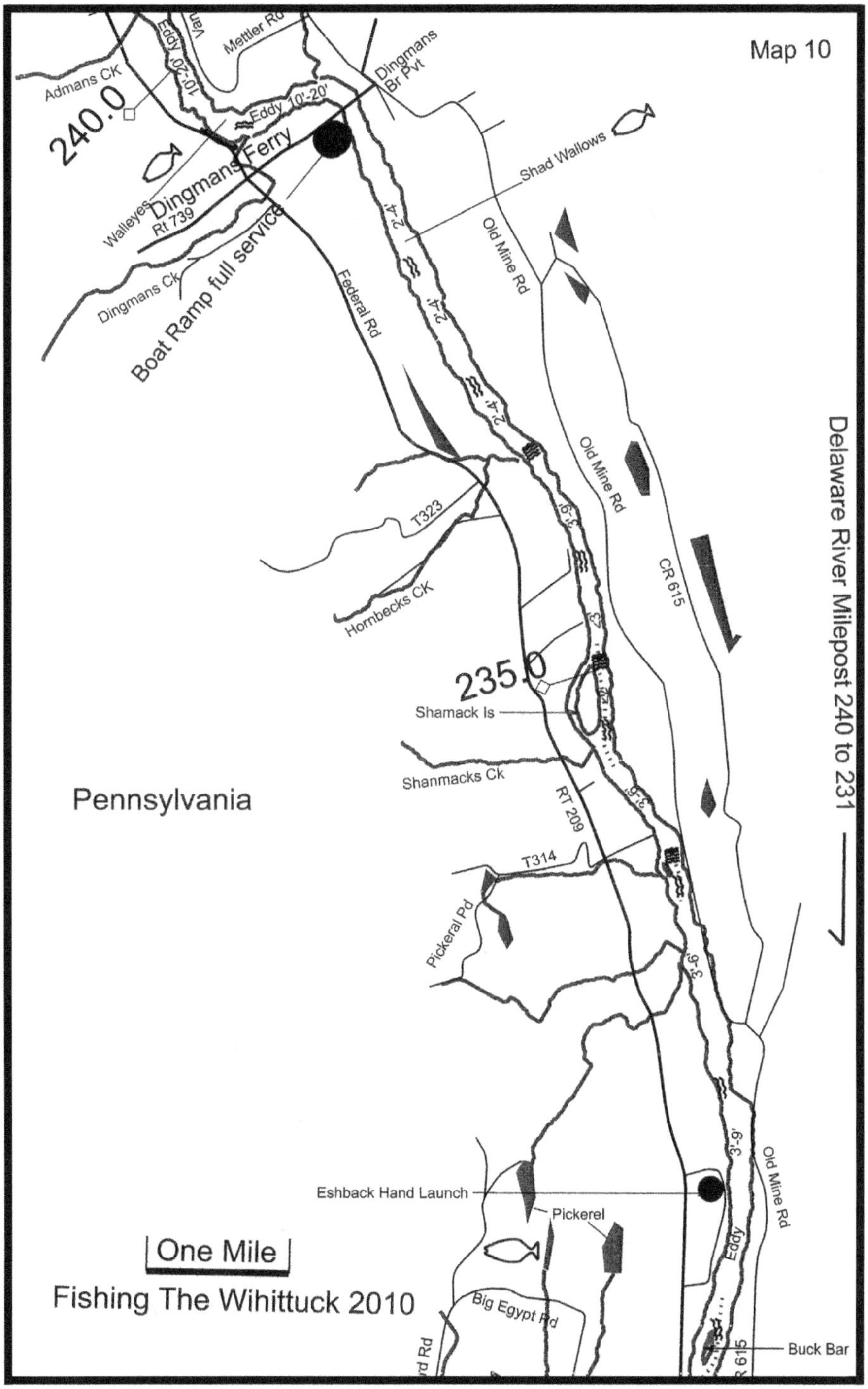
Map 10
Admans CK
240.0
Mettler Rd
Dingmans Br Pvt
Eddy 10'-20'
Shad Wallows
Walleyes
Dingmans Ferry
Rt 739
Dingmans Ck
Boat Ramp full service
Federal Rd
Old Mine Rd
2'-4'
Old Mine Rd
T323
Hornbecks CK
CR 615
Delaware River Milepost 240 to 231
235.0
Shamack Is
Shanmacks Ck
RT 209
Pennsylvania
T314
Pickeral Pd
3'-6'
3'-9'
Old Mine Rd
Eshback Hand Launch
Pickerel
Eddy
One Mile
Fishing The Wihittuck 2010
Big Egypt Rd
Buck Bar

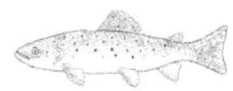

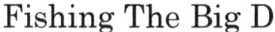

The Upper Delaware

To understand the movement and habits of the American shad one has to study them in a hatchery. What was discovered is what local Delaware Shad fishermen have known for years. When in captivity the fish are stored in a round tank with an injected current and a light system that is synchronized with the seasonal daylight. The fish swim in a formation against the current during the daylight hours. As the light fades they lose the formational swimming parade and seem to congregate in the slower center part of the tank. This daily pattern is repeated until the water reaches the 70 degree range and triggers the spawning ritual. As the water begins to warm and the lights fades in the evening the fish begin to bump into the sides of the tanks and each other to release the eggs and sperms into the water. This activity is continued well into the evening hours. Once daylight is injected back into the room the fish start to swim upstream again [150]. As the water is warm further the fish will start to show signs of stress, due to starvation, and begin to fall out of the upstream swimming formation, signaling the end of the run and time to return to the sea. If the fish in the tank have been injected with hormones they can be released to the river. The hatchery will tagged the shad cultures with Tetracycline for identification of the adult fish later.

Map 11: *At Wallpack bend, the river cuts, for a brief period, a narrow V-shape valley floor profile with a river grade typical of the upper section. Some good rifts at the mouths of Tom Creek, the back side of Wallpack Bend. This also has a good mixture of bottom types for different fish type. At the bend, good collections of camp sites can be found. The eddy below Poxono island holds spawning shad will into the summer. Shad run begins in early May late April.*

During February, they congregate in the Delaware Bay to become accustom to the fresh water. At this time the fish also begin to appear in the fish market department of local grocery stores indicating the presents of commercial fishing for the fish in the bay. When the water is in the upper 40 degree range generally around end of March, and thru April the reports of shad catches begin to appear in the river near Trenton and in the lower non-tidal sections. When the main run is in the river below Easton, generally the temperature is below 50 degrees, the river is high and the success and safety is limited. By mid April to mid May they should be in better river conditions and fishing temperature range of 52-60 degrees F between Easton and the Water Gap. As the water temperature passes 50 degrees, the fish become aggressive and the action starts. The month of May is the time for shad fishing between the Water Gap to Port Jervis, follow by June north of Port Jervis. These dates are not fixed and will vary from season to season, based on water flow and temperature. Depending on current, temperature and water clarity, the American Shad travel at a rate of six to fourteen miles a day. The Delaware Shad Fisherman's Association reports that if the Trenton flow rate is above 30,000 cfs the fish will be halted. A flow of 14,000 or below is ideal for good migration. At the Route 202 Bridge, a Hydroacoutic survey *(was)* set up to monitor this movement.

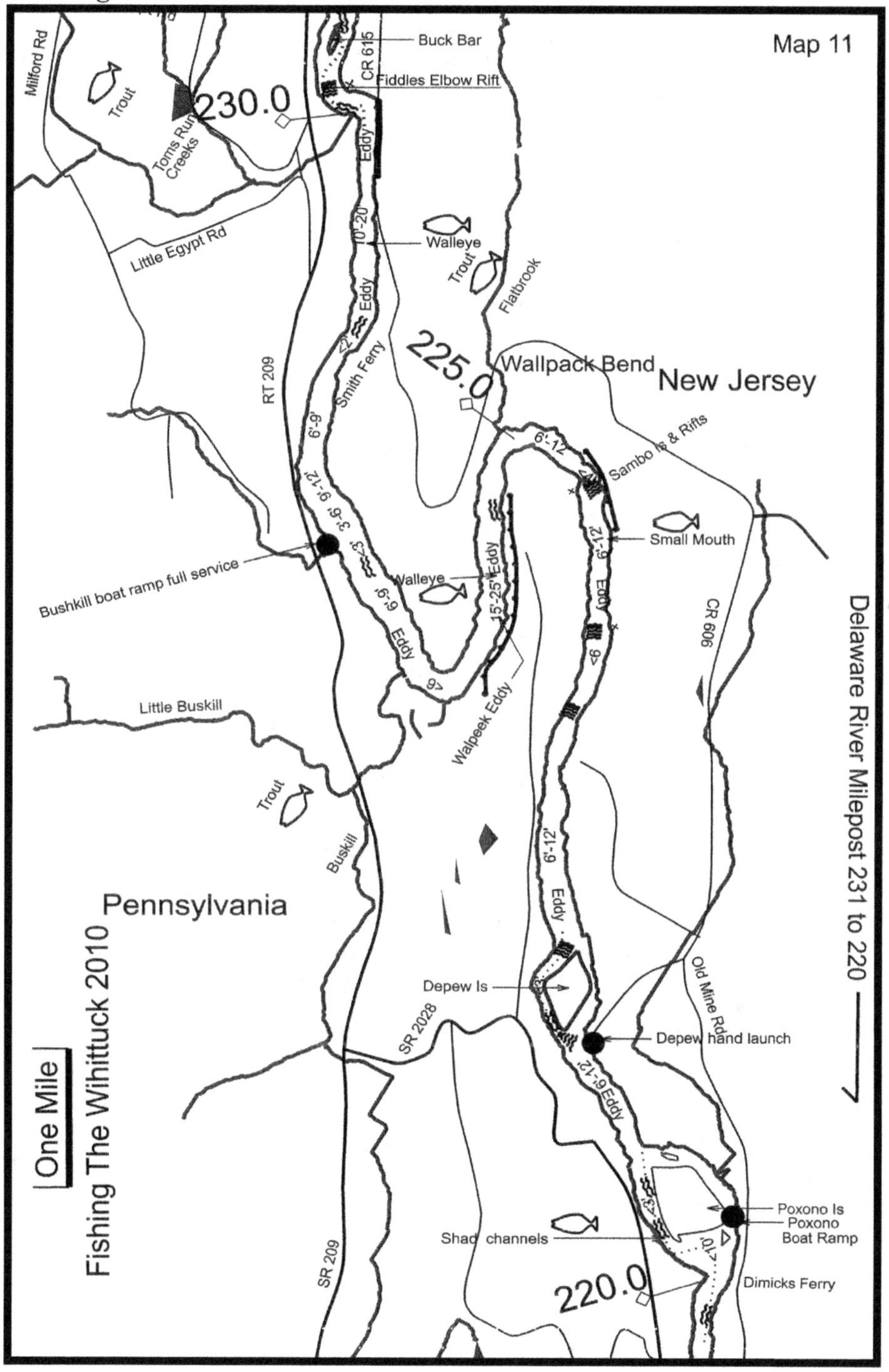
Map 11
Milford Rd
Trout
Toms Run Creeks
230.0
Buck Bar
CR 615
Fiddles Elbow Rift
Eddy
10'-20'
Walleye
Trout
Flatbrook
Little Egypt Rd
Eddy
Smith Ferry
RT 209
225.0
Wallpack Bend
New Jersey
Sambo Is & Rifts
6'-12'
6'-9'
Small Mouth
Bushkill boat ramp full service
Walleye
15'-25' Eddy
Eddy
CR 606
Walpeek Eddy
Little Buskill
Trout
Buskill
Delaware River Milepost 231 to 220
Pennsylvania
6'-12'
Eddy
Depew Is
Old Mine Rd
SR 2028
Depew hand launch
One Mile
Fishing The Whittuck 2010
6'-12' Eddy
Poxono Is
Poxono Boat Ramp
Shad channels
SR 209
220.0
Dimicks Ferry

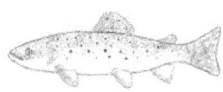

The Upper Delaware

Most serious shad fisherman keep yearly journals of results, showing dates, time, place, water temperature and river conditions. Fishermen soon learned, that once you hook the first one, more will follow. As confirm in the breeding tanks, they travel only in the daylight and rest in night in deep slow moving pools. Once the fish enter the warmer waters of the upper river the upstream movement begins to slow down and the spawning ritual begins.

Map 12: *The shallow river for crossing, good fishing and the gap for getting through the mountain made this a major early Indian home. Grounding at woodcock bar is common in this slow moving part of the River. Once in the gap the river begins to move with a mixture of mild class one rapids, deep turning pools and a spectacular view from below. Good access from both sides of the river, at the mouth of the Brodhead, makes this a popular spot to fish. Peak shad run is in early May late April.*

The fish will look for spawning pools or as locals call them "shad wallows" when the water nears 70 degrees. Shad wallows are slow moving shallow pools with rocky bottoms. In the evening the fish are visible as they move about trying to shake the eggs and sperm from their bodies. Here they are not just susceptible to the fisherman's hook but the archer's arrow. A good shad wallow can be found by the presence of a tree platform overhanging the water, much like a deer stand.

Life deals a bad hand to these fish. In the spawning process the fish's metabolism, for both male and female are unable to process food. After they spawn, these fish are weak, and near or at death bed. They are about half the size that they were at the beginning of the trip. Like all living creatures, when the fat is gone the mussels supply the last bite of protein that the body can use. Many fishermen comment, that the fish caught in the bay early, are tastier and fight harder than ones caught late in the season on the upper river. When the dead or near dead shad float down the river people will trigger reports of fish kills on the river. Many of these fish will have open wounds at this time.

The eggs are hatched in about a week and the young shad will remain in the river until early fall. As the water cools, the juvenile shad head southward looking for the warmer salt water and other shads of their own age group. On their trip downstream, they can cause a feeding frenzy as the local bass prepare for winter. You can take advantage of this situation with lures that imitate these juvenile shad in the early fall. They will remain in the saltwater environment until the fish reaches sexual mutuality at three years of age. At that time, the schools begin their journey back up the original freshwater river of their birth.

For early season shad fishing in the lower Delaware the most popular location is at the warm water discharge at power plants were the water can reach fifty degrees. By May the water should be warm enough to get the shad aggressive and they start hitting darts and spoons with more verger. As proven in the fish breeding tanks, shad

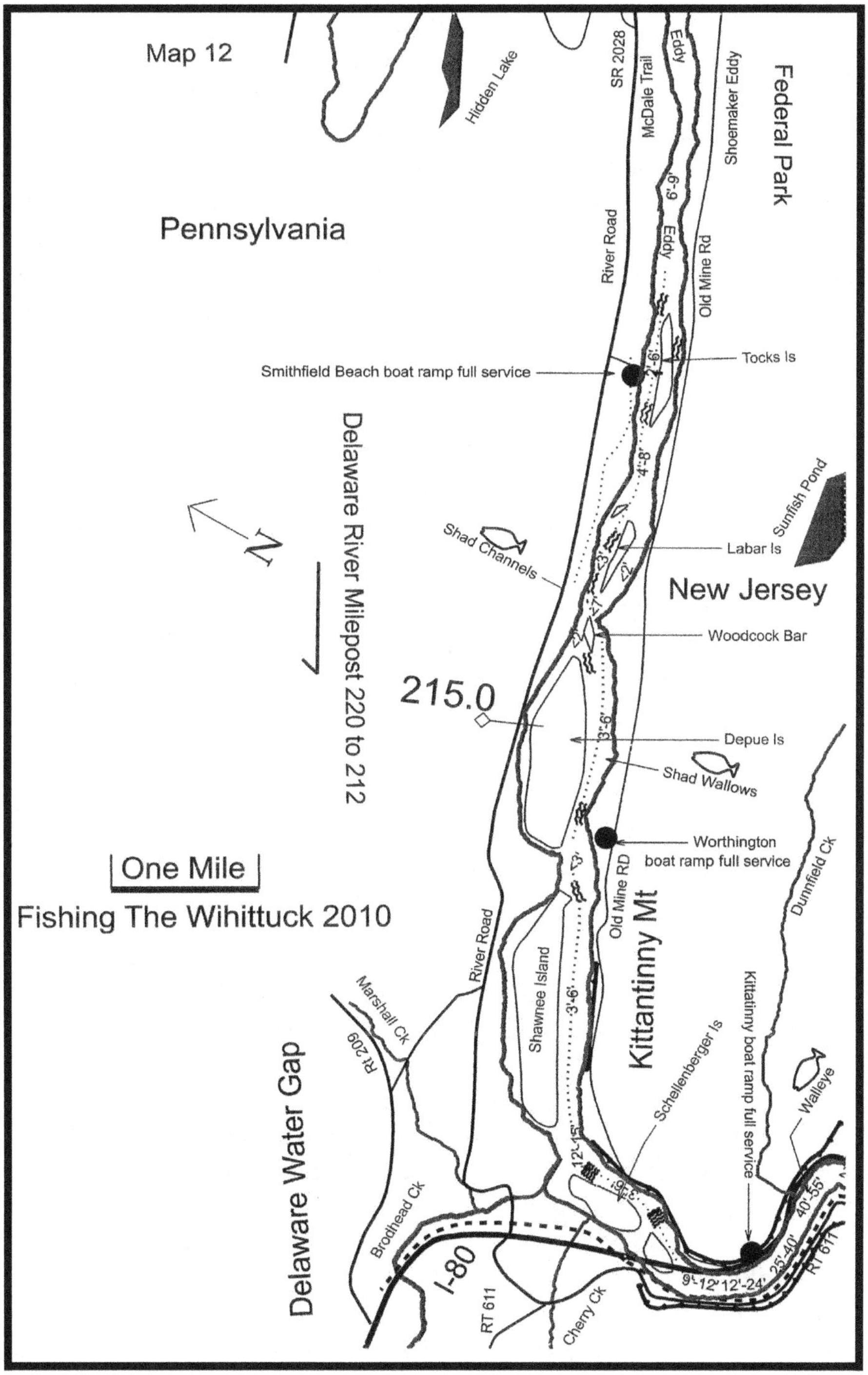
Map 12
Hidden Lake
SR 2028
McDale Trail
Eddy
Shoemaker Eddy
Federal Park
Pennsylvania
River Road
Eddy
Old Mine Rd
Tocks Is
Smithfield Beach boat ramp full service
Delaware River Milepost 220 to 212
N
Shad Channels
Sunfish Pond
Labar Is
New Jersey
Woodcock Bar
215.0
Depue Is
Shad Wallows
Worthington
boat ramp full service
One Mile
Fishing The Wihittuck 2010
Old Mine RD
Kittantinny Mt
Dunnfield Ck
River Road
Marshall Ck
Shawnee Island
Kittatinny boat ramp full service
Schellenberger Is
Walleye
Delaware Water Gap
Rt 209
Brodhead Ck
I-80
RT 611
Cherry Ck
RT 611

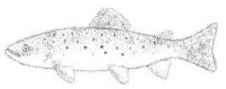

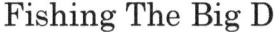

The Upper Delaware

tend to move in the day-time and like to rest in deep, slow moving pools at night. It's recommended to anchoring the boat on the headwaters of these pools in the morning. For some reason they tend to be more aggressive in the morning and evening with limited or no action at night. The fish like to travel in deep water with a current to give them direction. If you are fishing the bank, good spots to look for them are deep channels below and along islands, bridge abutments, and stream outlets in the morning and evening. Another spot to look for shad, particular in the day, are the deep channels cut into the bank on the outside meanders of the river. These channels might be close enough to the bank and within range of a good rod and reel combination. For those people fishing from the banks, a good guide to look for is to watch the boat traffic. On curves in periods of low flow, local boaters will try to keep the boat in the deepest part of the river.

Local tradition has it that the American Indian used fresh berries attached to an eagle or hawk talon to catch shad. The red and green head of the shad dart inmates these berries and the dart is placed in front of the fish to aggravate it rather than drawing a strike like bass. Like salmon and other migratory fish in the spawning phase they refrain from eating and as such they do not chase lures like tradition game fish. But shad and salmon do strike at bright objects placed in front of them. Fishing for them is much the same as salmon fishing where the egg or dart it places in front of them as they move up river. The key to this, like salmon fishing, is to know where the fish are, either by visual observation, general knowledge or by fish detector and get the bright color lure in front of them. Water temperature is critical so one must wait for it to reach the mid fifty degree range.

Today most people seem to be using spoons. If you are using the spoon always check the flutter action of your spoon. It must twist in a circular motion in the current. If it does not, try to bend the hook's shaft a little. If it still doesn't flutter, maybe the current is not strong enough to set the flutter action, and in that case, use a light dart or go somewhere else. Because of the twisting motion of flutter spoons, you need to set several swivel connectors attached to an inline sinker arrangement or a heavy lead shad dart with a four feet leader to the spoon. This should prevent the line from winding. The fish's choice of color is critical, so having a good selection of different colors and sizes of both darts and spoons is important. Bright red colors seem to be the most popular, but if the fish are fickle, which they do get, trying alternate colors might be the ticket to success. Some people will use multiple darts on the same lines. Keeping heavy debris of pollen pods from spring tree can be a problem this time of year. Some people tie strips of rubber bands just above the first swivel barrels in order to collect debris. It's recommended to use an eight-ten pound clear mono line.

One hard part in fishing for shad is guessing the depth of your spoon or dart. If you are fishing from a boat, you will want to hold the spoon or dart about a foot or two

Fishing The Big D

above the bottom. Once you think you have them close to the bottom but suspended in the current, bring them back only when the line starts to collect debris. The rod can be worked a little on a back and force method "jig it". Another popular method is down riggers. The advantage to the downrigger, over setting the pole in the back of the boat, is that it can take the guesswork out of the depth of the spoons and darts. Another advantage of using downrigger is that your rig is almost directly under you not twenty-five yards downstream and may or may not be in the channel. Setting rubber bands above the release clips for downriggers can also stop early releases due to debris collection. Fishing shad from floating kayak and canoes can be frustrating because you're casting from the front or side of the moving craft and the dart seldom gets and holds to the bottom. The most productive method instead is to the trail the dart as one floats downstream, unfortunately this will collects lots of snag. Instead it's best to beach the craft once a pod of shad is found and cast from the shore.

Fishing from the shore can be challenging. The shore fisherman must find a spot within casting distance across the channel. The lure must be cast at right angles to the current and let to sink to the bottom as it drift downstream before drawing it back. As the dart swings an arch across the current it might fall across the open mouth of a swimming shad. In salmon fishing terms this is called flossing. The fish will hit the lure when it is gets in their face. Fly fishing for running shad is can be done by stripping bright color streamers with sinking line cast across the current much the some as spinning rods. After the spawn the remaining health shad may start feeding on surface flies and small lures drawn across there faces.

The fish set the hook themselves so there is no need to "set the hook". Shad have a weak lower mouth and the hook can be ripped from its mouth rapidly. That's why darts have the hook pointed up instead of the normal down position. One should begin pulling the fish steadily toward the boat or shoreline. Beside the weight of the fish, you will also be pulling against the current as well so it is very important that the retrieval be steady and evenly pulled toward you, avoiding any sudden jerks or slack line that will rip the hook out. Set the drag so as to be able to pull the fish in an upward pull upstream but be able to permit some freedom for the fish if it decides to run. I don't have to tell you most fish are lost at the boat or the bank just before landing, so you will want to let it work out some energy just before you try to land it. This is the last place you want to tighten the drag. Always practice safety first. On small 12-14 foot boat, let the person in the bow reel in the last few yards of the fish, while the person in the stern nets the fish from the rear. The fish can stand the cold water better than you.

Trying to locate the path of these migrating fish with the help of a fish finder is easy when compared to getting the boat over the spot. The current is strong this time of year and the stronger the current, the harder it is to stay in the channel. This is where the anchor and rope come into play. The anchor must be the weight type, not the sand flute

The Upper Delaware

anchors that will trap itself under a rock after you have floated a few hundred yards down river. One of the locally made anchors is a two-foot long concrete filled tube with bend re-bar at the end to grasp and hold the bottom. If the anchor does not hold the bottom, you will have to pan out more anchor line until it holds. The more anchor line you have out, the more you will drift in and out of the channel. A good rule of thumb is to have the line length seven times the depth of the river. If you are fishing in ten-foot deep water, you will need at least 70 feet of line. When waiting for the anchor to hold, leave the motor running until it holds and you are over the channel. Some fisherman will use a secondary line secured to the primary anchor line that will permit them to swing the boat and hold it in the channel. This is done by adjusting the length and location of the secondary line and securing it to a cleat in the middle of the boat. For safety, never secure your primary anchor line in the middle or rear of the boat.

When State agencies went looking for American Shad stock they traditional went to the Delaware. Fish ladders are traumatic for the fish so stocking agencies still prefer to draw healthy fish, or broodfish, from open rivers for breeding. Transportation of broodfish is also traumatic and can result in high fatalities on long trips. The Pennsylvania center for anadromous fish is located on the middle of Pennsylvania. Because, of the issues of transportation most of the broodfish used for stocking on the East Coast today come from the Potomac basin. To say that stocking is producing high numbers of shad is incorrect. But the system is putting addition fish in the tributary. Studies show that about 20 to 30% of the fish

Delaware Shad Index New Jersey Game Non-tidal Delaware River

crossing the Easton dam are stocked fish. But the total amount of shad crossing the dam varies from 3,000 to 1,000 each year. The mortality rate is high.

Much research is spent on studying the return of shad and other migratory fish. Counting fish movement is an inexact process. The shad and other migratory fry fish were traditionally captured, in the fall at specific locations, both in tidal and non-tidal sections of the river. The count was than converted to a statistical means for the year by two methods (Peterson and Schaefer). On the non-tidal section of the river at the Route 202 Bridge, a hydroacoustics sensor was added in 1993. The Peterson method generated the larger count while the hydroacoustics yield the lower count. Even though the different processes yielded different results, they tend to project consistent agreements of good and bad years. The hydroacoustic count was the primary tool used to measure the runs. In

Fishing The Big D

2008 it went down with no plans to replace it. Instead the count will relay on the Lewis catches and fishing reports.

In the years from 1985 to 1995, runs of 800,000 fish were recorded and have yet to recover to that level. Many reasons were suggested for this drop. Commercial fishing is still done in the Bay and lower river. Striped bass numbers are up and they could be eating larger numbers of shad fries resulting in fewer fish. The acoustic equipment may have failed to count a large percentage of them and has been down on several runs. Recent spring river floods could be disrupting the hatching cycle. The most interesting explanation could be that more of the fish are spawning in the tidal sections of the river due to the cleaner water and not getting counted at the 202 bridge [129].

One way to determine why the counts are down from the good years of 1985 to 1995 is to compare the results of other watersheds. The Potomac is a good river to compare. The Potomac River has a natural dam just upriver in Washington DC and yet the number of shad type fish had remained a little more stable than the Delaware with 400 plus miles of open water. Both watersheds have aggressive restocking programs that are showing results of returning chemically tagged fished. Both suffer the same illness of pollution in the lower sections of the rivers and bays. All have fish ladders and dam remove programs on the tributaries. The one major different between the two is commercial fishing. In 1982 a harvest moratorium of American Shad was placed by Maryland and Virginia in the lower Potomac and Chesapeake. The numbers within 10 year increase exponentially as quoted by Michael Hendricks Director of the Van Dyke center for anadromous fish of Pennsylvania Boat and Fish Commission. The Delaware commercial catches peak at 500,000 pounds in the 10 golden years between 85 and 95 but now the total has been osculating between 100,000 to 200,000 pounds. To save the American Shad by banning commercial fishing in the bay and river would mean to lose another resource, a tradition of small scale family fishing. As per Mr. Hendricks suggestion, the real source of problems may lie in the open ocean and more study is needed there. In 2008 the shad counts on the Hudson, Delaware and Potomac were all down. With the ban on fishing in the Chesapeake and Hudson it might be more complex than we think.

In 2010, with the shad counter down fishermen began reporting better than normal catches with good results the following year. Could the stronger regulations on the taking of herring type fish in the Bay and Ocean for bait be having an positive effect on returning shad?

The Pike Family
Pickerel

Pickerel are normally not river fish but pond dwellers and the mountains have many ponds. You will most likely find them in small shallow ponds with lots of

The Upper Delaware

submerged trees, lily pads and grass. All pick family fish love to hide under and around these natural covers. Pickerel prefer muddy bottoms and can survive in mild, blackest water as well. In streams, they will be found in the slower moving section of the creek. Like most pike type fish, they prefer clear water to hunt for prey relying on eyesight. They are greenish gray to olive brown in color on the back with dark strips running vertical or horizontal or its side with a whitish belly. Look for the red fins for the redfin pickerel, which will distinguish it from the grass pickerel (Esox American us vermiculatus) which has ambler color fins. Both the grass and red fin will have vertical strips. The grass pickerel comes from the western basin of the Great Lakes, but has been stocked in the watershed of the Delaware. The New Jersey State record red fin is only one pound thirteen oz.

The chain pickerel is the fish of choice for ice-fisherman. The Pennsylvania state record for a chain pickerel is eight pounds 14 oz caught in Honesdale PA. The average good catch is two pounds. They can be easily identified by the chain pattern on the side of the fish. With the chain pattern, they are by far the most attractive fish of the Pike family. Because they live in the same areas as redfin pickerel, they have been known to bred and produce hydride fish in the wild. The normal life span of these fish is eight to ten years. They share the same solitary hunting habits, fast striking attaches, food and environments as the other pike family member. The reason why ice photos of chain pickerel are so common is that good chain pickerel fishing sites are generally over looked by summer time bass fisherman because of heavy weeds and lily pads environment.

Northern Pike, Muskellunge and Tiger Muskellunge

This family of fish may be the oldest in our waterways. The northern pike is the only one that is native to both North America and Europe. In the 1960's, Pennsylvania and New Jersey along with private individuals, started stocking northern pike and muskellunge in limited locations in the watershed. These long, narrow body fish with teeth resemble the scary Florida alligator gars of the south. Attitudes among fisherman toward these fish vary from great respect to don't return them. Many anglers believe that large pikes like northerns and muskellunge have a effect on competing game fish. Some marine biologist disagrees, on this subject. Still many notice a drop in bass and pan fish catches in waters that are reported to have large population of pike type fish in them. Today, tiger muskellunge, which are sterile, are stock in the river south of Frenchtown and muskellunge north of Frenchtown by New Jersey.

Chapter III
THE MIDDLE DELAWARE

Sections of the middle river were added to the list of Wild and Scenic Rivers. This section starts at river milepost 193.8 (North of Martins Creek) and extends southward for 67.3 miles to Washington Crossing. The sections are separated by Easton, Point Pleasant, Route 202 Bridge and New Hope. The act also includes part of the tributaries of Tinicum, Tohickon, and Paunacussing Creek. This section is classified as 25.4 miles scenic, 41.9 miles recreation and 0 miles wild [78].

The Gap to Easton

Once the river and car traffic clears the Gap, the river enters a world much different from its mountain origin. From Portland, the river descends into its own private gorge surrounded by gentle rolling hills of excellent farmland of the Lehigh Valley. This part of the river has its share of the usual small summer cottages and trailers parks that sit along its bank, complete with annoying "no trespassing signs". Due to new interstate connections with North Jersey and the Lehigh Valley, the most profitable agricultural products from these small farms today are new housing developments. This high urban growth rate has stressed the capability of local roads and the people who live here. Overall, public access to the river is poor.

The river depth south of the Gap averages 6 to 12 feet, in the pools at normal flows. The current picks up again with very strong rapids separated by slow deep pools. The river bottom is still full of large isolated boulders that can remove a lower unit from your outboard motor in a second. Notably fishing locations are near the warm water discharge spots at the power plants for shad and the rapids above and below Belvedere for small mouth bass. At Easton, do not get caught fishing inside the limits of the fish ladder entrance at the Lehigh River dam. Instead, try fishing for shad from the north bank of the Lehigh River before the dam. The river from the Gap south is not patrolled like the upper half so fishing licenses are seldom checked for.

Two important products that come from the geology of the region are the Portland Cement industry and limestone creeks. The horizon is dotted with white smoke stacks and tall cylindrical shaped silos with the interconnecting railroad tracks of the Portland cement industry. The limestone geology that supports this product produces excellent trout streams that in some places still support year round trout. One is now out of the acidic brown waters of the mountain streams and into the greenish cloudy waters of the farmland limestone creeks of the lowlands. On both sides of the river are small streams, some of which are not on the state stocking list, but one could pull a few native brooks or a hold over brown trout. Some of the well-known names creeks on the Pennsylvania side are Buskill, Little Lehigh, Saucon, Monocacy, Cook, and the Hosenack Creeks. The Saucon is the most well known, and rated now a class "A" trout stream, that empties into the

The Middle Delaware

Lehigh at the old Bethlehem Steel plant. The insects and fish's diet are different and as such, successful fly-fishing tactic will be a little different. Here the best seems to be the small Trico insects' presentations, which are the most common insects in the waterways, and lots of wet non-insect flies. These streams are full of the normal limestone aquatic vegetations, such as watercress, which the fish use for cover. On the New Jersey side of the river, just south of Phillipsburg, the Musconetcong River, and the valley that shares its name joins the Delaware. This river flows a 44-mile long journey from the New Jersey Skylands through a limestone valley. This river provides the angler with a variety of pools, lakes and rural stream type fishing. It is heavily stocked in places and generally has excellent access along its entire length. The river is more than scenic, its water and limestone base tributaries are considered one of the "Garden State Trout Hot Spots"[44]. Other nearby Jersey streams to try is the Stony Brook, Lockatong, and Capoolong Creek. All three of these streams are capable of holding left-over trout through the year [44]. So treasured is the Musconetcong Valley, that on December 22, 2006, twenty-five miles were declared and protected by the Wild and Scenic act [78].

Map 13:
This section of the river has a variety of different depth, from a 50 feet hole within the Gap to two feet depth at places near many islands. These shallow depths make for good wading near the islands and below the power plant at an old RR bridge. Warm water discharge draws Shad in the spring. Peak shad runs are early May and late April.

Walleyes

Fish have no eyelids; as such, fish are shy of bright, sunny, shallow waters. Fish with big eyes are even shier of the sun. For those of you who have served in the military and have experienced night vision goggles, you can appreciate the fear these fish have of bright lights. The refractive eyes of walleyes demonstrate how high level light is reflected from the eyes, thus blinding the fish. These fish can see very well at night, and in turbid water conditions proving its superior low level light vision. The term "walleye chop" describes a day that is overcast, windy, and the water has small waves on it. These creatures of the night are members of the yellow perch family. Sander vitreus, yellow walleye, is a coldwater fish that is native to North America. They are a very good tasting popular game fish and in the Great Lakes they were caught commercially. So highly prized, as a source of food the blue walleye disappeared from our world in the 1970's. Today, stories of people who have claimed to have caught them up north in Canada still appear, but it still has not been confirmed. Because of the good taste of these fish many that are caught are kept. Fortunately, the State fishing commissions are finding walleyes survive a wider range of environments then original thought and the stocking are on the increase. The other advantage is this fish is an all season fish. Depending on the basin and the original stocking sources, these fish come in a variety of colors with and without .

Fishing The Big D   55

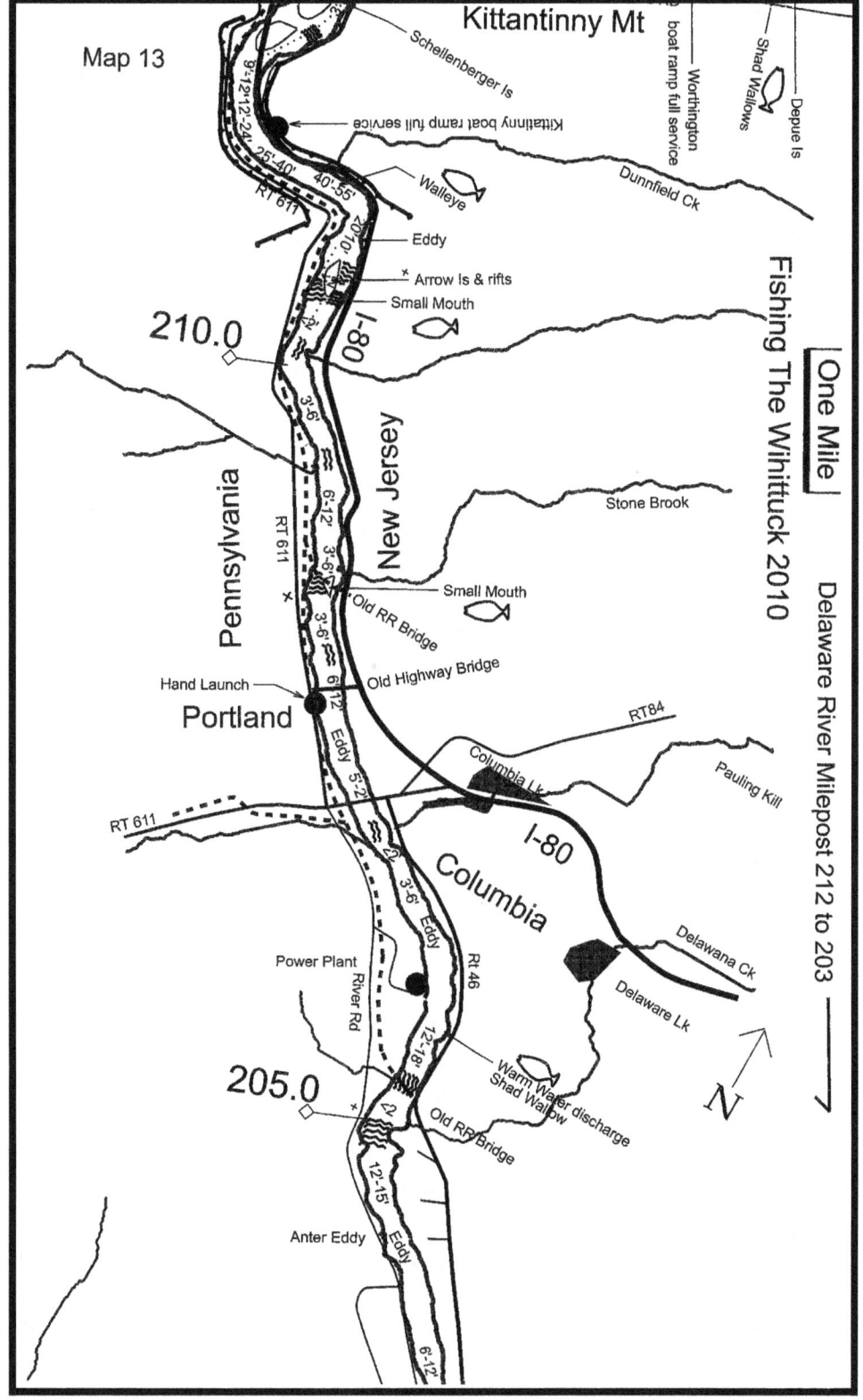

vertical strips to a golden color. Walleyes have been known to live up to 29 years with and but in heavily fished areas, they most likely will be one to six years in age. Currently the New Jersey record walleye is 13 pounds 9 oz caught in the Delaware River in 1993 [3]. The Pennsylvania record walleye is 17 pounds 9 oz, but was caught outside of the watershed [1]. These coldwater fish can be found everywhere in the Delaware basin and with increase popularity more lakes are being stock. They reproduce very well in most of the coldwater and deep warm water lakes and waterways of the regions. From year to year, the New Jersey and Pennsylvania fish commission share the stocking of the fish in the Delaware River north of Easton/Philipsburg but I have seen many fish caught as far south as Trenton.

Because walleyes eat much the same meals as bass and pike type fish, the bait is the same. It is more of how, when and where you fish for these fish that counts. In summer, fish deep holes with moderate flow and rocks, working a worm or leach along the bottom. If you get snagged a lot you are fishing for them correctly. In the fall they become very aggressive and love bright colored lures such as bright green, yellow and red along the shallow edges of the holes. As it gets colder, they start building up fat for the winter and will be hungry. When the water freezes, you might want to go back to live bait because they will not want to use up energy chasing food. As the water begins to warm up, they will go shallow and spawn along the edges of ponds or up into feeder streams. In early spring on river, fish them in the shallow water upstream from deep holes. While fishing for bass or trolling for trout, and a minnow is cut in half, it most likely was a walleye hit.

Map 14:
This section has strong rapids separated by deep slow moving pools or eddies. Since some of these rapids can only be transverse by jet boats, pools without public launches are very productive. A population of spotted bass is present in the pools here. The second most hazardous rift on the river, Foul Rift can be found here. Once the river passes Belvedere, it drops 22 feet in a half mile through a narrow ravine. It is classified as a strong class II rapid during moderate flows. In floods, it can be much more and people have been killed here. What make this one of the most hazardous set of rapids in the river are the repeating lines of large downstream limestone rocks with submerged ledges. These rock lines can collect trees after floods which can trap and drown floating travelers. In the late 1700's, a channel was cut through these rock lines so the log rafts and Durham boats could get through. Even after the efforts of the early rock removers to make the ravine safer for river traffic, people still drown here. The power companies wanted to build a dam here once. By following the main channel and avoiding down trees one should be able to transit this. Start the journey in the center of the river at the first set of rapids than move to the right of an island on the Pennsylvania side, after the island, move quickly back to the center of the river before crossing the third and final set. One can scout the conditions of this rift and locate any fallen trees from an observation post on the PA side. Peak shad run is in early May late April.

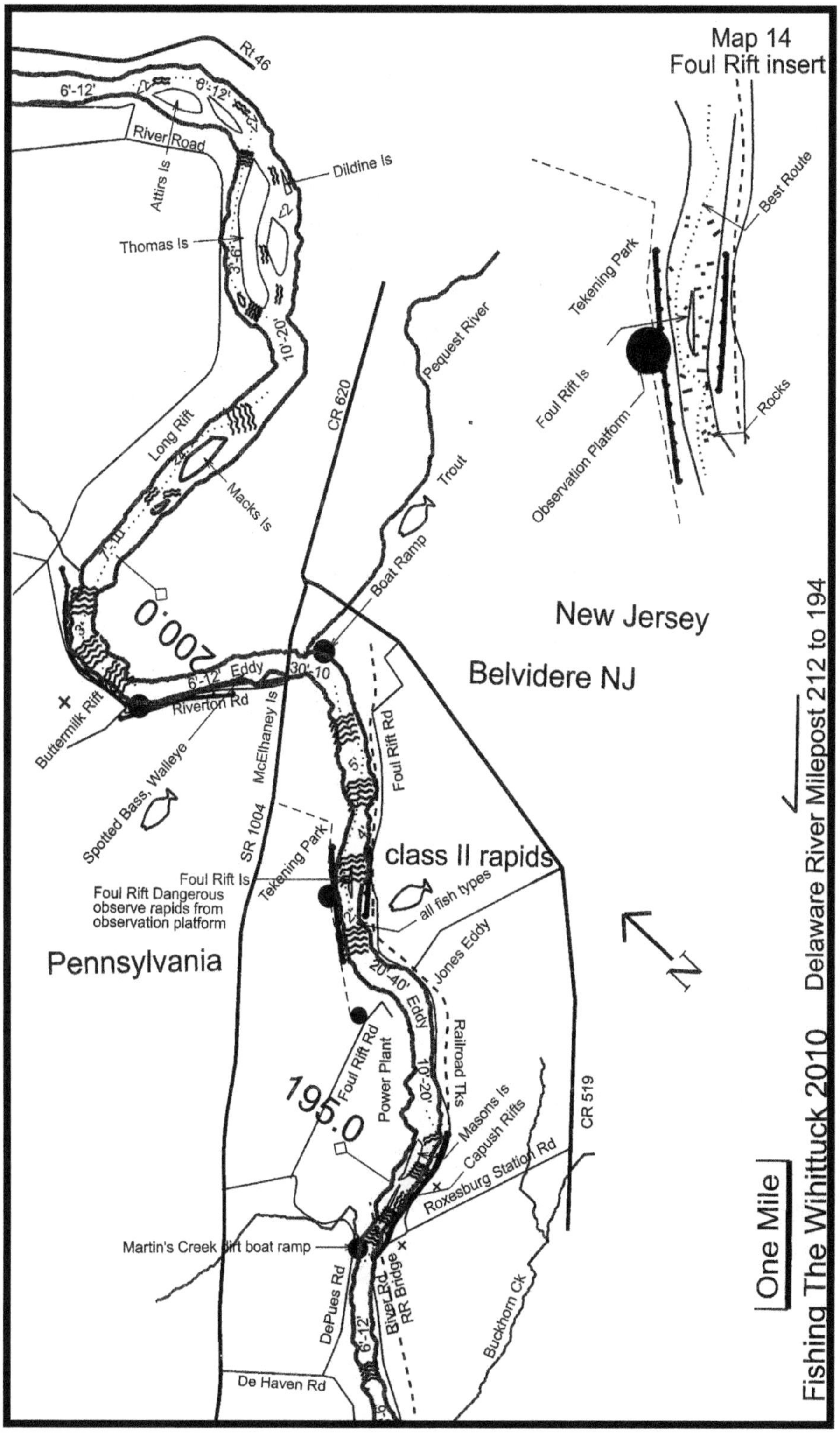
Map 14
Foul Rift insert
Best Route
Tekening Park
Foul Rift Is
Observation Platform
Rocks
Rt 46
6'-12'
River Road
Attirs Is
Dildine Is
Thomas Is
3'-6'
10'-20'
Pequest River
CR 620
Long Rift
Macks Is
Trout
Boat Ramp
200.0
New Jersey
Belvidere NJ
Eddy
Buttermilk Rift
Riverton Rd
McElhaney Is
Foul Rift Rd
Spotted Bass, Walleye
SR 1004
Tekening Park
class II rapids
Foul Rift Is
Foul Rift Dangerous
observe rapids from
observation platform
all fish types
Jones Eddy
Pennsylvania
20'-40' Eddy
Railroad Tks
Foul Rift Rd
Power Plant
195.0
Masons Is
Capush Rifts
Roxesburg Station Rd
CR 519
Martin's Creek dirt boat ramp
DePues Rd
River Rd
RR Bridge
Buckhorn Ck
De Haven Rd
One Mile
Delaware River Milepost 212 to 194
Fishing The Wihittuck 2010

Yellow Perch

The yellow perch has many of the same qualities as the walleye. It loves to spend the summers in deep, dark holes. The fish is classified as a pan fish with a record catch of two pound 9 oz. from the Beltsville Reservoir in 2000 [1]. In 1865, a four pound 4 oz yellow perch was caught in Crosswicks Creek, New Jersey [3], a world record Yellow Perch. If you know where they can be found, they make an excellent game fish for the youngsters. The best time to fish for them is through the fall and into the winter. From my own experience, if you catch one in the summer, it will most likely be an isolated catch. During the colder seasons, they will congregate together. Look for areas with overhead trees branches or near creek outlets. The best way to find them is by trolling around weed beds with a spinner and minnow rig and a fish finder if the lake is not ice covered. If they are hungry, they can be caught on just about anything you drop in the water.

Map 15:
This ten mile section has only a few public access points to the river; still many anglers illegally trespass on railroad property on the New Jersey side to wet their lines and feet. Be careful of Merrill Creek water outlet pipe a mile below the Martin's creek boat ramp. Good locations for small mouth bass can be found below Kiefer Island, a RR Bridge and near the many large rocks downstream of Hog Rapids at Frost Hollow. The Gap at Frost Hollow was another proposed dam site. Good wading at the mouth of Martin Creek, Kiefer Island and Hog Rapids. Peak shad run is in early May late April.

Foul Rift

Fishing The Big D

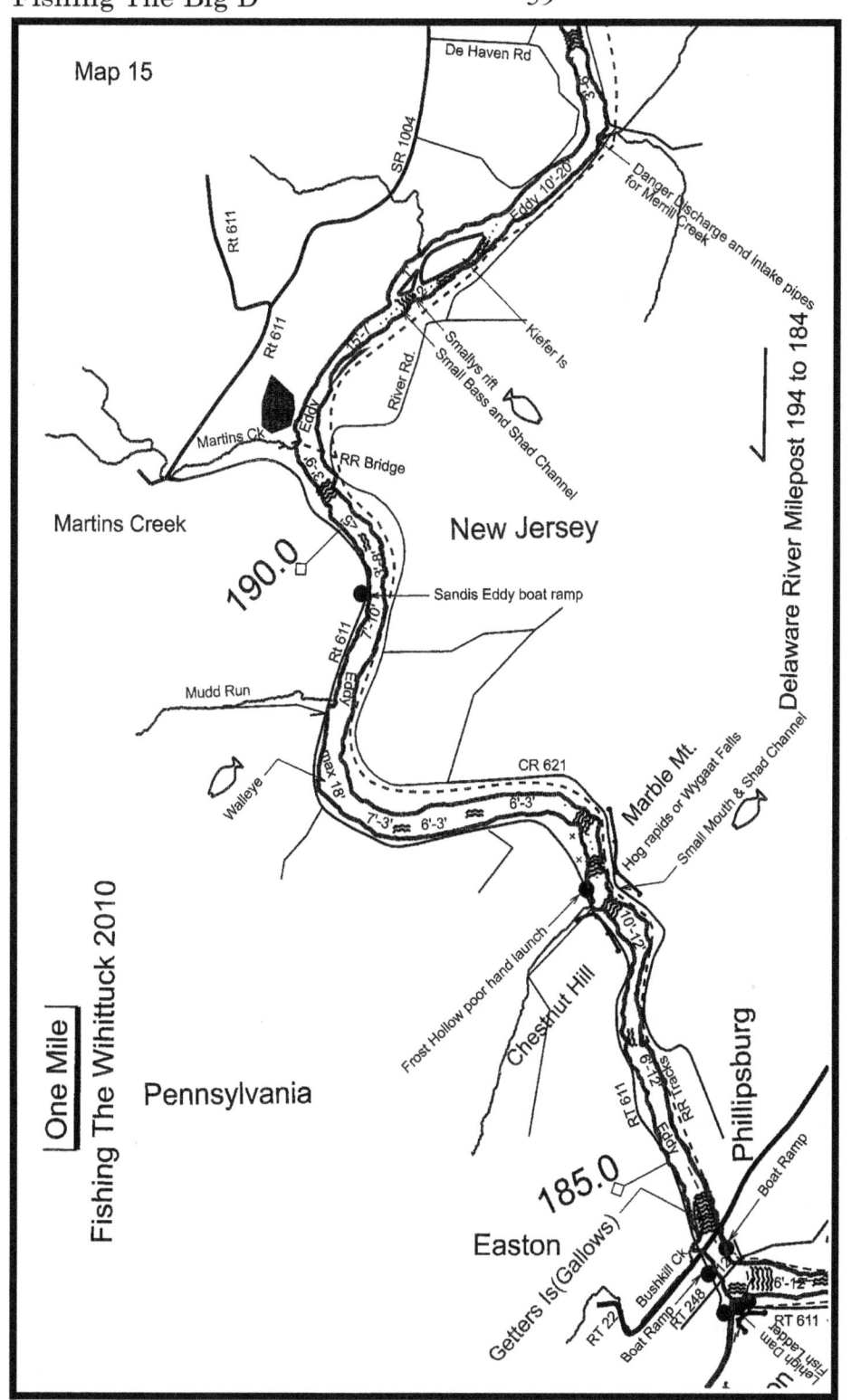

The Middle Delaware
The Lehigh River

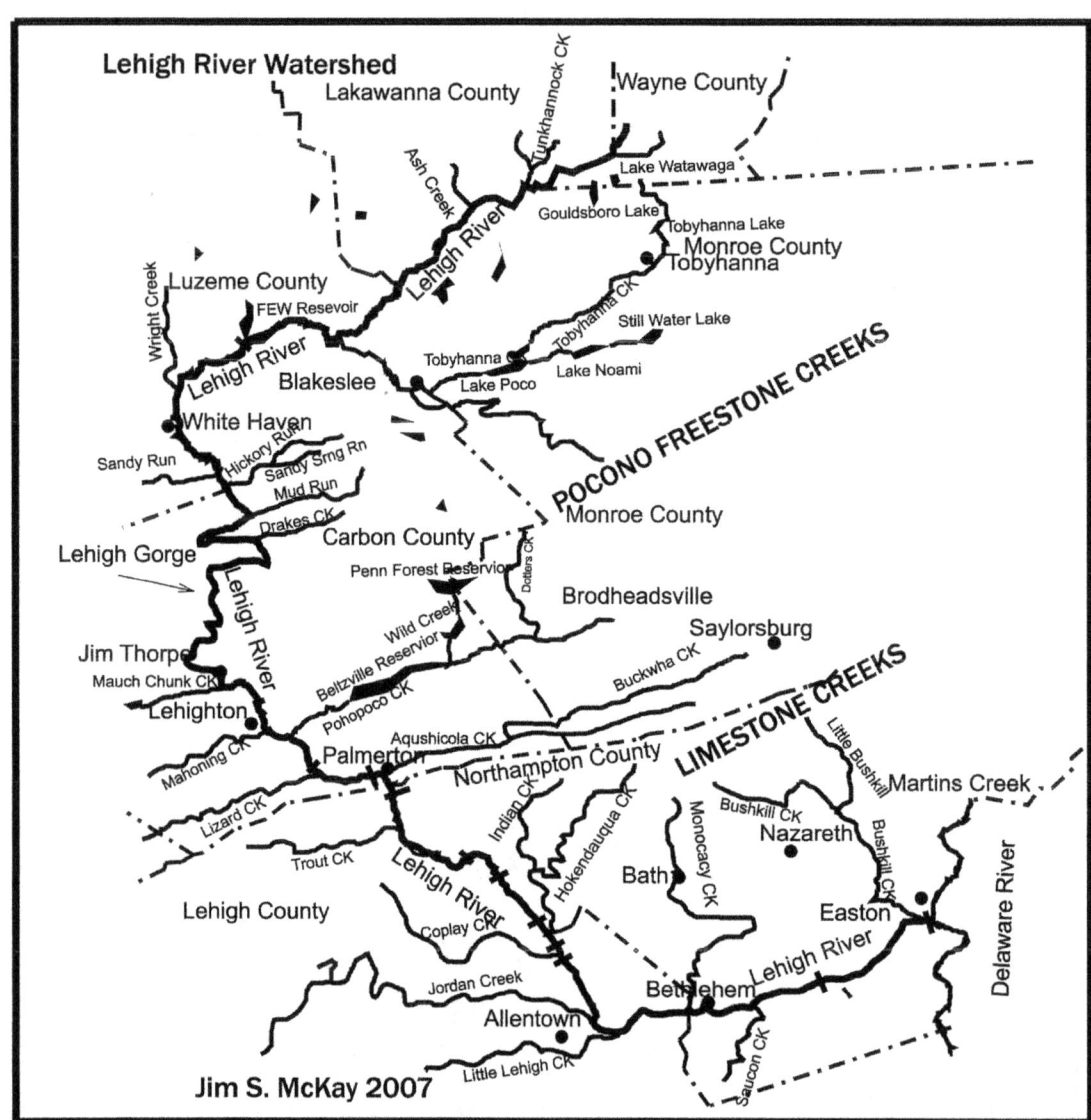

The Lehigh had a very different history than the peaceful waters of the Catskills. The Lehigh was a working river by every meaning of the word. What happen to the Lehigh, happen to all of the Eastern Rivers. The Lehigh Coal and Navigation Company owned the river at the heights of the coal exploration period. Today the upper half is a watershed of contrast. On one side it is a play ground, the other side it is a world where the land has been turn inside-out. The east side of the upper river has private clean lakes with summer homes. On the west side, are old mining towns with names like Macado and

Fishing The Big D

Hazelton, with neighboring deep brown pits. The mountains on the east side are rich with green vegetations and ski runs while the west side has brown slag piles and bare rock cliffs. Even the streams are different. East side streams are full of life while the west side creeks are clear with sulfur colored bottoms and little else. The upper river also divides a culture of people as well. The people on the east side talk with a northeastern accent, while the west side, the southern Allegany twinges or coal county brogue is heard.

The fishing history of the Lehigh River was discovered by local angler and historian Dennis Scholl. His research on the history of shad fishing in the Lehigh River, centered on the Moravains, in Bethlehem, who learned the technique of pulling shad from the rivers from the local Indians. The Moravians kept careful record of the amount, locations, dates, types of fish and price they sold and caught in the Lehigh River. On average, they pulled about 100 to 200 hundred per netting on a good haul, with an average of several thousands in a good season. The dates of the netting were between the second weeks of April through the first week in May in the Bethlehem area. Not just shad but the river had multitudes of other fish that fed the inhabitants of the river valley. One can easily image they used systems that relied on the local conditions of the riverbank and bottom. They may have had to build walls made of rock or tree branches and brush (before woven nets were available). They then drove these fish into this corral or "pond" using nets or a primitive woven collection of vines and sticks. Once in the corral or "pond" they talked about forcing the fish further into a "lock" or wood box. The technique differed between the people, location, and time. In the research of early shad fishing, there were also accounts of arguments or disputes over who was in charged, or who had the right to use a special place in the river [15]. Accounts of arm conflict were document when the entire tribute was block.

Why then was this spring movement of fish such an important part of our heritage? Please remember you had another two months before your crops became edible. No wonder the religious leader called for fasting in the months before the shad runs. Food was always in short supply from February thru April so fasting in the season of Lent by the European settlers was a practiced to insure food remained in the community until crops came in. The blooming of the juneberry tree was the tradition sign that shad were in the river. To the Moravians, this spring gathering may have grown into a religious ceremony where a tradition of serving water crest with the fish developed. The shad were cooked on wooden planks set near the fire or in clay ovens. A large fire may have been going on the bank, but not just to cook the fish, but to warm the people who had been in the water. If you think about it, this must have been a welcome occasion. If the catch was successful, it was the end of the winter hunger and solitude, plus the enjoyment of warmer weather and a gathering of friends. Some years, according to the Moravians, the river was too high to net fish and none or few were caught, meaning another month or two of old food and maybe starvation [15].

When coal was discovered in Panther Valley in 1791[85], the nation entered into a new area of development. Prior to that, the only coal the new nation knew came from

England. This new local coal was harder, more difficult to light, and with the cost of getting it to cities and iron smelter sites, it was more expensive than the English coal, but the demand was there for this new product. Three canal companies would compete to bring the coal through the watershed. The D&H would supply the coal to New York City by means of the upper river system. The Lehigh River route planned to supply coal to both New York and Philadelphia. The Schuylkill Navigation company would route it to Philadelphia by the Schuylkill River. These early navigation or canal companies were issued by State legislation "God like powers" to condemn property, dam rivers, relocate small creeks, alter river channels, and monopolies fees, all in the name of a private corporations for the betterment of man-kind.

The Lehigh Coal and Navigation Company under the direction of Josiah White & Erskine Hazard, started by building a system of wing dams and "bear trap lock" to assist with the navigation of one-way wooden barges or "Ark like rafts" full of coal from the coal fields to Easton and then onto Philadelphia. Once the coal reached Philadelphia, the rafts were sold and dismantled for the wood [92]. A "bear trap lock" patented by Josiah White, was a lock built in the river that lowered the raft or boat across the rapids. It was an ingenious system using trap doors and water pressure to permit crafts to descend the rapids. This temporary one-way system of moving coal gained time until the two-way canal was built. The open river system could only operate during a particular flow rate, causing many periods of no delivery. By 1829, a two way canal system, which is still visible today and open to the general public, was finally completed between Easton and Manch Chunk with plans to construct two more canals: (The Delaware Division Canal to Philadelphia) and the (Morris Canal to New York City). Because the Lehigh used 100-ton barges and the other two canals used smaller boats, all loads had to be transferred at Easton making for a very inefficient operation [92]. The Lehigh Canal later expanded up to White Haven, and then to an incline plan system. This later stretch was an engineering marvel with 29 dam and 29 locks but was quickly destroyed by a flood in the 1860's and sold to the Railroads who filled in what was left of the canal and placed rails over the canal bed [92]. Before the steam engine arrived in the Lehigh Valley, the coal was originally brought down from the mines by an early gravity and mule power rail car system to Manch Chunk [86]. The original loading point for the coal was the parking lot in the lower section of the town filled in by the railroads. Today, the mining company that still operates here, operates under the "old name" of the Lehigh Coal and Navigation Company "LCN"[85]

By the 1860's, the Lehigh Valley rivaled Pittsburgh in iron and steel production. The stretch of the Lehigh River, beginning at the Town of Catasaugus through Easton, was a collection of small iron and steel mills that were scatter throughout the length of this river valley. In between the two Lehigh River towns was a transportation network of roads, railroads, and canals that tied it all together. Other industries quickly sprang up supplying services or receiving services from the iron mills. Well-known large manufacturing companies such as Mack Truck, Bethlehem Steel, and Air Products sprang up in the Allentown area at the heights of the industrial phase of the Lehigh Valley. A

local graphite source supplied a growing market in pencil manufacturing which still operates today. Other industries that flourished were textile businesses, tanneries, and lumber mills.

Much has been written about trout fishing the Upper Delaware, but many writers forget about this diverse character of the Lehigh system. Whereas the Catskill and Upper Pocono's Wallenpaupack streams are exclusive tannin-stain, freestone mountain creeks, the Lehigh also has a good section of limestone creeks. Trout anglers who live in this watershed are doubly blest.

Within its 130 mile trip to Easton the river starts at an elevation of 2,100 feet and drops to 200 feet above sea level, making it one of the fasting moving rivers in the northeast. Because of the rapid discharge of water, the Lehigh River at its upper limits has been able to fight off the toxic material of the early coal, steel, lumber and tannery industries. Unfortunately, it now has very recent water born pollution element for us fishermen to deal with, "recreational white water rafting".

The river originates from the same glacial created ponds and swamps of Allegheny plateau. It is the second largest tributary of the Delaware. Its main source of water comes from a series of man made reservoirs in the heart of the Pennsylvania Pocono resort region. The river starts as a small tannin-stained creek in lower Wayne County and flows southeast toward White Haven. Before it gets to White Haven, it flows into the valley of the Francis E. Walter reservoir. It is here, that it connects to the Tobyhana Creek. The Tobyhana Creek is found in every local fisherman's conversation as a good place to fish. The creek connects the Gouldboro, Tobyhana, and the Pocono Lakes and is known to be the primer watershed for all types of regional fish. All of these lakes can be found on the State stocking list and most of the ones have small marinas with boat rentals. The Lehigh's western tributaries, the Quakake and the Nesquehoning Creeks have had to deal with the history of the early coal explorations [83] [4].

One of the biggest bodies on the upper Lehigh is the Francis E. Walter Reservoir, F. E. W. Like the Cannonville reservoir in New York the FEW can enhanced or restrict the downstream coldwater fisher of this section. A flood control lake is normally kept at low levels, but through careful regulations, it could be to permit cool water discharge [4]. A conflict between white water rafting and coldwater release has develop between trout fishermen and rafting here. Rafters want a strong flow on weekend where trout need a consistent flow 24-7. The fast moving water and deep gorges below the dam help to retain lower temperatures all the way to Palmerton. Trout can be caught the entire length of the Lehigh to Palmerton in the fall and spring, but the best location is believed to be between the FEW and Sandy Run near White Haven. Just south of the F EW survey request forms were sometimes posted for anglers to report successes. According to some fly-fishing guides, it has the same general hatches and seasons similar to the Catskills but with a heavier dependence on the Caddis aquatic insect family. In May, one should have some green body Caddis, March Browns, Grey fox and a collection of yellow sulfurs flies. In April, bring some black green and tan body Caddis, along with some Hendricksons and Grannoms flies. Over the years, fishing clubs have tried to restricted people from fishing

the upper river but the Pennsylvania State Supreme Court ruled that the Lehigh is a navi-gable river and people have a right to be within the river.

The most scenic and visited part of the river is the Lehigh Gorge State Park, which sets between Jim Thorpe and White Haven. The park became popular with the transfer of some of the abandoned Railroad property to hiking trails. Prior to transfer, only outdoorsman with four-wheel drive vehicles, Railroad workers and early white water canoeist had the ability and knowledge to access the river between Jim Thorpe and White Haven. Because of the rapids and easy access to the general public, it has become a mecca for local kayakers. Numerous rafting companies ferry people in big yellow school buses back and forth through the gorge in this section. Even in the colder seasons, the section between Drakes Creek and the Town of Jim Thorpe will be filled with kayakers. The upper section of the park discourages kayaking for us fishermen and is heavy stocked just below the R. E. W. When the F. E. W. sets high discharge rates this section of the river is better fitted for white water raffling than fishing, so plan your visit with that in mind. Unfortunate for trout, water discharge from the F.E.W is geared for white water rafting on weekends not year around which is need for a healthy trout population.

Just below the Lehigh gorge is the town of Jim Thorpe. During the early 1800's, the town of Jim Thorpe, first known as Coalville and later East and West Manch Chunk, was noted as one of the wealthiest towns in the United States. Its fortune came from the removal of the hard black energy that lay in the vertical seams to the west and the transportation network to remove it. This was the closest energy source for New York and Philadelphia. By the early 1950's, the town was on the list of the poorest communities in the Commonwealth. Today the economy comes from the river and views of it's mountains. Our early transportation impact has yet to disappear from the landscape and banks of this river. Eleven low canal dams are still visibility on the Lehigh River south of Manch Chunk so one should know the location of these dams before floating the river.

Before leaving its mountain beginning, the river picks up more water from the Pohopoco Creek, which is a tail water of both the Beltzville and Penn Forest Reservoirs. The Beltville Reservoir is another flood controlled lake built by the Army Corp of Engineers in the 1970's. It comprises 949 acres with approximately 20 miles of shoreline that sits in the middle of a 2,972 acre State Park. The special attraction to this lake is that it permits large powered boats. Like Lake Wallenpaupack, this lake is busy and noisy on the weekends. Because of the loose motor restrictions, this is another popular place for bass fishing tournaments. Both lakes also supply a coldwater discharge to the tail water trout below. Above the Beltville lake is the smaller Penn Forest Reservoir that is connected by Wild Creek.

At the town of Walnutport, the river loses its time capsule atmosphere and cold water fishery and begins its trip through the Allentown metropolis. In this 20 miles urbanized run, the Lehigh still retains its fast moving grade but finds itself in an urban environment until it meets the Delaware main branch at Easton. In this section, it picks up water from many limestone creeks. The most popular creeks in this region are the Buskill,

Little Lehigh, Saucon and the Coplay. The special treat in this area is the overall quality of these streams for trout in a fast growing urban and suburban environment. Even isolated pockets of brooks trout can found in some of the limestone streams that are not on the state stocking list but are generally on private property. One stream that produces a self-sustaining trout population comes from a water amusement park.

At Easton, a fish ladder permits the movement of migratory fish to the Lehigh. Shad and other migratory fish are using it and making it past the second dam (Chain dam) further upstream [5]. Plans are underway to make the river accessible to all fish from Easton to White Haven. The Easton Fish ladder has had problem in recent years with silting on the up-streamside and flood damage forcing it closed on occasions.

Easton to Trenton

Early explorers and local Indians once named the Lehigh River as the west branch of the Delaware River. Thus, the Delaware doubles in both width and flow as it pushes its way toward Trenton and the sea. In this stretch between Easton and Trenton, the river flows once again through a narrow valley with many rock embankments on both sides. The rock walls we see today are more pronounced due to mans action rather than the river. The low rocky hills that border the river are the remaining foundation of an early mountain system that has eroded away. These hills are littered with small bare boulder fields. Removing hard bedrock stones for construction material has always been an important industry here and quarries dot the cliffs along the entire length of the river. The bedrock also provided an easy source of iron for the early iron industry that flourished. Slag found on the banks of the river at Cook Creek is a testimony to this being the birth place of the industrial revolution in American along with the early canals and railroads that accompanied this section of the River. These early transportation systems today serve little purpose except to provide or restrict access to the water. The Pennsylvania Delaware Canal, that ran uninterrupted from Easton to Morrisville before the 2005 and 2006 floods, provided an excellent trail for river access by foot and bicycles. The path today is under construction and almost completed. The New Jersey's D & R Canal between Bulls Island and Trenton is used to carry water to central New Jersey, and as such, has a source of funding for repairs. The walking trail for the D & R canal has remained in good conditions, in part because it's an old railroad bed that was elevated above the original canal towpath. The problem with this section of the river is inadequate parking on the Pennsylvania side and outrages river access fees on the New Jersey side. On a nice weekend afternoon, one might not be able to find parking at any of the canal parking lots. Even boat ramps areas have limited parking such as Upper Black Eddy, which only has spots for five vehicles without trailers. The New Jersey side has better access to the river in this section but charge an outrages boat ramp fee for access. As for fishing in the

canals along the River, the D&R must not be overlooked for large mouth bass. The best spots, in D&R are the isolated sections far from the over fished trout stocking points.

In the Town of Lambertville is the home of the Lewis Shad Fishery. This is the last of the commercial fisherman that still uses net to catch shad. The Lewis family has been doing it since 1888 from Lewis Island, just north of the bridge that crosses the river at Lambertville [18]. The April event draws a crowd of people into the town for the spring shad fest. A great deal of attention is paid to the netting results by environmentalists, State Game agencies as well as local fishermen. Family members and volunteers do the netting in the evening. Results are announced on the local internet fishing sites and hot lines. Across the river is the Town of New Hope with its rich history of artists, actors and numerous art shops, restaurants, playhouses, and bars that would make your wife or significant other happy. As for us fishermen, we would rather be helping Mr. Lewis row his netting boat across the river. Many of the local paintings that made this place famous by starving artists come from the landscape of the river.

Some of the best fishing spots between Easton and Trenton, are locations below wing dams. Wing dams were built, as a compromise between the canal and logging companies and have become a Delaware oddity. They kept the river open for early navigation and, at the same time, provided a water control system for the canal company. They could raise the water elevation several feet upstream and at the same time keep an open channel. The early ones were constructed with logs anchor with iron pins at the base, and then flat rectangular 1 x 2 foot size stones lay vertically behind the base. Such early construction can still be seen at Scudder Falls. They were constructed as two separate walls in a V formation that pointed downstream. An opening on the downstream side allowed water, log raft, boats and fish to pass through. Over the years, the major dams were repaired by covering the original rock walls with concrete, not so much for the old logging companies but to keep the now established water level able to operate the canals, mills and water intake upstream. Today, these choke points provide a great place to catch the seasonal migration of fish, while the downstream end provides an excellent environment for small mouth bass and channel catfish. Wing dams also provide a location for kayakers to congregate. The first wing dam is at Bull Island (Lumberton) (Raritan) and has a very easy chute to go through. This was built to feed water to the Raritan Canal on the New Jersey side. The New Hope/Lambertville (Wells) dam is still in good shape, but has very strong hazardous downstream rapids with large rocks at the end of the chute. This is the most dangerous falls on the river and should be portage. Wading below the dam is very hard and should only be attempted during periods of very low flow. The wing dam at Scudder Fall is in poor condition, but the original foundations of rocks, wood logs and iron pins can still been seen. This is a favorite site for spring shad and stripers.

After Washington Crossing the flow remains strong and hard to navigate with a boat due to shallow summer time depths. This section can be deceptively shallow. You will still see many larger rocks in the river with the white crossing marks of propeller

blade hits. One can still find the usual cycle of long pools separated by wade-able rapids and long islands all the way to Trenton.

At the start of the tidal influence at the "What Trenton Makes the World Takes" bridge, boating and wading is difficult for either party but the reward is high. The rocks protrude just below the water line at this tidal zone and what was accessible at one hour may not be the next. The rocky bottom here will destroy a lower unit in a second, but this will not discourage many boaters. Trenton/Morrisville is an excellent place to fish. The holes under the three bridges contained the biggest selection of fish types in the Delaware River. Walleye, small mouth, large mouth, striped bass, both types of perch, catfish, herring, and eels can be caught under these bridges. The Route 1 bridge, used to be the legal separation point of striper regulations and fishermen have been observed walking or trolling their fish north of the bridge before landing the fish so as to take it home. The legal separation line is now the Calhoun Bridge just north of the falls. One word of caution for those who wade below and under the bridges here; you are now in the tidal limits of the river and one can be left stranded on rocks. When the tide starts coming in, it comes in fast at a foot in less than half an hour.

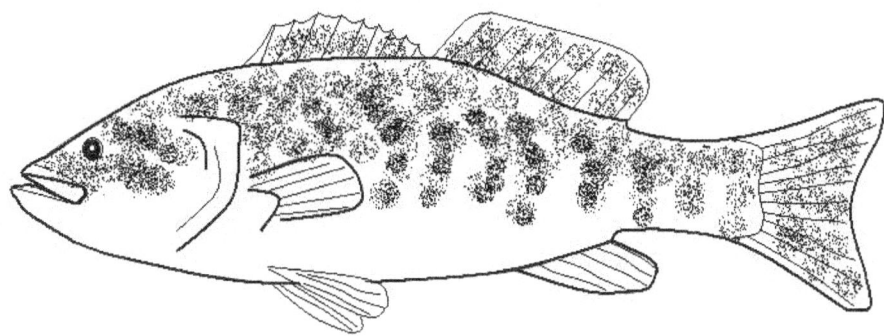

When you tighten your line and a fish jumps to the sky you know what you have for nothing jumps and dances like a Delaware Black Bass.

Small Mouth Bass

Micropterus *dolomieu*

The locals call them smallies, but that is a very insulting name for a fish with such a fighting spirit. Zane Grey would roll over in his river side grave if he heard that description of his favorite fish. Surveys conducted by the Pennsylvania State Game Commission on the River, states that the small mouth is the most caught fish in the River. All most any lure will draw a strike from a hungry small mouth and that is the wonder of these fish. The best time to fish for small mouth is when the river flow is moderate, water is less than 75 degrees, the days are long, and one can wade the river well up into darkness. Many of the other popular game fish seem to have a migratory season or special stocking windows of opportunity for one to be successful. With these small windows of

opportunities come the usual strong fishing pressure, crowded streams and boat ramps. But, the small mouth is everywhere and its voracious appetite is only matched by the channel cat. They are, by all accounts, the perfect fish at the perfect time of year. There is something about a sultry solitary evening, with a rod in hand, on the river when the bass start to feed you realizes that it doesn't get any better than this in life. You, don't need expensive fish finding equipment to seek them if you know how to read the river.

These fish seem to enjoy shallow, fast moving water and the downstream holes that accompany ripples. The bigger ones do seem to be plentiful in deep channel runs of the river. As a general rule, small mouths are few in numbers in lakes; but in rivers, they are easier to locate and the fish are more plentiful in clean, fast running water. The fisherman that is willing to get his feet wet and wade along the ripples, islands, and downstream holes will have the major advantage to catching small mouth over the person who abhors wet feet.

The average size of the fish in the River is under a pound. Small mouth in lakes tends to be larger and many are caught in the two to three pound size range. The Pennsylvania record stands at 8 pounds 8 ounces, and caught near Havertown in Berks County [1]. Color varies greatly for bass from olive green to brown but the common ones in the river are brown. To tell the difference between large and small mouth, look for the mouth to end before the rear edge of the eye. The large mouth lip will extend past the rear edge of the eye. Small mouth will have vertical lines while the large mouth will have horizontal lines. Black bass begin spawning when the temperature reaches 55 to 65 F in shallow waters with gravel bottoms and will actively feed to 75F. The males guard the nest and it is unethical to fish for them when they are guarding the nest. Legal and ethical practices dictate that the bass must be released when fishing for them this time of year (check regulations). Sportsmanship suggests that other species should be targeted during the spawn.

Map 16:
This is a scenic section of river with high rock bluff, many islands and a strong flow. The river is full of rock ledges that bass love to hide under. Two good eddies to fish at is the one above Whippoolwill Island and at Pinchers Point Eddy. Good wading locations can be access at Raubs Island, Lynn Island and Crosswater Island. Many fishermen are finding access to the river from the New Jersey side by crossing over a rail line. Peak shad run is in early May late April.

Spotted Bass

Another black bass type in the local waters is the spotted bass. This is generally known as a southern fish, but has been stocked in the Delaware River. This bass has the mouth and eye configuration of a small mouth but the markings of a large mouth.

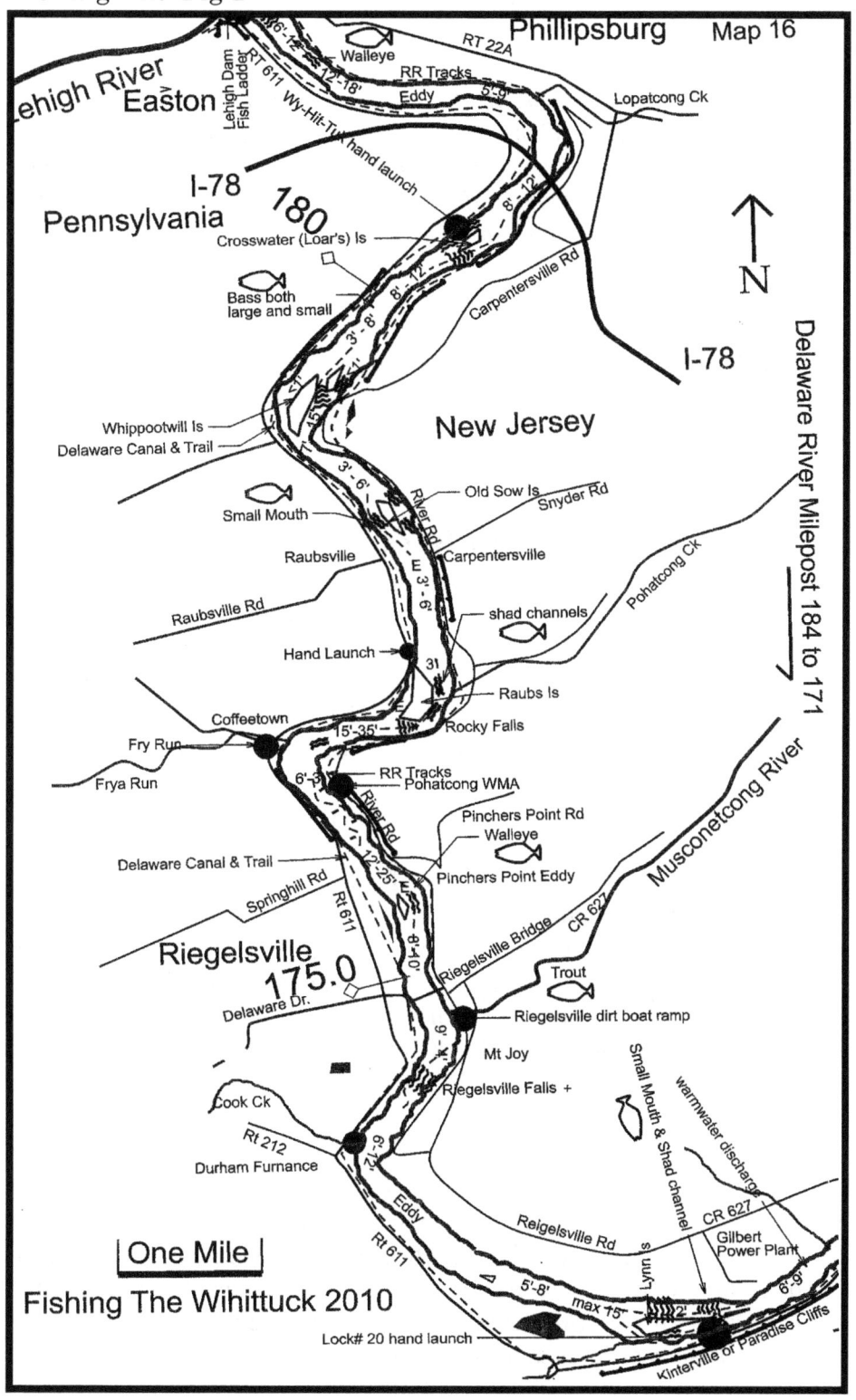

Map 17:
This section has two warm water discharge point, if operating, Gilbert Generation station below Lynn Island and the Riegel Paper Company to attract shad in the spring. Slow moving pools between Lynn Island and Frenchtown, make this a slow trip. The river becomes very shallow after Milford and travel is difficult. At Frenchtown the commercial rafting companies control the river. Peak shad run is in April.

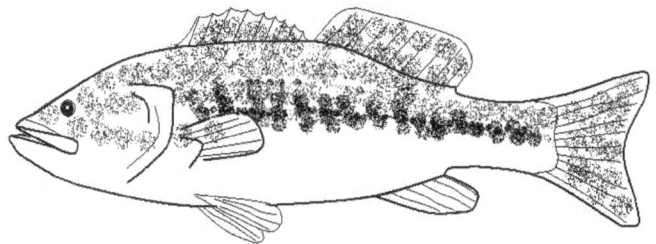

Large Mouth Bass
No other fresh water fish attach so much attention as the large mouth bass

    The large mouth is the king of the local warm water lakes, ponds, and reservoirs of the region. These fish love lakes and slow moving sections of rivers. The fish will get slightly larger than the small mouth with an average size of 1 to 3 pounds. The local state record large mouth was taken near the Maurice River in South New Jersey at ten pounds 14 oz. in 1980 [3]. The best fishing holes may not be the large mega lakes but golf course size ponds that you can find in your own back yard. The experts on large mouth bass state that the optimum fishing temperature is 65 to 75 degree. They like to patrol the edges of the lakes, so you don't need a boat to be successful for this abundant game fish. Look for them in and around lily pads, rock structures and logs. Large mouth bass love to hide from the sun under these structures. In the summer time when the water gets hot, look for large mouth bass in deep sections of the lakes, shady places and any spot where the water may be cooler such as underground springs and cool water stream outlets. In the winter search in warmer spot such as sunny areas near banks, and deep holes when the thermal temperatures turn. In the spring and fall you should find them at there usual spot, near the shore lines.

Lures

    All Black Bass hit basically the same lures, it's the size and where you use the lures that bring success. As the name of the fish implies uses larger lures and hooks for the large mouth over the small mouth. There are hundred of lures but most can be divided into Spinner, Plugs and Plastics all with one purpose, create movement that will set a fish off. What can be said about these bass lures is universal for all fishing lures.

Fishing The Big D

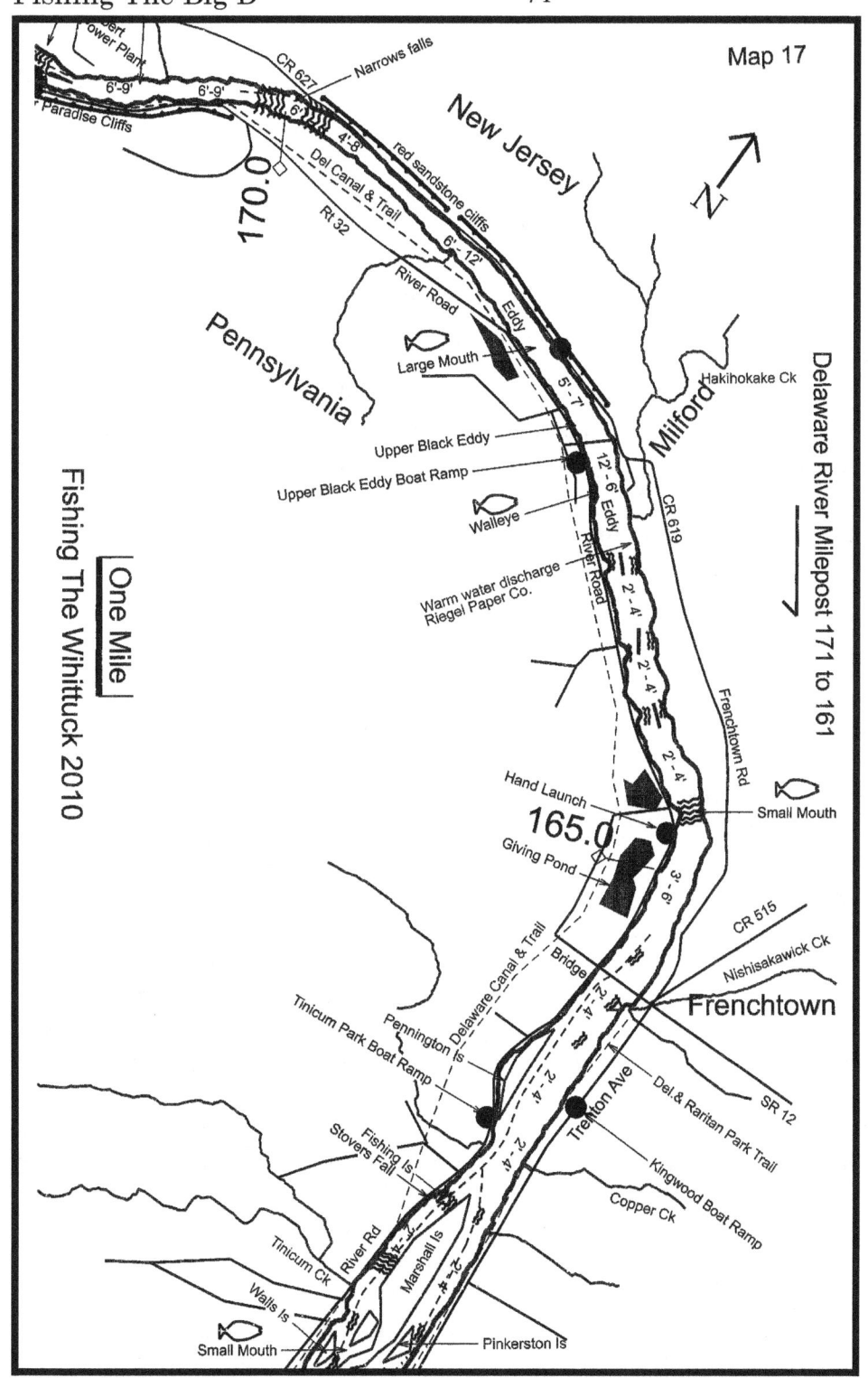

The Middle Delaware

Spinner

Spinner Lure

Spinners are the most effective lure for small fish on the River. They require little skill in throwing and retrieving and colors seem to have little to do with success for the novice fisherman. When using spinners, always keep an eye on the hooks, straighten any bends, or if you are missing parts of the tri-hook, replace it. The trick to using a spinner is to get and keep the blade moving. After every cast give it a quick jerk, to get the blade turning, and then quickly start bringing it in steady. The rotating blade is the trick as it sets up a vibration that attracts fish. The cheaper spinners lack the smoother movement than the more expensive ones. On each cast, try a different speed, but never stop the speed in the middle of the retrieval as this might cause the blade to stop. If you see fish following the lure but never strike it, try a different speed, replace it with another, check to see if you still have a hook on the end, or add some live bait to the end. They have a very keen smell and your scent might be on the fabric tail of the spinner. The only problem with spinners is they seem to catch small fish.

Map 18:
Here the river has a consistence moderately fast flow that meanders between many islands. The depth is shallow with mild ripples that surround the islands. The constant flow, shallow depth and mild ripples create a perfect place for rafting companies and novice river people to operate. Because of the multiple islands and channels, one needs additional visits to see the entire river, insuring repeat visitors for the rafting companies. The abandoned rail bed on the New Jersey side, now a hiking & biking trail, also provides an avenue for bicycle return trips for the lone rafter. The rafting companies put in at a public launch below Frenchtown, New Jersey and pick up at Point Pleasant, PA. The Point Pleasant landing on the Pennsylvania side is private. Public access is on the New Jersey side behind the old bridge abutment use to avoid river access fees. The bank is steep but kayaks and canoes can be carried up. To find the next public landing requires a long slow paddle to Bull's Island Park. At the end of this eddy is the Bulls Island wing dam, which can be dangerous to the unaware victims. Bulls Island has two ramps, one above the wing dam and another just below it, both on the New Jersey side. Good places to wade are below the wing dam at Bulls Island, around Hendrick Island and in the rift upstream from Stockton. The shallow Stockton falls can be tricky to navigate in low water. Peak runs: April for Shad, May for Striped bass.

Crank bait

For larger bass diving plugs or what some call "crank bait", are productive. This is also a good lure when water visibility is poor or at night. The vibrations will bring fish from some distance away even without them seeing it at first. The movement or action,

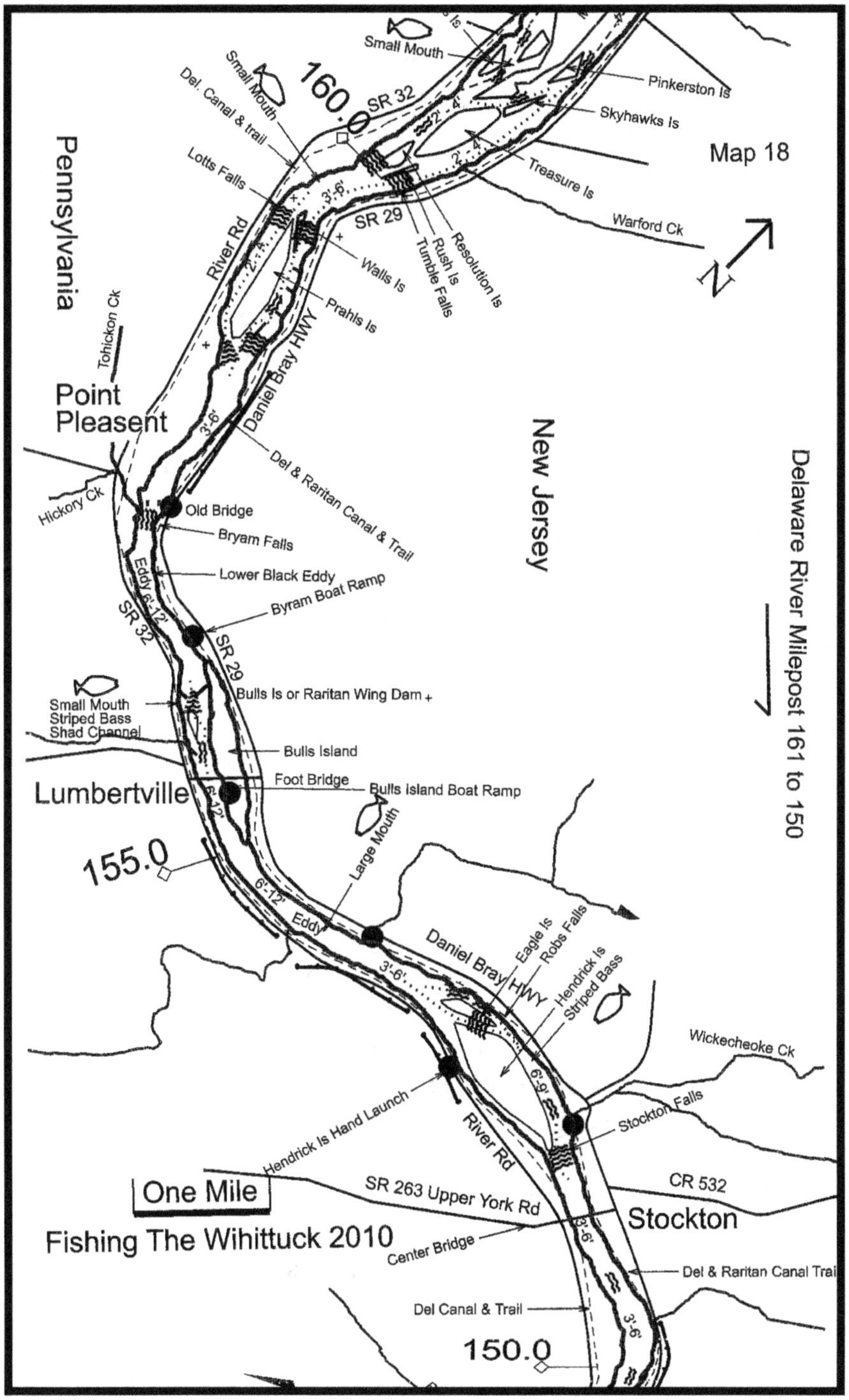
Map 18
Pennsylvania
New Jersey
Delaware River Milepost 161 to 150
160.0
155.0
150.0
Small Mouth
Pinkerston Is
Skyhawks Is
Treasure Is
Warford Ck
SR 32
SR 29
Del. Canal & trail
Lotts Falls
Resolution Is
Rush Is
Tumble Falls
Walls Is
Prahls Is
River Rd
Tohickon Ck
Point Pleasent
Daniel Bray HWY
Del & Raritan Canal & Trail
Hickory Ck
Old Bridge
Bryam Falls
Lower Black Eddy
Byram Boat Ramp
Bulls Is or Raritan Wing Dam +
Small Mouth
Striped Bass
Shad Channel
Bulls Island
Foot Bridge
Lumbertville
Bulls Island Boat Ramp
Large Mouth
Eddy
Eagle Is
Robs Falls
Hendrick Is
Striped Bass
Wickecheoke Ck
Stockton Falls
Hendrick Is Hand Launch
CR 532
SR 263 Upper York Rd
Stockton
One Mile
Fishing The Wihittuck 2010
Center Bridge
Del & Raritan Canal Trai
Del Canal & Trail

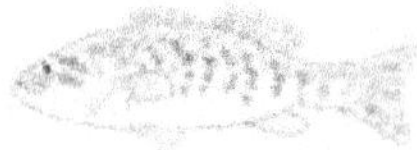

The Middle Delaware

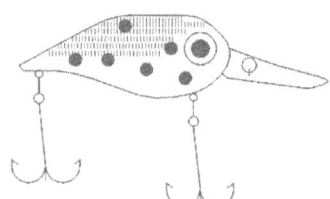

of diving crank bait is based on the length and size of the bill. If you are fishing in deep water, you want one that will dive deep. The diving depth of the lure is based on the weight of the lure, angle of the blade, and type of line. Most good lure manufacturers will post the diving depth of the lure in feet. To achieve the maximum depth of the lure, the line should have as small a diameter as possible. The larger diameter mono line will float and not permit the plug to dive properly. Some of the serious crank bait fishermen use fiberglass rods with bait casting reels. These same people will use sand paper and heat to modify the bills to achieve the desire action. A good lure is balance and once that balance is lost, it will not operate property. If you replace the hooks, you might have to add weight by wrapping wire or melting lead onto the hooks. If the lure is acting erratically, check it for debris and remove any excess line on the knot ring of the lure. Plugs that run on the surface, are best thrown at or after the sun sets on the water. Most fish are light sensitive and they will not look up at the surface until the sun is out of the sky. Surface plugs are exciting to use in the evening when the fish are feeding the surface. The jutted bug type plugs are a good night time lure to use.

Map: 19: *What makes New/Hope Lambertville Dam the number one worst fall in the river? Large downstream rocks cause three to four foot waves. Unless one likes to ride waves the trip is to short and brutal to be enjoyable. Portage and access is best from the New Jersey side. Many good place for river access, Bowman towers, Keelers Island, Titusville Falls and the canals*

Plastic

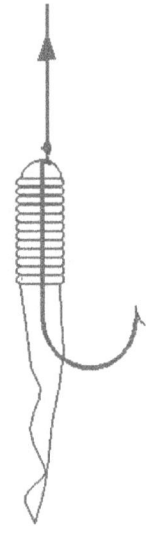

To be successfully with plastic lures for bass or any other fish, the presentation counts and to get a good presentation means getting the correct line, weight and hook combination. Clearly fishing with plastics takes more time and skill to learn then other lures. As in using any lure, observe the action, if it looks unnatural it might not work. The traditional four to six inch plastic worm is a good general lure for largemouth bass. For small mouth the shorter twister tail worms or a short hollow type of plastic called a tube are good. The more expensive scented lures are productive but need to be change regular. Worms are best used as a Carolina rig, which employs a sliding bullet shaped sinker above an offset hook. In order for these rigs to be productive, the hook needs to be very sharp and as such, you will pay more for a pack of these hooks. If the hook is rusted or blunted, don't use it. The sliding bullet type sinker that rides the line up and down will provide a slower more natural diving action for the worm. When tying the offset worm hooks wrap and secure the line to the shaft of the hook,

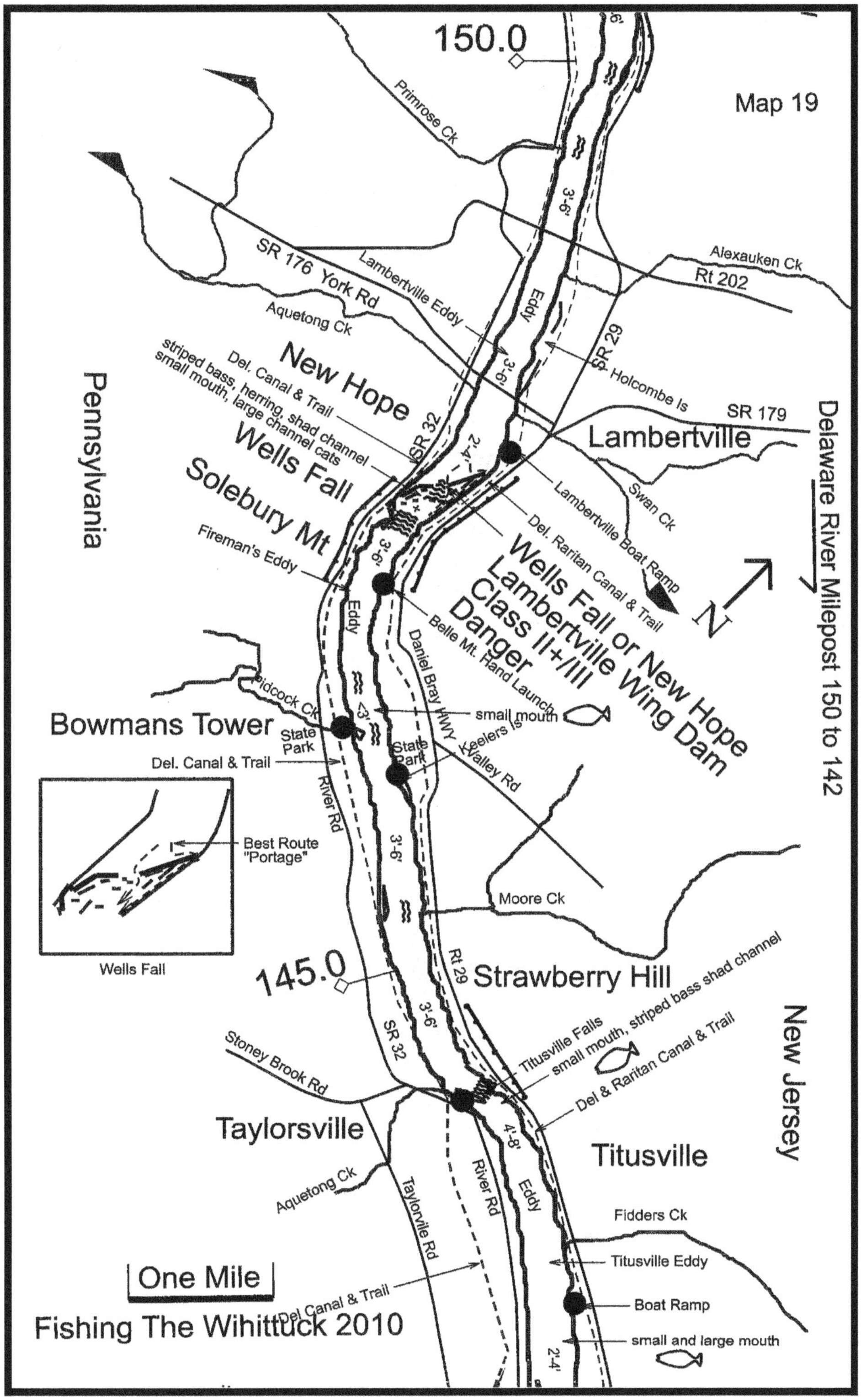
150.0
Map 19
Primrose Ck
Alexauken Ck
Rt 202
SR 176 York Rd
Lambertville Eddy
Eddy
Aquetong Ck
New Hope
SR 29
Holcombe Is
striped bass, herring, shad channel
small mouth, large channel cats
Del. Canal & Trail
SR 179
SR 32
Lambertville
Wells Fall
Solebury Mt
Swan Ck
Lambertville Boat Ramp
Del. Raritan Canal & Trail
Wells Fall or New Hope
Lambertville Wing Dam
Class II+/III
Danger
Fireman's Eddy
Belle Mt. Hand Launch
Daniel Bray Hwy
Pidcock Ck
small mouth
Keelers Is
Bowmans Tower
State Park
Del. Canal & Trail
Valley Rd
River Rd
Best Route
"Portage"
Wells Fall
Moore Ck
145.0
Rt 29
Strawberry Hill
SR 32
Titusville Falls
small mouth, striped bass shad channel
Del & Raritan Canal & Trail
New Jersey
Stoney Brook Rd
Taylorsville
Titusville
Aquetong Ck
Taylorvile Rd
River Rd
Eddy
Fidders Ck
Titusville Eddy
One Mile
Del Canal & Trail
Boat Ramp
Fishing The Wihittuck 2010
small and large mouth
Delaware River Milepost 150 to 142

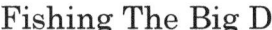

The Middle Delaware

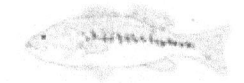

not the eye. When the line is tied to the shaft of the hook, it provides two advantages. First, when you "set the hook", the hook is pulled on an angle where it is most likely to catch the inside of the fish's mouth rather than a pull directly out. The other advantage is that after what might seem like a hundred casts with the same set up, the consistent hitting of the sliding sinker against the knot will weaken the string. Say goodbye to the big one you had been fishing for over an hour. The color of the worm is almost always a dull green and brown. When using plastics the presentation can vary and it's best to have multiple types of retrieval, much like a baseball pitcher. Many use a drop, slow drag and quick pull retrieval method. If that fails to bring a strike a quick steady retrieval might work. Be creative in your use of plastics is the key to success.

Map 20:

Washington's crossing has good access from both side of the river along with nice places to wade above the bridge. New Jersey will still try to collect money for kayak access to river.

Two strong falls can be found on this last section of the none-tidal River. The first is Scuddars Falls, an old wing dam with three breached openings. The center can be navigated with a powerful boat. The channel on the New Jersey side has large waves at it mouth and classified as a strong class II. Fish stack up in a pool just below the just below in the spring. Good parking and river access can be found on the New Jersey side of Scudders Fall. Pennsylvania has good access to the river from Islands but no parking. There is a shallow boat ramp on the Pennsylvania side about a mile down river of the Falls

Trenton Falls marks the division between tidal and non tidal river. The Trenton falls strengths vary greatly due to seasonal flow and daily changing of the tides. At high tide, in summer low flow, rocks and the current of the water disappear to form an eddy. But when is changes, it becomes a raging rapids with visible rocks. Beside the native bed rock, the bottom is loaded with concrete blocks exposed rebar, car parts and shopping carts, all of which can puncture holes in kayaks and canoes. On the New Jersey side, a mile long pier blocks any attempt to beach a craft. A small dam between the mouth of the Assumpink Creek and an island on the Jersey side does not help the journey. Stay to the west side of the island. The current here can become very strong and can carry one some distance. The Pennsylvania side is a little friendlier but at low tide the banks are covered with slippery mud coated rocks and mud holes. River access can be found just above and below the falls on the Pennsylvania side, and expects to pay on the Jersey side. This section is much better suited as a fishing spot than white water rafting. This location has many good places to wade for small mouth bass. It is shallow above the falls with access along the New Jersey side from a river walk trail and from the levee on the Morrisville side. Best fishing is during outgoing tide under the bridges at Trenton/Morrisville.

Fishing The Big D   77

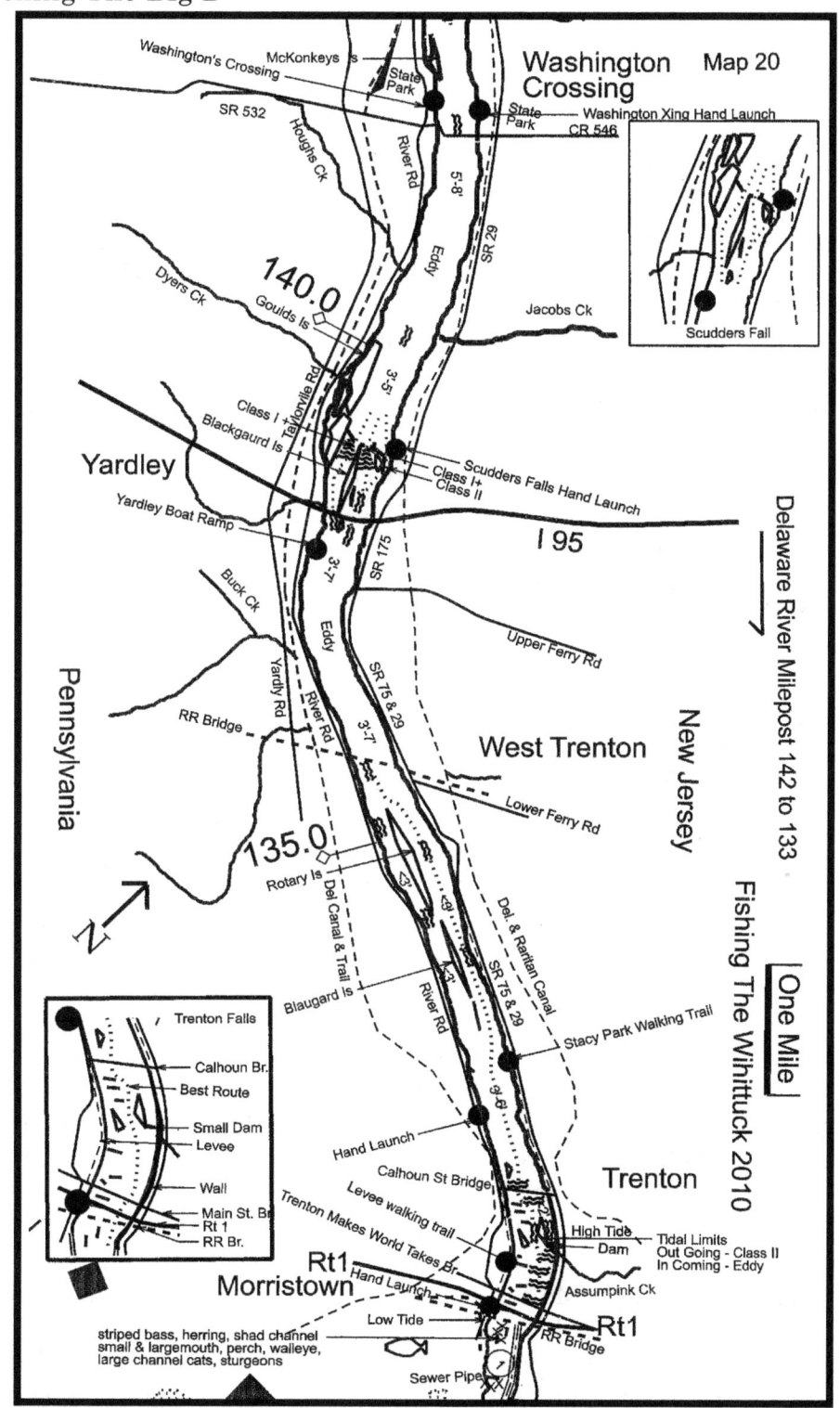

Live Bass Bait

The Middle Delaware

Fishing is big business and most of the shows and articles that engulf us in our day to day life are trying to hook us like fish. A general rule is live bait is always more productive than lures, especially in heavy fished waters. The most common minnows or bait found in the water you fish are the same ones the fish are feeding on. The best live bait for small mouth is the black ugly hellgrammite. These aquatic insects are the nymph stage of the Doomsfly which are very plentifully under rocks in the shallow ripples of good small mouth bass territories. They go by a variety of different names such as pincher, clippers or ugly bugs. They stay on the hook very well so one can catch multiple fish from one insect and if you run out you can always get some more from the river. Not just bass, but every fish in the river, loves to eat these bug so you never know what fish will strike it. Their pinchers will draw blood from your fingers but once you learn how to handle them, by holding them behind the head, its not so bad. The best way to present the hellgrammite is to place the hook through the hard shell behind the head and then through the abdomen once. Do not ball the insect up on the hook, but let the tail hang out and it will draw attention from any nearby fish. If you are fishing for bass, use a light split shot sinker about a foot above the bait and do not let it rest too long in any one spot or a catfish will most likely smell it first. Throw it upstream and let the current carry it down as a normal dislodge hellgrammite might float down stream. Once it's at the limits of the line, retrieve it slowly, you might get a strike on the retrieval. The bugs are full of juices and when they are opened up, they can attract fish by smell so of course the fresher ones work best.

Few bait stores sell them so you'll have to get them yourself. To catch them use a two X two foot wooden frame sieve, (max legal size permitted in PA), with a quarter-inch heavy galvanize metal screen placed inside the wood frame. Place the screen in strong current downstream of foot size rocks that can be flipped over. The current will wash the hellgrammites out from under the rock and into the screen. Don't get discourage if the first dozen rocks you turn over yield nothing, they seem to be in clusters, so once you find the first one, more will be under the next rock. The most productive time is during low water flow. If the water level appears to be at or below summertime normal, you should have a very productive hunt. It's best to use two people, one to hold the screen while the other to flip the rocks and pick the bait from the screen. When flipping the rock, it's a good idea to wear work gloves because there are all kinds of sharp objects lying under the rocks, like broken glass and dark hidden things with pinchers and teeth that will scare the heck out of you. Never flip a rock that is only partially submerged, these rocks are excellent hiding spots for snakes. Judging from the different sizes of hellgrammites, they live in this nymph stage for two years. Most of the ones you will find may be too small to fish with so please return them. You will be looking for the large, meaty ones, about half an inch wide and about two inches long. I believe they can be over harvested, so looking for them at ripples near parking lots can be frustrating. In the final stage of the nymph stage in late August or September these three to four inch insects will develop wings and

Fishing The Big D

can be seen on rocks and trees along the river and should be left alone
to breed for next season's supplies. After their aerial hatch in early fall hunting for the insects can be a little frustrating.

Be warned, hellgrammites will craw out of cans and buckets without lids. they should be stored in covered minnow buckets with flowing water through it with grass, or in dry, covered, bait buckets with lids and damp grass or leaves in the bottom. Hellgrammites will suffocate and die in stagnate water within a few hours. Outside of that, they can live in covered containers with a damp grass bed for days. Grass or leaves have to be put into the container because these bugs like to have space and if they are crowded, they will fight and kill each other.

While searching for Hellgrammites, you will find other fish-bait or bait-fish in the water like crayfish, minnow, eels madtoms, stonecats and leeches. All of these can be excellent bait. Crayfish are another common food for bass. If you find some crayfish, hook them through the abdomen so when you pull the crayfish, it will swim backwards as it normally does. Leeches are not a popular bait on the lower half of the River. I seldom see them in the bait stores here, but if you do find them, try them. I have used them on far northern fishing trips and they were very successful. I was told for best results to stick a finger into the can, let one tack on and permit it to fatten up with blood before hooking them. "Draw's more fish that way", I was told, but I was not that desperate for a fish.

Madtoms, or what some call stonescats, resemble a finger size small catfish. Many fishermen state they are better than hellgrammites for bass. They tend to draw strikes from the bigger fish. True stonescats, are on the unauthorized bait list and should not be used. The madtoms, on the other hand are authorized, and plentifully in the rivers and streams of the watershed, but most people commonly call them stonecats. These small catfish like fish have poisonous barbs and will infect your hands if not properly handled.

YOY

Delaware River small mouth bass are now infected with a new disease. The disease is commonly called the Youth of the Year (YOY) which infects a single age group of a fish species rather than the entire specie. It's a silent killer that is seldom notice because it doesn't produced highly published fish kills. Thus one can find a large amount of a particular size or age group of a fish in an effected area but over time the entire population will disappear. For years Susquehanna anglers have been complaining about decreasing small mouth catches in the lower Susquehanna River system. The Pennsylvania game commission in 2000 did an intensive survey of the Susquehanna River and determines that it was infected with Youth of the Year disease. The most affected area was downstream of Sunbury to the Maryland State Line. The Pennsylvania Game Commission went on to say that the small mouth bass population's drops were due mostly to the YOY and not increases numbers of predator fish like pike, flathead catfish and walleye. In 2011, Pennsylvania Game Commissions surveyed the Delaware River and

found the same YOY infection. The highest infected area was the lower non-tidal section from the Water Gap to Trenton, with Yardley being the highest. The Schuylkill River was tested as well and found positive for YOY with high concentrations in the Hamburg section of the River.

The disease hits the first year fish with lesions on fins and loses of scales which later leads to the fish's death. The YOY is brought on by the columnaris disease which is secondary infection that health fish can fight off. The Susquehanna surveys determine that the columnaris disease outbreaks are brought on by summertime low water flows, high temperatures, and low oxygen counts. In all of the ten plus years of surveys a strong correlations was establish showing years of low flow rates and increasing outbreaks. The columnaris bacteria is common in soil and harmless to human and normally health fish. Pennsylvania Game commission claims that only small mouth bass are victims but the author thinks that all the members of the Black Bass Fish Family which includes sunfish blue gill and largemouth bass may be affected in the same way to the disease. The commission goes on to say that it is a growing problem that it exceeds normal fish mortality rates. The commission has provided little advice on how to halt the YOY and admits it is still studying the problem. Why than is this disease now killing our most treasured game fish. The State could provide little guidance other than stating strong flow rates are needed to offset the disease.

To draw water from our river have we been slowing the natural flow rates down? The Delaware watershed supplies water to, New York City, Philadelphia and the growing urban areas in between. Much of that water is never returned or comes back further down stream into the tidal section of the river thus by pass small mouth habitat. Besides the consumption of water to outside watershed, thousands of gallons are lost daily to evaporations from reservoirs. About 8 out of 10 gallons of water that flows down the Delaware River gets used in some way. When the average flow rates between the first and second haft of the last century are compared the difference is small. But it becomes obvious after looking at the yearly Trenton flow chart that flow rates have become more erratic in the second half of the last century with more than average floods and droughts. It can be quick to point out that these erratic flow levels can be attributed to poor storm water management from growing urban areas, better recording devices and possible global warming. But regardless of the reason the fact is that extreme droughts and floods are stressful to all fish and any living creature under stress is more acceptable to disease, infections and lower reproductive numbers. Thus will small mouth bass become a stocked fish in the Delaware River?

Large Urban Lakes

Below Easton, only two lakes the Merrill Creek and Round Valley Reservoirs are considered coldwater lakes because they support year around lake trout, only the Merrill Creek Reservoir is within the watershed. But, Round Valley is within easy driving distance of Phillipsburg. All other lakes and ponds should be considered warmwater, south of the Water Gap. Some of the larger ones have strong coldwater attributes of deep water with gravel or stone bottoms and vertical temperature structures with collections of year round coldwater fish except trout. The Army Corp of Engineers built many of these lakes during the dam boom years of the 1950's through 1970's. The 650 acre Merrill Creek Reservoir and the 2,000 acre Round Valley, which is 180 feet deep, both have been successfully stocked with lake trout. The sister lake of Round Valley, Spruce Creek, which is a little shallower, as such, is a warm water lake[80][81]. In Pennsylvania, the 1,450 acres Lake Nockamixon is the biggest on the Pennsylvania side and known for its non-marine stripers [82]. All of the above lakes have small marinas for boat rentals and a rich variety of fish, which includes walleyes, hybrid bass and pickerel. On the internet, there is a wealth of information on these large regional lakes advertising fishing hotspots, tournaments, maps and chat lines well beyond the scope of this book. When making a special visit to one of these lakes in a boat, try fishing for something that is unique to the particular water body, such as lake trout in the New Jersey lakes or stripers at Nockamixon. This region is dotted with many other smaller, named and un-named, water bodies which can be very productive if you can get to the water. Lake Galena (Peace Valley) which is typical of the smaller warm water lakes south of the Water Gap is owned by North Penn Water Authority, but Buck County Park Service controls the recreational aspect of the lake. As with most lakes that is use for water consumption, gasoline engines are prohibited. This lake was a product of the Point Pleasant pumping station. All of the state built lakes have retained public access and as such many have been stocked with fish. Some private lakes, like Springdale Lake near Churchville PA are privately owned and not open for fishing. Private water companies will buy some of these public lakes and post them for fishing. The smaller flood control lakes or impoundment ponds should be looked for on a topography map and visited in the spring or cool fall. By the time, the days become hot generally by June; most of the very small ponds used for flood control will become over choked in algae blooms and hard to bass fish. The phosphorous and nitrates we use to make our clothes and lawns bright also add colors to our ponds. Somehow, the fish can survive these nutrient rich, oxygen poor ponds.

Fundamentals of Lake Fishing

It would be easy to classify lakes into two simple types, cold and warm water lakes. Warmwater, sometimes called Eutrophic, lakes need to be repeatedly stocked with trout and other cold-water fish. Coldwater lakes, sometimes called Oligitrophic lakes, on the other hand, can handle a healthy, self-supporting coldwater fishery such as trout.

The Middle Delaware

Coldwater lakes here are deep, man-made reservoirs normally originating in mountain regions. Warmwater lakes may be man-made but are generally shallower, supporting a smaller variety of fish species but larger numbers of fish per volume. Whereas coldwater lakes generally have a stronger vertical and thermal gradient, warmwater lakes have a more uniform, vertical temperature throughout the year. Another factor is the water quality. Warmwater lakes have a higher nutrient, lower oxygen ratio; while coldwater lakes have a low nutrient, high oxygen ratio. Thus, coldwater lakes tend to have higher water clarity than warmwater lakes. The bottom type is a factor as well. Warmwater lakes have muddy bottoms and coldwater lakes have stone or gravel bottoms. Whether a lake is cold or warm, the fishing quality is based on the balance of nutrients and oxygen level. High nutrient levels will produce algae blooms in the summer, while low nutrient levels will produce limited food production. The age of water bodies is a factor that can't be overlooked, as the older lakes will lose its depth and have to be de-silted from time to time. The truth of the matter is that few lakes fit perfectly in these two categories and that is a good thing for us. If a lake is truly cold or warm, at the strictest limits, then it would have no life or very little at all. Most lakes are a mixture of the two and termed Mesotrophic lakes [105]. Lakes used for water consumption, like the reservoirs of New York City, will come as close to a true Oligitrophic that one can find because that is what the city wants - a super clean, sterile water body. What we as fishermen need to recognize is the features these Mesotrophic lakes have and what our best tactic should be. Warmwater fish such as bass, catfish, and carp can live very well in coldwater lakes. Some coldwater fish, such as trout, may not survive very long in a warm lake. Pikes, pickerel plus crappies, perch and walleyes can live and reproduce in both warmwater and coldwater lakes and rivers very well. These fish are called coldwater fish because they reproduce very well in coldwater and all lakes in this region get cold and experience periods of ice cover.

Shallow Ponds (Euptrophic)

Temperature profile is unform all year around
Mud bottom - high nutrient - low oxygen - heavy vegetation - cloudy water
Fish in shallow channels, near tree stumps, under overhanging bushes and at the dam breast
Can be diffucult to fish in the summer and winter

Deep Coldwater Lakes (Oligitrophic)

Spring and Fall Fish Depth — Mixed Layer
Extreme Winter and Summer Fish Depth
Summer Temperature Profile - water gets cooler with depth
Winter Temperature Profile - Water gets warmer with depth

Temperature profile non uniform different summer or winter
Stone bottom, low nutrient - high oxygen - low vegetation, clear water
Fish with water temperature in mind -
Fish the tail and head waters
Can be diffucult to locate fish

Fishing The Big D

The two most stressful times of year for any lake, or any water body for that matter, is late summer and late winter. These two periods are when most fish kill will happen. The dog days of August and the old ice of February are when oxygen levels are their lowest. During these two events, one might find the fishing also at it worst because of the stress this placed on the fish. Oxygen levels will increase in water due to aeration, (water movement over rocks, wind on the water surfaces), diffusion (the process of oxygen passing into the air), photosynthesis (plant life producing oxygen), and the cooling of the water (cold water can hold more oxygen than warm water). Oxygen levels will drop with little or no movement of water, lack of winds, ice cover with snow, high amount of oxygen demanding agents, warming of the waters, and cloudy or dirty water, which leads to the stop of the photosynthesis process. When oxygen levels drop below 5.0 mg/l, fish and other aquatic life will begin to experience stress [124]. To see how much photosynthesis plays on oxygen levels, look at a summer time dissolved oxygen chart of the river from one of the reporting stations that monitor it(Trenton). In the warmer months, a daily fluctuation can be seen with the lowest levels in the morning and highest in the evening. During flooding, one would think that the dissolved oxygen levels would be high, but they are actually lower because of the lack of sunlight that enters the water. It becomes very easy to see, that a correct mixture of aquatic plant life is very important for a healthy water system. Patches of green colored plants that are rooted in the bottom of the lake is a good sign of a healthy lake or river and a good place to fish. Lack of green rooted plants are a poor sign and will lead to poor fishing in hot summer months and under cold winter ice. Any non-green colored floating aquatic vegetation signifies a high oxygen demand agents and an over fertilized environment.

Over the year we have populated our highly pressured water bodies with more than sport fish we have dump various bait fish to feed our prized quarries along with our dreams of increasing our growing eagle population. The result is many of our popular urban lakes are now over populated with gizzard shad, alfwife and carp type fish or minnows. Our hope was that with such a massive amount of easy picking food our game fish should be large and plentiful in our local public lakes. One problem is that many of the larger foraging fish disrupt the reproduction beds of our bass thus decreasing first year bass number. The second problem has to do with the feeding habit and fishing pressure. With such a large amount of natural food in the water are these adult bass more lightly to suck down a live tasty minnow that swims by or chase an artificial lure? Another question to ask, with our growing fishing pressure are we conditioning these fish, both in an environmental and genetic way to be less aggressive. Face it, the more aggressive fish has a higher chance to get caught. With the aggressive fish slowing disappearing are we promoting non-aggressive genes in the local aquatic gene pool, some marine biologist think so.

The Middle Delaware

Common rules for lake fishing:
- Look and fish near structures
- Fish in the shadows
- Work the weed patches
- Look for rocky bottoms
- Work the inlets hard
- Watch for steep, submerged grade changes
- For small pan fish, look and watch the local diving birds (loons)
- Fish the channels on low water
- Watch for surface activity
- Get away from the parking lot and boat ramp, unless it was just stock or a fishing tournament was recently held and they release the fish at that spot.
- Avoid days with heavy boat traffic
- Don't forget to fish the tail waters of lake.
- Fish deep water 10' to 20' in hot Summer and cold Winter days
- Fish near the banks or in shallow water during Spring and Fall
- Lean to catch the local bait fish in the Lake and use them

Chapter IV

THE TIDAL DELAWARE
Trenton to Wilmington

Under the golden dome of the New Jersey State Capitol, the river flows over the last set of rapids, marking its end of the flow through the Atlantic hilly piedmont plain to the flat Atlantic coastal plain. This is the industrial heartland of the river. It is here that the Delaware has matured to a functional important waterway. It also marks a clear sharp line between fish type and techniques to use. A small fishing boat can easily be swamped by the wake of the commercial barges and shipping traffic that prowl the water regularly from this point on. This is where boating skills are required for safe handling. Channel markers and tugboats with barges start to appear in the commercial shipping channels below the falls. It is also here that whales and other ocean wildlife been observed in the waters.

Between Trenton and the northern edge of Philadelphia, the river is surrounded by green thick tree lines, low tidal mud flats, and exclusive old mansions that hide the highly urbanization world just beyond. Hidden from the main channel are the hundreds of acres of urban wetland marshes and ponds that were formed from the creeks that empty into the river from both sides. Just below Trenton, a 1700- acre wetland filters the water that enters the river. It is estimated that twice that number of acres reside along the river between Trenton and Philadelphia. When one passes the Palmyra-Tacony Bridge, the west side of the river is now lined with old warehouses and vacant weed lots where once heavy manufacturing facilities like the Frankford Arsenal and Cramps Shipyard in Kensington were. These buildings are now mostly unrecognizable from their glory days. The barriers to urban-renewal for this section are our needs for the petroleum–chemical industries, sewage treatment facilities, power plants, storage for junk car, and Interstate 95. The fish in this section of the river also carry the highest concentration of PCBs, according to studies done by the DRBC.

Today in this urban section of the Delaware it is hard to image that at one time commercial fishing took place here. Information on this subject comes from a variety of sources, but the most important are the recorded catches of operating fishing companies such as Fancy Hill Fishery located south of Philadelphia, the Howell Family Fishery at Woodbury NJ, and the Moravian settlements on the Lehigh. Commercial fishing was done on the fresh water river section from the 1600 to early 1900s hundreds. Their records all show one recurring theme, how man's acts affected and influenced the river and catches. An anchored net on the bank was the first system used in the lower sections of the river. The boats would row the nets out into the river then a team of horses would haul the nets back. At the height of this shoreline fishing practice, these part-time fishing companies [6] could collectively haul an estimated 20,000 fish within 24 hours during the

The Tidal Delaware River

spring shad runs. In order to haul fish from the shore in this matter, fishing rights were inherited through land titles at key locations. Like mineral rights, this riparian fishing right could restrict the new owner from fishing the waterway. In a 1909 interview, Charles H. Cramp of Cramp's Shipyard, recalled how his family fished the river for employment. At one time the river banks were full of fishing companies with fishing rights to fish from the banks or skips to catch fish from within the river. Not just spring shad but "catties and eels" were caught for consumption by these companies. Mr. Cramp recalled that the center of the fresh water fish market was between Berks (Cherry), Aramingo (Gunner's Run) and Richmond Street (Old Point Road), today this part of Kensington is called Fishtown. Most of the skip or " gillen" were docked at Otis or Susquehanna Ave. The smoking of fish also took place here. In an 1875 report by the New Jersey commissioners it was noted five major fishing companies controlled this part of the urban tidal river and were all from the Fishtown area. Due to the declining catches in the mid 1800's the commissioners recommended that Pennsylvania needed to enforce its fishing regulations on these companies [147].

Map 21: *Start of the tidal Delaware River. The average channel depth is between 20 to 25 feet. Underwater obstacles such as rocks and submerged wooden piers outside of the channel are hazardous to high speed boating. The many freshwater lagoons and lily pad grove provide excellent places for both large and small mouth bass to hide. Popular location for spring striped bass is Landreth Channel under the Turnpike Bridge and Trenton Channel just below the falls. The power plant at Duck Island when pumping hot water has access to bank fisherman and is popular during spring shad runs. Shad and herring can also be pulled from the river at the Trenton ball park and a spot on a desiderating unsafe wall between the ball park and the last bridge crossing the river. Van Sciver Lake is a privately own lake for member only. Best fish here is outgoing tide. When the water is high, it's best to fish on the Pennsylvania side. When the water is low it's best to fish in the New Jersey side in Moon channel. Expect the fish to stack up just below exposed rocks line on the tidal flows at Trenton Falls*

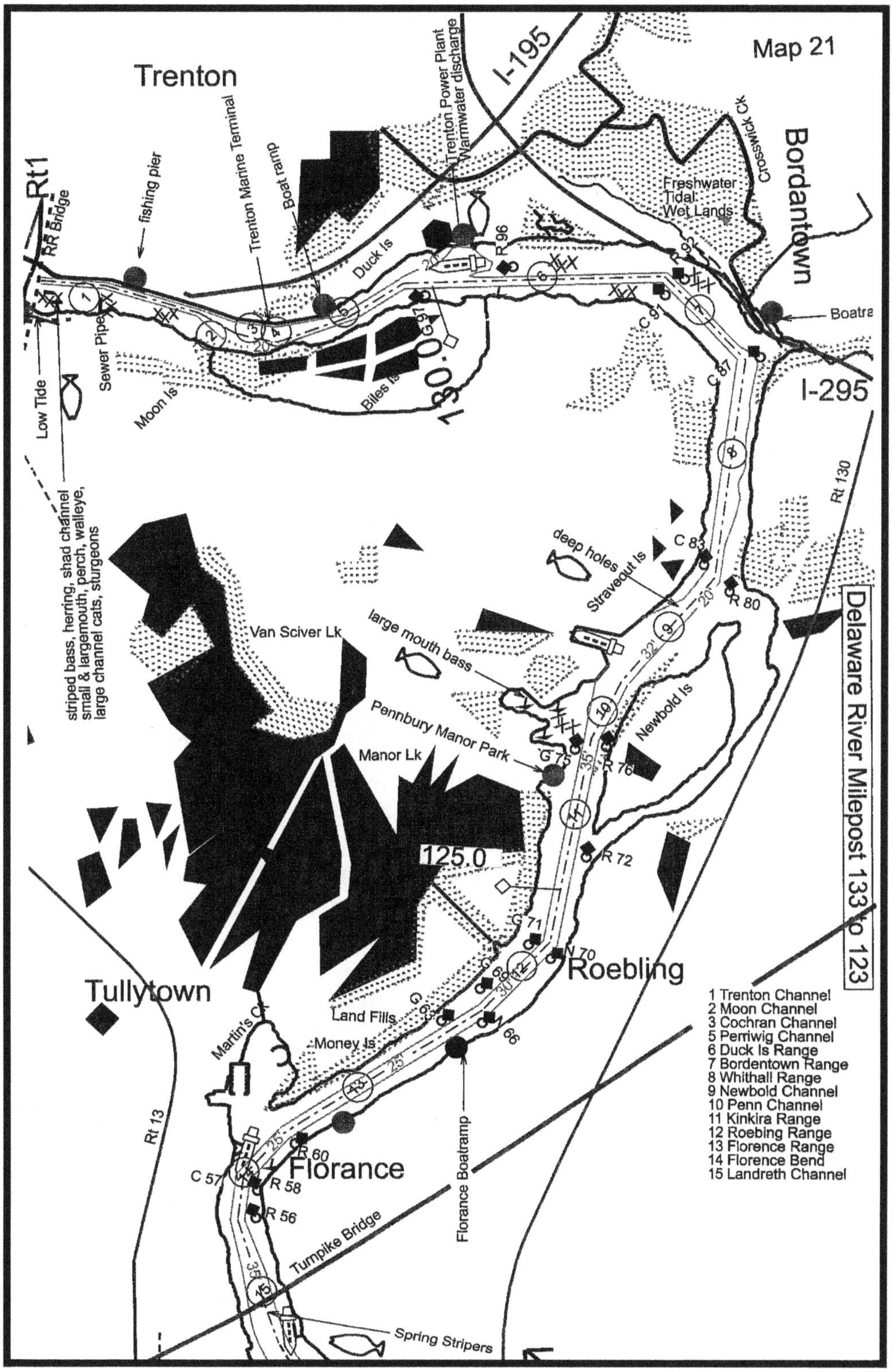
Map 21
Trenton
I-195
Bordantown
Rt1
RR Bridge
fishing pier
Trenton Marine Terminal
Boat ramp
Trenton Power Plant
Warmwater discharge
Crosswick Ck
Freshwater Tidal Wet Lands
Duck Is
Biles Is
Moon Is
Sewer Pipe
Low Tide
130.0
Boatra
I-295
Rt 130
striped bass, herring, shad channel
small & largemouth, perch, walleye,
large channel cats, sturgeons
deep holes
Straveout Is
large mouth bass
Van Sciver Lk
Pennbury Manor Park
Manor Lk
Newbold Is
125.0
Delaware River Milepost 133 to 123
Roebling
Tullytown
Land Fills
Money Is
Martin's Ck
Rt 13
Florance
Florance Boatramp
Turnpike Bridge
Spring Stripers
1 Trenton Channel
2 Moon Channel
3 Cochran Channel
5 Perriwig Channel
6 Duck Is Range
7 Bordentown Range
8 Whithall Range
9 Newbold Channel
10 Penn Channel
11 Kinkira Range
12 Roebing Range
13 Florence Range
14 Florence Bend
15 Landreth Channel

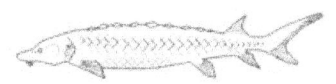

Map 22:
Ocean going ship traffic wake can swamp a small boat. Another warm water discharge point, if operating, can be located on the New Jersey side just downstream of the Burlington Bristol Bridge but without access by shore. The boat ramps at both Burlington and Croydon have fees but people can access the river for free at hand Launch places near Croydon and Bristol. Neshaminy Park and a small park near Station Road both provide fishing access to the river in the daytime. Not just large mouth bass but both perch (white and yellow) will come up from the deep channel and spawn in the many shallow creeks in spring. The private Burlington Island has a unique inter lake and is a popular place kayakers.

Between 1880 and 1910, it appeared that the river was making a comeback in migratory fin fishing production. Most of the catches for shad by this time were in the bay and lower tidal water section of the river south of Gloucester, not the fresh water river systems. The process of catching shad changed from anchored shore nets to a system of nets laid or planted in channels between mud flats with the help of gasoline engines. In 1900, a peak record of sixteen million pounds of shad were landed in the bay and lower river compared to one million pounds 20 years before [6]. By the turn of the new century, the low water dam at Lackawaxen was not needed for the defunct D&H canal system and the fish could now travel way into New York State. Reports of good catches would only last a short time. Shad catches soon decrease to an average of three to seven million pounds in the years following 1900 [6]. The fishermen noted that the catches had a lot to do with the alternating yearly flows of the river. By 1916, the catches decreased to back under a million pounds of shad marking the end of a rebounding shad fishery, which has yet to recover. Fred Lewis, a commercial shad fisherman, who's family had been operating since 1888 reported catching only 3 fish in 1949 year and by 1953 he reported none at his netting location in New Hope [15].

By the start of the 1900s, the population of Philadelphia and surrounding area would reach a million and a half people [115]. The waste generated by such a large population must have been unbearable along the lower river. Approximate 200,000 tons of solid untreated raw sewage, mixed with storm and creek water, was dumped into the river each year at the start of the twentieth century [6]. In the tidal section of the river, during periods of low flow, floating sewage floated up and down the river twice a day. It must have taken several days for a single piece of trash to float from Philadelphia to Wilmington because of this back and forth tidal movement. This slow movement of sludge could only add to the problems by creating massive amounts of sulfuric dioxide and hydrogen sulfide gases that would make living and working along the rivers unbearable. The port developed a nasty reputation as the foulest smelling port in the country. Philadelphia's native son, W. C. Fields called it the armpit of the world. Even early airline pilots complained about the smell of the armpit from the largest freshwater port in the world.

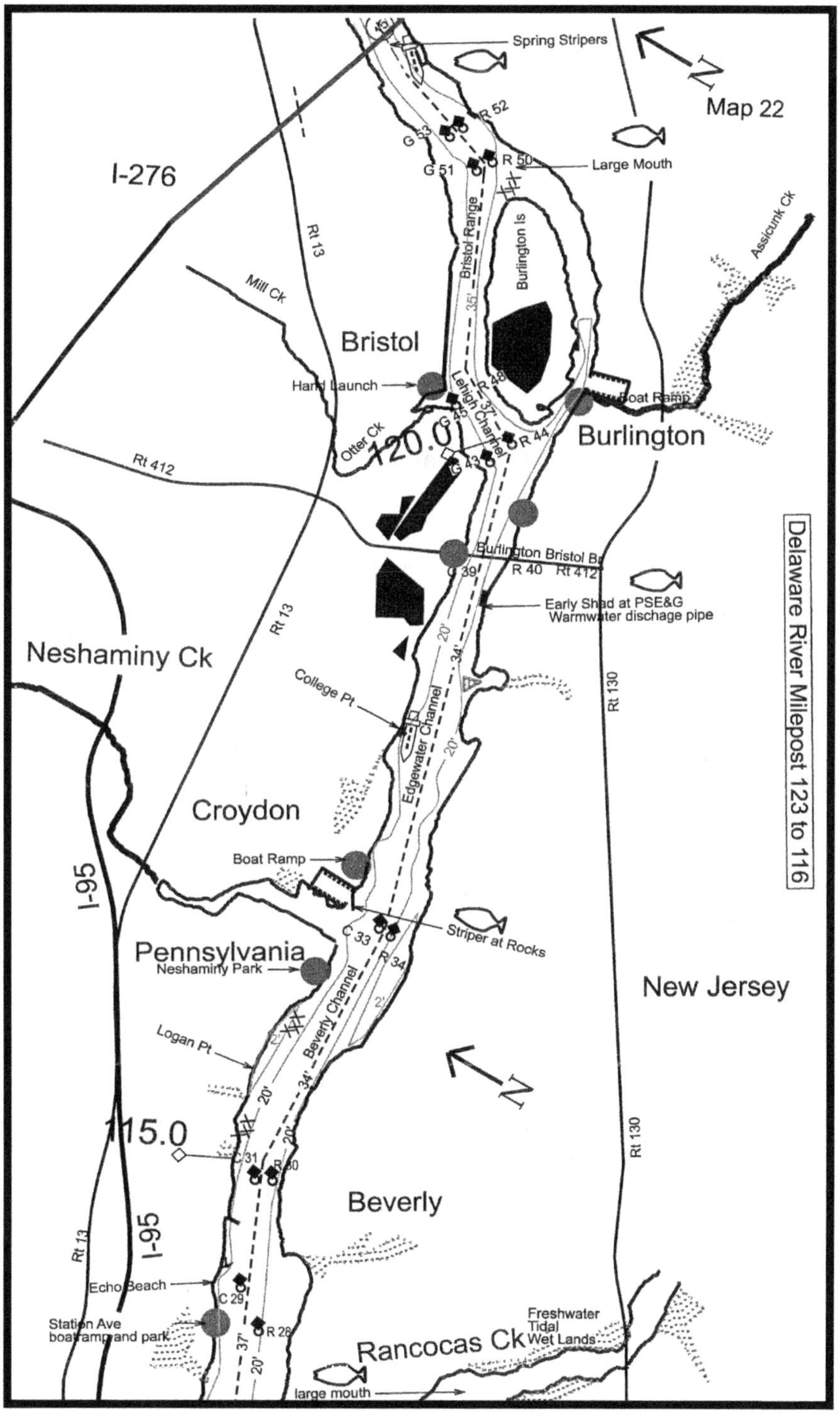
Spring Stripers
Map 22
Large Mouth
I-276
Rt 13
Mill Ck
Bristol Range
Burlington Is
Assiscunk Ck
Bristol
Hand Launch
Lehigh Channel
Boat Ramp
Burlington
Otter Ck
120.0
Rt 412
Burlington Bristol Br
R 40
Rt 412
Early Shad at PSE&G
Warmwater dischage pipe
Delaware River Milepost 123 to 116
Neshaminy Ck
Rt 13
College Pt
Edgewater Channel
Rt 130
Croydon
Boat Ramp
I-95
Striper at Rocks
Pennsylvania
Neshaminy Park
New Jersey
Beverly Channel
Logan Pt
115.0
Rt 130
Beverly
Rt 13
I-95
Echo Beach
Station Ave
boat ramp and park
Freshwater
Tidal
Wet Lands
Rancocas Ck
large mouth

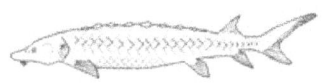

Map 23:
Several good places to fish for stripers can be found near the entrances of the Rancocas Creek Pennypack and Pennsauken Creek. Excellent public boat ramps can be found at Tacony, Frankford in P.A., and the Derouse Ave. Ramp in NJ. At low tide the beaches along Palmyra cove and down stream can be fished from the banks .At high tide fish the shallow mud flats in the evening

This type of water environment was not just bad for fish but for people who lived there as well. By the second half of the ninetieth century, the city's sewage waste removal system employed a state of the art process of taking open flowing streams like Frankford and Mill Creek and totaling encasing them into a closed system. Sewage was directly dump into them and flowed into the Delaware or lower Schuylkill River. The maps of the sewage system showed a radical different underground "Philadelphia sewer shed" than what was there before the streams were covered over [64]. This system did eliminate the unsightliness and smell of a raw sewage from the neighborhood where it started but it had to end up somewhere. Philadelphia had two cholera outbreaks in 1891 and 1899 which helped to fuel the drive for cleaner water sources. Even though Philadelphia was the first city to use chlorinated (1912) and sand filtrated water systems, for potable water, it still had problems in it source water [64]. The tidal flow at the city's second water plant at Torresdale (1908) would at times receive contaminated water caused by the returning flow [64]. By 1914, the city started plans for three wastewater treatment plants. It was not until 1923 that the first of three planned wastewater treatment plant began operations in Philadelphia [64]. The City would have to wait until the mid-1950s before all three plants were on line. The wastewater that was discharged from the hundreds of open unfiltered sewers from the start of the twentieth century to the mid 1950 blocked the migratory fish runs better than any dam that we could have built. The primary blocking agent was the lack of oxygen, causing the fish to suffocate in this thirty-mile run of water, which now extended from Trenton southward. The rate of flow determined the severity of the blockage. During periods of strong spring flow, fish could get through the blockage. In the fall, the flow was generally low and as such, the low oxygen level prevented any young fish from moving back to the bay. The heights of this stagnation must have occurred in the 1940's during the Second World War when shipbuilding and all other forms of manufacturing reached its heights. In the Second World War, little or no environmental restrictions were in place. During the first half of the twentieth century, in order to generate much needed tax funds and to gain support, the term "**Philadelphia Black Sag**" was adopted to describe this black zone of oxygen poor water[64] [6].

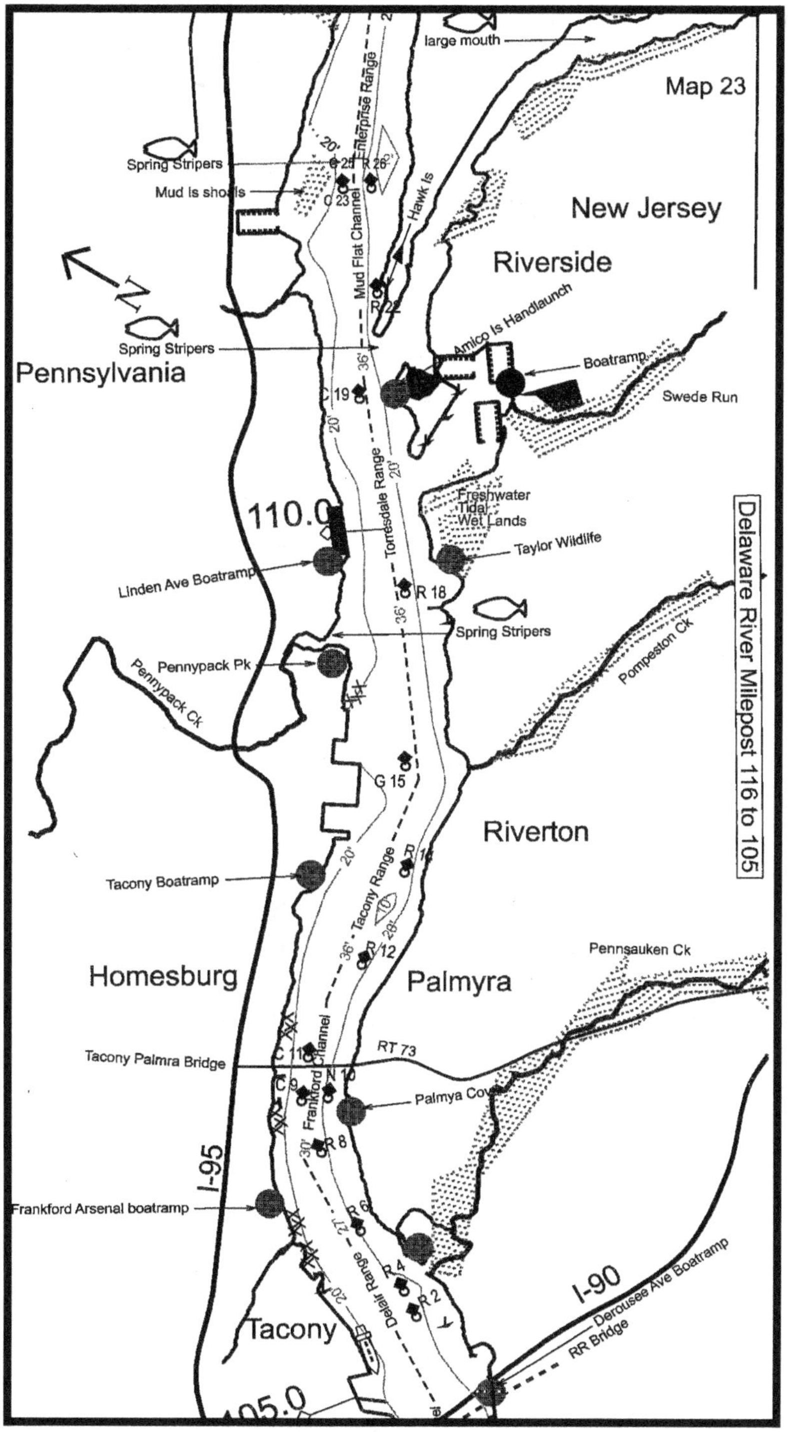

Fishing The Big D   91

Map 24:

The Tidal Delaware River

Map 24: *Tiago Terminal marks the beginning of the shipping industry on the river. This is a busy section and recreational boating for fishing should be done with care. Still the back channel of Petty Island holds underwater structures that provide shelter for a variety of fish. Besides the sunken ships behind Petty Island, abandoned piers on the PA side does the same. It is hard to find spots to fish from the bank. The Camden Water Front and Penn's Landing permitted it but the rules change frequently. Once the industrial lease is up on Petty Island it will be open to the public in 2020.*

In 1936, INCODEL (Interstate Commission of the Delaware River) was formed by the four states boarding the waterway. Later in 1961, INCODEL would become known as DRBC (Delaware River Basin Commission) which would include the Federal Government. The formation of the INCODEL commission was to pressure the four bordering state legislations to generate funds and pass regulations for water management and clean up. Funding is always the major roadblock of any environmental project. In the 1940's because of the war, INCODEL was helpless in cleaning the river. What it did accomplish was to buy time and enlist the support of the Army Corp Engineer to provide studies to prove the need and offer solutions to fix the state of the river. INCODEL's master plan involved not just improving the sorry state of the water quality but the need for flood control and monitoring future water requirements. After the Second World War, the money for public improvement came rolling in. In 1946, the Pennsylvania Commonwealth Supreme Court approved a tax or rent for the funding of a sanitary sewer system for the City of Philadelphia [64], which would finally enable the City to have a complete sewer system. Two years later, the Federal Pollution Control Act became law, and federal money was authorized for sewage facilities. The 1948 Federal Pollution Control Act opened up money for all communities along the waterways in the 1950's.

In 1972, the Clean Water Act was reluctantly passed by Richard Nixon. The Clean Water Act would amend the original 1948 Federal Pollution Control Act, which continues to change yearly now. The revised act provided new and more rules for wastewater discharge levels with money to implement the improvements. President Nixon's legation would clean our water way more than any other legation. Prior to this act, sewage discharge was regulated for solid waste material only.

The old plants used a system of filtration and sediment tanks to remove particular matter from the water called a primary treatment. The first method removes only about one third of the Biochemical Oxygen Demand agents (BOD) and no dissolved minerals. High BOD level was what caused the oxygen blockage that the Delaware experienced during periods of low flow. The new required secondary treatment would use aerobic microorganisms with the help of injected oxygen to break down the organic matter to a safer material and $CO2$. The secondary process would reduce the BOD by ninety percent. The wastewater would then be treated with chlorine to kill bacteria before release into the waterways. A third stage (tertiary) is used in some locations to remove nitrogen and phosphorous (soap products) from the water which adds to algae booms. The Clean Water Act would control The Total Maximum Daily Load (TMDL) and limit

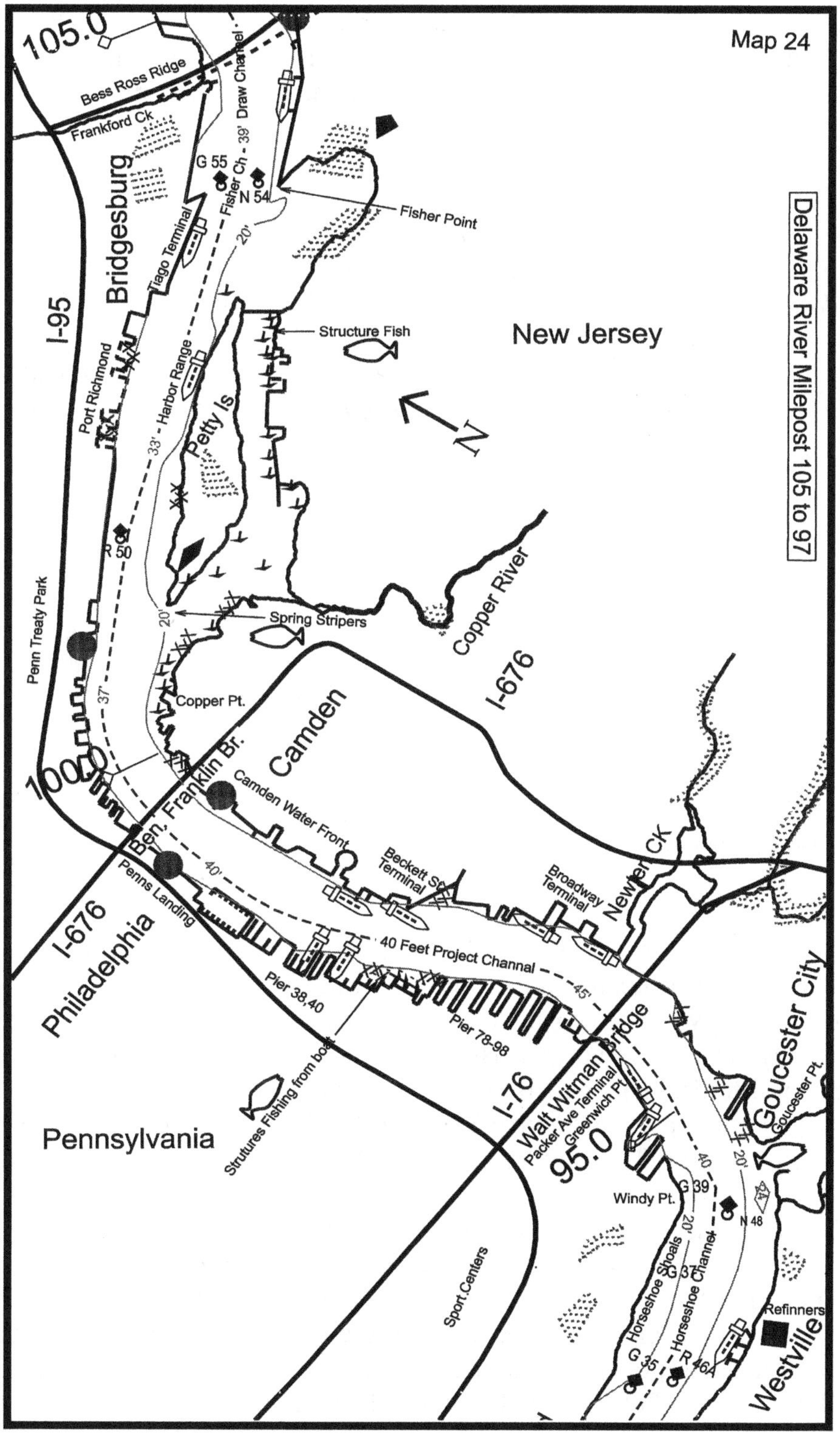

Fishing The Big D

Map 24

Delaware River Milepost 105 to 97

The Tidal Delaware River

excessive discharge of pollution in our rivers. Items that are monitored from each discharge point are fecal coliform, sediment, and nutrients. In 2002, the DRBC reported that 76% reduction in BOD discharge in the estuary with an increase in dissolved oxygen [112]. In the writer's opinion, this monitory second stage had more to do with the cleanup of the river than any other regulation.

Map 25:
Only a few places to fish from shore such as the old Philadelphia Navy ship yard, and Hog Island behind the Airport can be found. With the closure of refineries river access should increase Deep water holes at the mouth of Woodbury Creek and structures along lower Hog and Tinicum Islands should produce some good fishing spot for boats. The future Philadelphia airport expansion plan many radically change the shoreline and river use. Since 2012 snakehead have been reported caught in this section of the River.

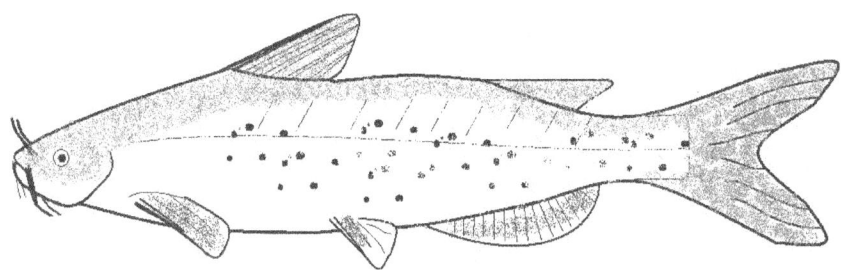

Catfish

A channel cat is one that your child will want to catch and once hooked you have a fishing partner for life.

Any fresh water fish that has no scales and barbets (whiskers), with a sharp spine in the pectoral and dorsal fins can be classified as a catfish. To understand why they are so plentiful world-wide, you need to understand their sensory capabilities. No other fresh water fish comes close to what a catfish has going for it. The ability to smell food is based on the nasal folds. The catfish olfactory pit has 140 folds compared to trout which has 18 and largemouth bass which have 8 to 13 [98]. Cats can detect one part of food per 10 billion parts of water [98]. Another sensor for food detection is the taste bud system of this fish. Of course the barbells (cat whiskers) and the mouth have taste buds but the entire fish has taste buds on its skin at a density of 5,000 taste bud per square centimeter for channel cats [98]. The hearing of catfish, like most fish, comes from two locations, the lateral line along the body flanks for low frequency detection and the swim bladder through the inner ear for high frequency. What the catfish's swim bladder has over bass and trout is that the swim bladder and inter ear is connected by a bone structure much as our inter and outer ear. While bass and trout can hear at 20 to 1,000 cycles per second, the

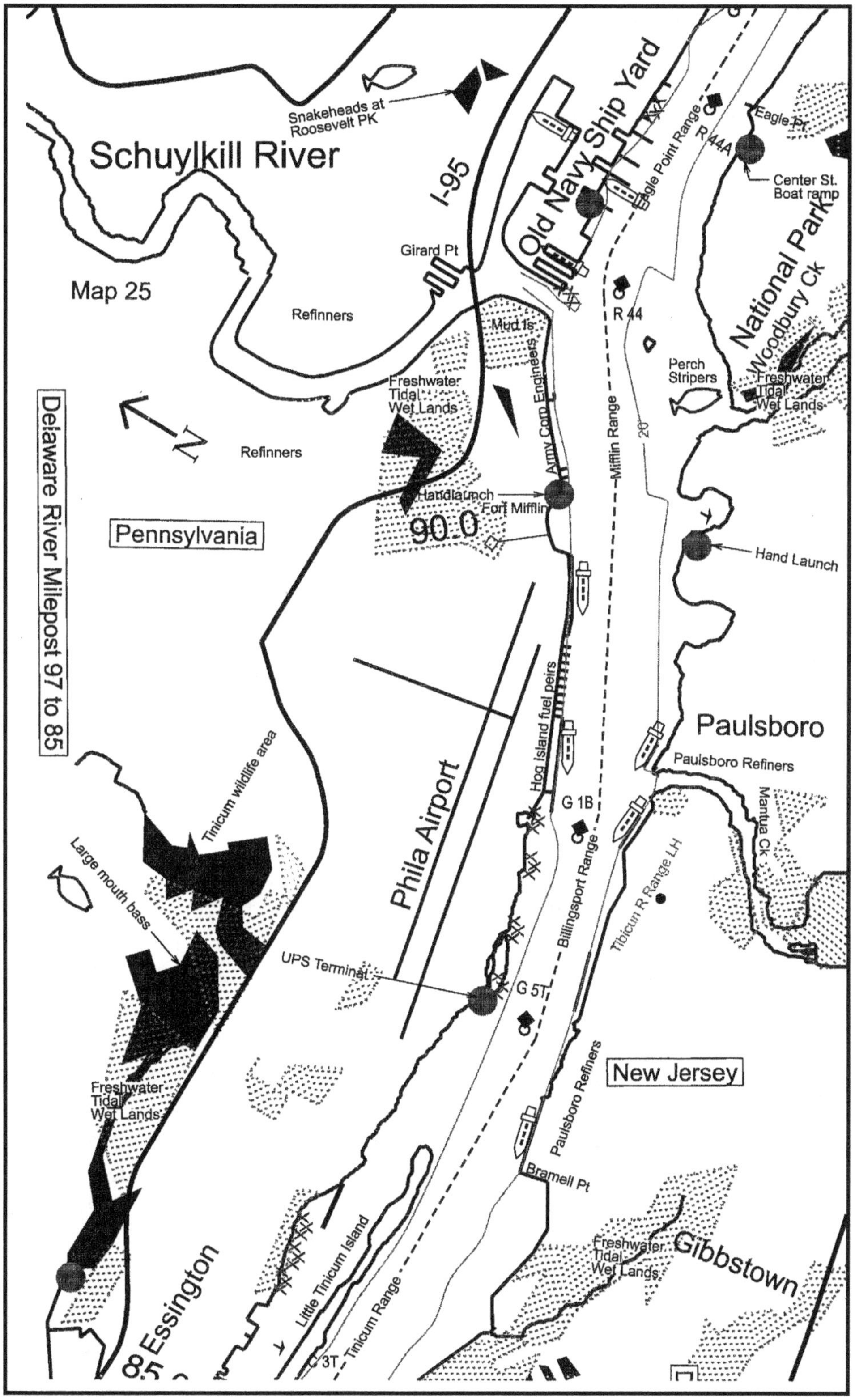
Schuylkill River
Snakeheads at Roosevelt PK
I-95
Old Navy Ship Yard
Eagle Point Range
R 44A
Eagle Pt
Center St. Boat ramp
National Park
Woodbury Ck
Girard Pt
Map 25
Refinners
Mud Is
R 44
Perch Stripers
Freshwater Tidal Wet Lands
Army Corp Engineers
Mifflin Range
20
Delaware River Milepost 97 to 85
Refinners
Handlaunch
Fort Mifflin
90.0
Pennsylvania
Hand Launch
Hog Island fuel peirs
Paulsboro
Paulsboro Refiners
Tinicum wildlife area
Phila Airport
G 1B
Mantua Ck
Large mouth bass
Billingsport Range
Tinicum R Range LH
UPS Terminal
G 5T
New Jersey
Paulsboro Refiners
Freshwater Tidal Wet Lands
Bramell Pt
Essington
Little Tinicum Island
Tinicum Range
C 3T
Freshwater Tidal Wet Lands
Gibbstown

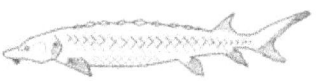

cat can hear up to 11,000 cycles per seconds [98]. The ability to hear underwater low frequency sounds for the cat as well as the Navy is survival. Low frequency sounds travel greater distance than high frequency, that is why you hear only the bass part of a song coming through a cars sound system from the outside of the automobile. Low frequency will be sounds from someone walking on a bank or oars banging on the hull of the boat. The cat picks up this frequency through hair like projections that rest in pores within this lateral line that travels the length of this scale-less body. They were so good at low frequency detection that the Chinese used bullheads to detect earthquakes. Even though catfish eyes are small, they can be relied on to caught food by sight, both day and night. I have caught many on lures and live bait while fishing for bass in just about any water conditions. They also have excellent night vision possible second only to the walleye. Take a picture of this fish at night and you will see the eyes glow. Cats are the only fresh water fish that have the same electrosensing as sharks. Electrosensing is the ability to detect the electric energy from all living animals. With this entire food and protective sensors, as long as there is food out there these fish will find it. Even if the water is muddy or one of the senses, like eye sight is gone this fish will still eat. Truly, this fish is at the top of the evolution of fresh water fish.

Every continent has their collection of 100 lb plus monster cats. In North America, we have record size 100 pound flathead and 150 pound blue cats. Blue and flathead catfish are native to the Mississippi and the adjoining western basins. In Asia, the biggest is the 600 pound mekong cat. Europe has the 150 pound wels cat. South America has several 100 plus cats known as redtail, jau and azulejo. Indian has the 100 pound goodan and Africa has several 60 pound cats by the names of the vundu and sharp tooth cat.

Of the 2,200 species of catfish world-wide, the Delaware basin may only have three native cats, the white cat, yellow and brown bullheads. The channel cat may have been brought in by the early canal system with the small mouth bass.

We are blessed, to have the one that by all accounts is the perfect recreational game fish – the channel cat. The channel cat's average size in the river is from one to four pounds but reports of ten or more pounds are common in the lower section of the river and in large warm water lakes. The Pennsylvania State record stands at a fish caught in Northampton County Pennsylvania at 35 pounds 2.5 oz in 1991. The name, "channel cat" came from a mixture of what was thought, at one time, to be three regional North American separated species of catfish, until it was determined to be one general fish to be classified as a channel cat. Channel cats come in a variety of colors but the standard is a silver gray to bronze and dark blue with a white lower half and bottom with black spots on its flanks. The warmer the water, the greater the growth rate of the fish. Their life expectancy is about ten years but reports of twenty have been observed. Channel cats are most active in the summer months with a peak temperature range of 70 to 75 degrees.

Yellow, brown and black bullheads can be caught in this water. These fish seldom exceed one pound. Both New Jersey and Pennsylvania record catches of brown bullhead where taken at four pounds eight oz and four pound four oz respectively. They can be identified by a larger then normal head or tadpole shape body, wide ugly month and soft

fleshly body. Most people will give up fishing when they start catching them in quantities, me being one. Before you look down on these ugly little fish, they can outlive any other fish in a poor oxygen water environment and deserve a place in the system.

White cats are rarer, but you might have caught one and not known it. They are light in color with a gray molded appearance. The fish's anal fin has few rays (under 25), and is smaller with a slower growth rate than channels. They average between one to two pounds in the river and lakes, but are known, to be better fighters with a slimmer and more attractive body appearance.

Flatheads may have been brought in by mistake or by illegal bucket biology but by what every method they are in our waterway to stay. Originally they were most noted in the Schuylkill River above and below the Fairmont dam. But today they are found in both the Delaware and Schuylkill and weighing as much as 50 pounds. Clearly they are the biggest sport fish in the region. Flatheads are brown in color with a bullhead appearance. To distinguish it from the channel cat, which can be brown in color also, look for the lower jaw to extend pass the upper jaw. The Commonwealth of Pennsylvania Game Commission recommends that if you catch a flathead do not return it to the water. Both the blue and flathead are eating machines. The stocking of these fish can bring strong controversy in the local fishing community.

I have not seen an official report that a Mississippi blue cat was caught in the river, but have heard of lots of people claiming to have caught them. Because of the similar appearances of channel and blue cats, I'm not sure if reports of caught blues cats are always correct. Blue cats are light blue on top with white colored lower flanks and bottom without spots with 30 or more rays on the anal fin. Large channel cats can get pretty big and can have the same color appearance as blue cats, so take any report of a true Mississippi blue cat with caution. Large channel cats can lose their spots but will be darker in color than a blue cat. If you catch a truly big cat, count the anal rays. If the cat has 30 or more rays on the anal fin keep the fish and contact your game commission.

Popular place for river channel cats to hide in are the same locations as small month bass, in ripples, and shallow channels of the rivers around island, below wing dams, under bridges, log jams, and under eroded banks, and in holes down stream of large rock. In the lower navigational part of the river they can be found just about anywhere you can get access to the river. Favorite spots are along banks near the mouth of tributaries within casting distance of the main shipping channels or on the edges of lily pads A good general rule for cats is the deeper and warmer the water, the bigger the cats while shallow water will produce more but smaller cats. Because of their excellent arrays of night sensors, this is a great sport to take your kid out at night and introduce them to the sport. The nice thing about fishing for cats at night over various other fish is that it is a very sedentary practice where you are not continually throwing lures into trees or dealing with snag lines. This is an ideal way to introduce kids to fishing. The action is hot and the level of skill is just right for them. Just throw the bait out in the river and listen for it to hit the water. If you hear two splashes, you might have lost your chicken liver bait. You can catch them on bait other than chicken liver, but for night fishing, or in

muddy water this is the best. There is today commercial stink bait on the market that will remain on the hook better than chicken liver, but I have used little of it that did better than chicken liver. It's more of a regional demand. Worms, leeches, minnows, and hellgrammites will all put cats on your line as well. Use a number # 2 bait holder hook that has barbs running along the shaft to hold the bait. The sinker arrangement depends of the bottom type. For rocky bottoms, use split shots attached about a foot above the bait so as not to get hung up on the bottom as much. For sandy hard bottoms, the one-two oz tear drop sinker about a foot above the bait and hung from the main line is good for letting the fish set the hook themselves. I have caught them on plastic and crank lures as well, but never on surface plugs. The barbets on cats are harmless but the sharp dorsal fin and pectoral bones cause cuts and infection. Care should be taken when handling these fish. Always brief your kids on the proper handling of cats. Teach them to drag the cat unto the bank gently. Grasp the fish from behind and slide the hand forward until it is behind the dorsal bone and side pectoral bones before trying to remove the hook. Never use nets on these fish, the sharp bones will get fouled in the net. Catfish don't have teeth but have a sandpaper mouth. After a good day of fishing your thumb and fingers may become raw from removing hooks which could lead to infection, so using pliers on a busy fishing trip.

    Flatheads seem to be very territorial. In the daytime they hide under banks, around log jam or in deep holes. In the holes they will ambush food that floats by them and if hooked it may become impossible to get them out due to the surround logs and debris. At night they move from their nest to open shallower water to hunt prey. From the people that are successful the best time is at night on shallow sections of the river just outside of their daytime hide out. Small one can be caught on chicken liver but most of the big ones are caught on live bait fish such as suckers, small sunfish or large minnows. Large circle hooks with a sliding sinker tie to heavy 50 pound line is the rig of chose. Like channel cats sometimes they will strike artificial lures but the recommended bait is live bait fish.

Urban Hot Spots

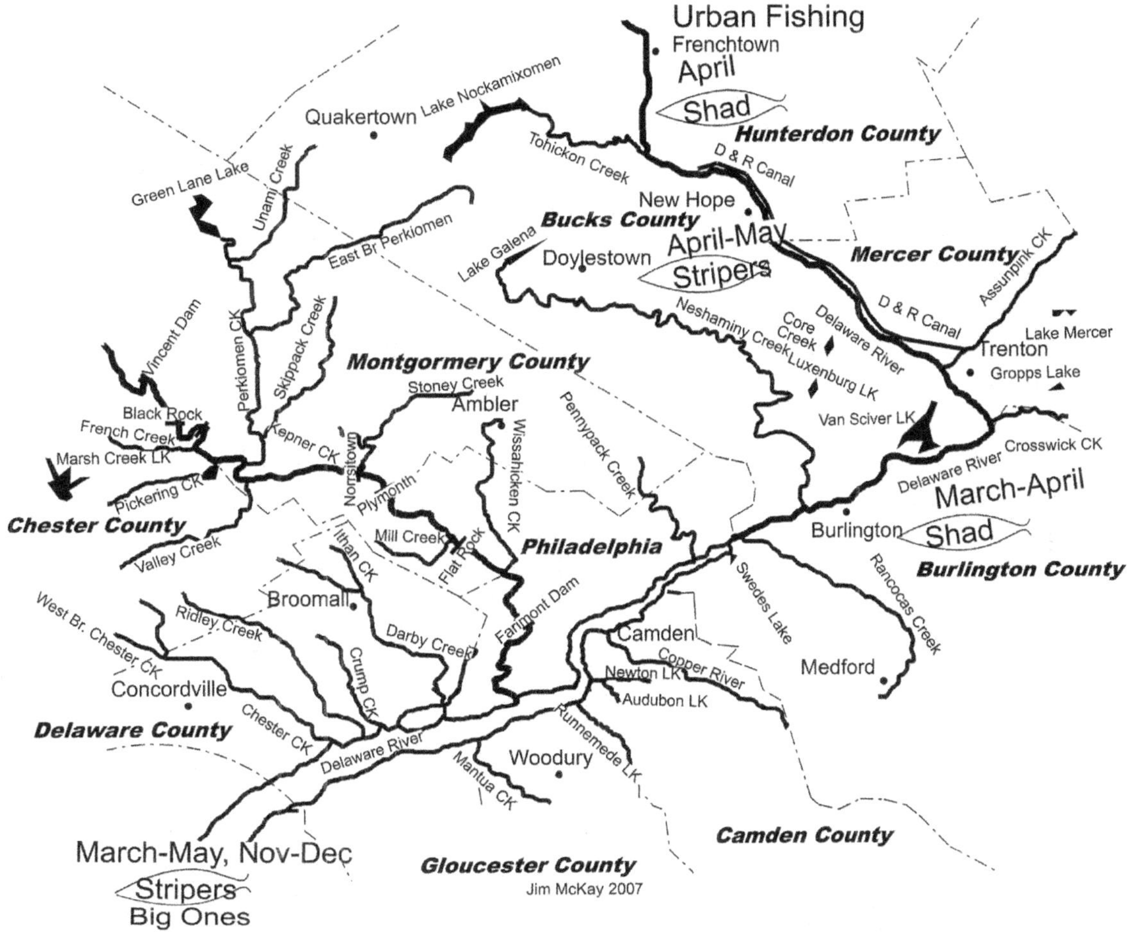

- The number one rule in fishing the Delaware freshwater tidal section is the outgoing tides will provide the best chance for a catch. On incoming tides the water doesn't flow up river it builds, turning the water environment stagnates and for some reason most fish appetite will do the same. On outgoing tide the water moves carrying food and temperature fluctuation which excite the appetite of bass type fish.
- The second rule is to expect all bass type, fresh and marine, to move with the water level. Look for fish at the edge of deep channels, along steep banks and at mouth of creeks at low water levels. At high water levels expert action from fish looking for food in submerge mud flats, lily pads and up into creek channels. The lures you use will depend on water depth, surface plugs and spinner in shallow water, deep diving crankbait and plastic worms in deep water.

The Tidal Delaware River

The quality of life in a river community can be measured in part by access to the water front. If you look at any towns where water front access is restricted, generally real estate prices are low. Where access is good, home values are high and urban planners across the country are learning that rule. In an area that has the highest population concentration of the entire watershed, the urban Delaware is the worst for public access. There are no places on the urban Delaware section where one can walk or jog any distance along the River. The piers and refineries that border the riverbanks make it almost impossible to achieve that goal for any significance length. On any given summer evening, the few Delaware River waterfronts that the general public has access to are packed. Many of the government own public land or parks, ban fishing and have very restrictive hours. The only public areas on the center city waterfront that openly permit fishing is the Camden waterfront. As for fishing the river from the bank, most fishermen are left to search for secluded locations like the UPS terminal or some isolated pier that has not yet been fenced off. The UPS spot will be fenced off once the airport expansion takes place.

Both cities are working hard to open up river access to people, even for us fishermen. Currently Philadelphia and private developers are working on public walking trails along the river bank both north and south of Penn's Landing. Venezuelan President Hugo Chavez, who owned the Petty Island under Citgo has donated the land to New Jersey and should be open to the public in 2020.

Fortunately, for the ones that have boats there is plenty of good potential. Fish love structures and the river is full of abandoned piers and man made underwater items. Bottom dredging for shipping has dug deep channels and holes for fish to collect in. The water temperature can also vary greatly here as well. Thousands of storm water pipe empty cold storm water into the river creating pockets of cooler water that can get bass feeding on hot summer days. Many warm water discharge pipes from power plants can attract fish in the cooler seasons.

Several locations in Philadelphia that deserves a word about fishing are the Wissahickon Gorge, Fairmount Park and Pennypack Creek. Fortunately, the entire length of the Schuylkill River is available for fishing from the bank in the largest city park in the United States. Different types of catfish and bass fill the Schuylkill above and right below the dam. Below the dam striped bass and shad are commonly caught. Inside the park is a creek that cuts a 100-foot deep gorge through Wissahickon schist bedrock (the building stones of thousands of Philadelphia homes). The eight-mile long ravine creates a remote mountain stream environment filled with rapids and deep pools fed by underground springs. The headwater of the Wissahickon comes from a limestone source that has the potential to support a trout fishery if pollution and water temperature permit. The game commission has started stocking trout in the creek and it has been discovered that holdover trout are starting to appear in the deeper, seldom fished holes within the ravine. While the stream will never be able to compete in a list of world-class trout streams, it could provide a rewarding experience for local fly fishermen if the State and City would promote a catch and release policy or delayed harvest. A visit on a rainy, weekend, spring day, and several weeks after opening day of trout season can be a rewarding experience.

Strong aerial insect hatches are rare here, streamers fly types or a beady-eye black wet-fly, will produce a tight line if not for trout maybe a small mouth bass. At the dam where the Wissahickon enters the Schuylkill there is always a group of fishermen with reported good success.

The Pennypack, another scenic stream that flows through a city park has good access and scenic trails. The dams have been remove on the lower Pennypack with the hope of making is a good stream for striped bass, herring or shad.

On the New Jersey side of the river, trout stocking is limited south of Trenton NJ, but, what the Garden State has, and many people overlook, is the fishing potential of the lily pad ponds and lagoons that protrude from the river into the Garden State. In the spring, large mouth bass like most fish will search out shallow moderate flow water to spawn. The tidal movement in small creeks provides an excellent place to spawn and build nest. These shallow urban wetlands naturally restrict large boat access. With the un-accessible banks and foul smell most fishermen over look these hidden channels near our city. Because of the lack of fishing pressure, unlike their black bass cousins that live in the heavily fished public lakes, the large mouth bass that live in these urban wetlands are not afraid to hit the first plastic lures and spinning bait that are thrown at them. It is best to access these fishing paradises with a kayak or canoe and follow the tide. When working these lagoons, take into account the tidal cycle. For some reason the fish bite count is highest when the tide is moving out. It is best to enter the creek from the river several hours before the heights of high tide is reached and paddle out with the out going tide. Be sure to paddle out before low tide sets so not to get stranded. Since you will be fishing in areas of lily pads, your fishing technique will be different. You can not play them when fishing near lily pads. Make sure you have a strong line in case you get tangled here. Be prepared to take something big for you are fishing in between deep river channels and shallow muddy bottoms, a favorite hide-out for muskies. Most of these pools have hazardous waste sites nearby so don't eat anything caught in these waters.

Philadelphia Fishing Clubs

To promote the comradeship within the fishing community a number of fishing or angler clubs have always been present within the Delaware Valley. Most are specific to a particular fish or fishing techniques such as bass fishing from high performance boats, fly fishing for trout or ownership of private fishing piers and ponds.

Schuylkill Fishing Company or the State of Schuylkill

Of all the sporting social clubs along the bank of the Delaware River the one that needs to be brought attention too is the Schuylkill Fishing Company or the State of

Schuylkill. It's the oldest men social club in American, founded in 1732 under the name of the Colony of Schuylkill. Under the original charter the club was an independent country founded on the banks of the Schuylkill River. The solvent nation status was granted by the Lenni-Lenape Indian, Chief Tammany, who was the same grantor of land to William Penn under the classic conditional statement "until the water stops flowing-."

The original members or "citizens" as they prefer to called themselves were affluence local Quakers with more than a common passion for fishing and eating they dominated both the political and the economics environment of the region. The roster included names of governors, signer of the decoration of independence, mayors and parents of future industrialist. The following is a list of some of the early members: James Logan, Joseph Wharton, Thomas Stretch, William Bradford, Clement Biddle, Anthony Morris, Thomas Mifflin, Samuel Morris. These members would become the driving force for independence from British rule. The original location of the colony was at the "Falls", or where Fairmont Dam and the Schuylkill Expressway are today. The colony's club house or "castle" would become a meeting place with good food and drink to discuss important issues of the time. One story goes that General Washington spent an evening in the castle once and was incapacity for three days after drinking the clubs famous fish punch. After the Revolutionary War it changed its name to the State of Schuylkill. As a self-styled political entity where they establish their own rules of fishing and later refused to adhere to prohibition of liquor laws.

After the Fairmount dam was built and the fishing ruined the club and its house or castle was move to Rambo Rock across from Bartram Garden on the Schuylkill River and remain there until the fishing dropped off in 1887 and replaced by petroleum refineries. Today, after several relocations the State of Schuylkill club house now rest on the bank of the Delaware River at the Andalusia Estate in Bensalem Township. The nation's membership is limited to the original membership numbers: highly selective and private. After 250 years of existence the club collected a treasure-trope of memorabilia and rituals. Some of the collected memorabilia was destroyed in a1980 fire, but the secretive citizen's ritual of catching; cooking and eating fish is still carried on today. On the other hand the State of Schuylkill neighbor Philadelphia Gun Club, and their pigeon shoots cannot enjoy the same seclusion.

Bassmaster Elite

Between the rocks at Trenton and the saltwater line at Chester, a regular group of fishermen with fast boats and big hopes of competing in national bass fishing contest meet. The American Bass Angler group meets here regularly to compete in bass fishing. Most regional lakes will not permit these high powerboats on their waters. Within the watershed, Lake Wallenpaupack, Harvey's, Tobyhanna, Beltsville, and Hopatcong are the only ones that will permit these high performance boats. The lower river is ideal for them. It is wide, deep, with plenty of access, and few people along the riverbank to complain about the noise. The winners of these local club compete for a place in the regional

tournaments and then on to the national tournaments where cash prizes are presented. The biggest award is winning sponsorships from boats to fishing line manufacturers. The rules seem to center around the boat specifications more than fishing. Each fishing event ends with a recorded weigh in where a winner is announced and presented a plaque. All bass must be returned to the river with dead fish adding negative points to the count after the weigh-in. You can only record fish that are within the state limits and size. All fish become the property of the association. A practice called culling is permitted where a fish can be replaced with a larger fish if the limits have not been reached. All fish must be caught on lures with normal casting rods from the boat. Fly fishing with fly rods and fishing from outside of the boat is prohibited. The point system is based on the total weight of the catch from the contestants [34]. The big problem with this type of fishing is you can become very restricted in fish location, but it provides an excellent opportunity to fish with a great group of people.

In 2014 the Bassmaster Elite was held on the Delaware River. This was the first time that a bass contest at this level was held on such a large urban tidal river. The results were disappointing to the average observer, but to the experience contestant the word was challenging. Some of the pros would end a day with zero catch and many failed to turn in the max limit of 5 fish. At the end it proved that fishing tidal urban river is much different than fishing southern rural lakes for black bass. Here you had to know tides and structures and where the fish go during the tidal stages. The structures were not tree stumps and rocks but drainage outlet pipes, sunken ships, docks, and mud flats. It was clear that local knowledge and experience would win the tournament. Local bass-pro Michael Iaconelli knew the river better than anyone. He has fished the river from the Pocono to the pinelands of South Jersey. His fishing education from the Delaware has earned him the title of 2006 Bass Angler of the Year. He continually earned top finishes in national championship since 1994. In the 2014 Bassmaster Elite, as the favorite Michael Laconelli took first place with 40 pounds of fish. Proving that while this urban river may not be the easiest river to fish the challenge of it will generate great fishermen.

Trout Unlimited
Don't throw that rainbow back it will only die or worst yet someone else may catch it.

Each TU Chapter takes a watershed and stock trout in sections that are rich in oxygen and within public access. The stocking locations and times are only known to members. Many of the stockings take place in the fall and provide fish throughout the winter and into the spring.

Unlike the upper Delaware the lower urban valley of the Delaware is not known as a rich environment for trout. Most people consider the high water temperatures, fishing pressures and selfish attitudes prevent any of the tributaries from supporting a year around trout population.

The Tidal Delaware River

Facts:
- The earth is round
- Cold water can stores more oxygen than Warm water.
- Hatchery water is not much difference than the steams that trout are placed in.
- Fish tend to shallow hook with live bait while they tend to spit out the artificial lures.
- Tri hook lures can be just as traumatic for fish as swallowing a hook.
- Fish tend to die when they shallow hooks or have their lips ripped from their bodies by removing tri-hooks
- Trout can survive in our streams if left along in oxygen rich zones in the summer and fished with respect the rest of the year.

Catch and Release is more than chucking the fish back into the water, it's the way one fishes.

Therefore what kills trout is not just warm water alone but combination of poor summertime oxygen levels and the stress of being caught during those times. Trout Unlimited promotes the retuned of trout and other fish back into the environment where they came from and with attempts to improve that environment. Members promote the use of artificial flies with small single barbless hooks. Member refine from fishing in hot months instead they hit streams in the spring, fall and winter when trout can stand the stress of being caught. Trout Unlimited has proven that some of our urban stream can support year around trout if properly managed and protected from abusive fishing techniques and greed. Many chapters provide private fishing opportunities for youth. Another project for TU is promoting Delay Harvest a concept of no closed seasons on designated trout streams but all trout must be returned in the cooler season and fished with artificial lures and barbless small single hooks.

Fresh Water Mussels

A good indication of a river's condition is it shellfish population or lack of it. In most of the freshwater streams of the Delaware the lack it is the norm. Fresh water mussel can live for 80 years or more. They require certain native and migratory fish to spread themselves throughout the watershed for reproductive needs. Like their saltwater cousins the oyster they are the cleaning machine of the river. One must see what the cleaning action of zebra mussels have done to the vertical visibility of water in the Great Lakes. Vertical visibility of depth of 25 feet or more are common in the Great Lakes. Because of the longevity of mussels and the thousands of gallons of water that flow through their gills they have become very sensitive to pollution and have disappeared

through much of the system. With the additions of dams and the disappearance of certain fish population particular mussels like the alewife floater were thought to have disappeared. With the introduction of certain manuals to North American like the raccoon, which came from South American, mussel populations were further threaten. Prior to a 1919 survey of the fresh water mussels it revealed a system full of mussels with five to seven species in each stream. Today the surveys found only five of the original seventy streams that had mussels in them. The surprising find of the 1999 and 2010 mussel surveys found a high concentration of mussels in the tidal section of the Delaware between Trenton and Philadelphia. Another important find was the Alewife floater was found in streams within the city. Today the Partnership of the Delaware Estuary is busy with mussels restocking programs with the hope of making the longest un-dammed River on the east coast one of the cleanest. [168]

The Schuylkill River

The Schuylkill River with its eight active dams and five breached dams may be the most dangerous waterway in the watershed. The location of the dams should be known to all floater and boaters before getting on the water.

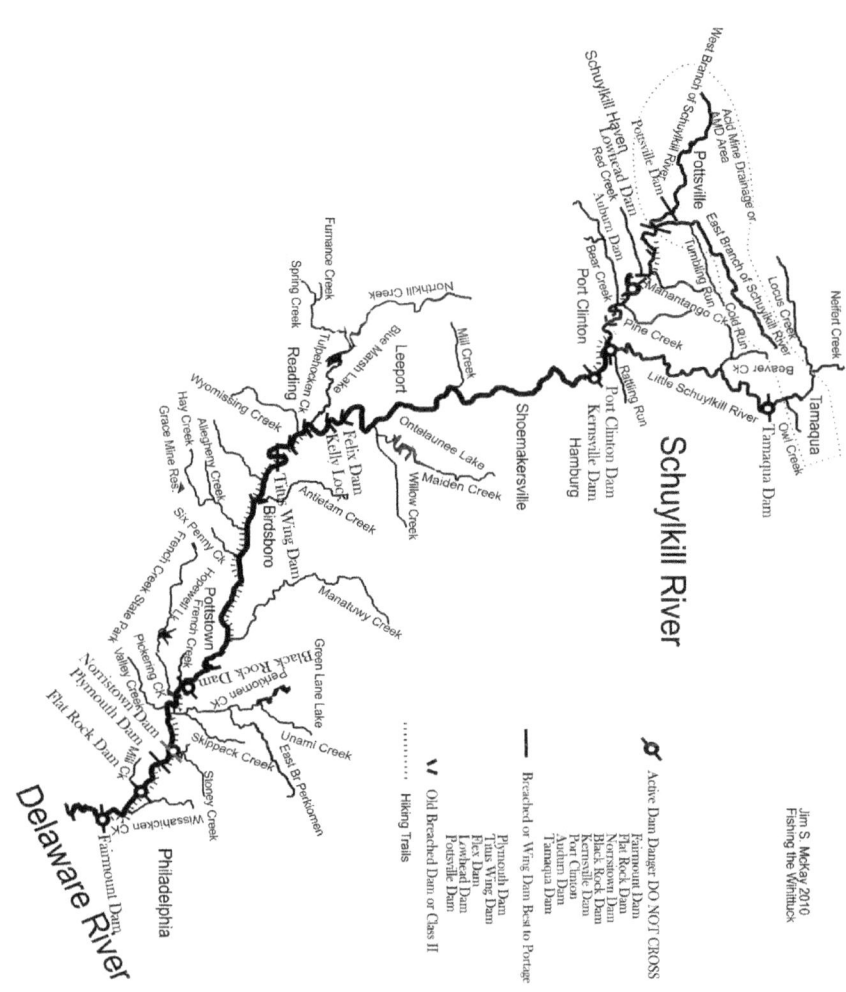

The Schuylkill River was the jewel of the City of Brotherly Love. Between Manyunk and where the Fairmount dam is today the river drops 30 feet. Before the dams were built the steep drop in elevation created a fast flowing river with a fall where Fairmount dam is now. Early account stated the water was colder and cleaner than the Delaware and as such it became the early source of water for the city. The City of

Philadelphia in the late 1700s and early 1800s, was the largest city in North American and following several serious epidemics of water born diseases, getting clean drinking water would becoming a major project. The Yellow fever epidemics would force the fledging nation's capital to another newer and clearer city. The Fairmount water works was built in 1820s, and was an engineering marvel for the time [64]. It used a process of pumping water, first by steam and then later by a gravity driven water wheel to a high reservoir where it was filtered and permitted to flow in wooden pipes to the rest of he city. Not only did it start a crude process of purifying and transporting water through the city, it purchased massive tracks of land along the Schuylkill River to halt development along its banks. In order to insure safe drinking water, the city bought 1,480 acres of property south of Manyunk [Lenape Indian translation "Place to Drink", and still true today] to the tidal limits along with the Wissahickon Creek Gorge. The Schuylkill was also the home of the colonies' first appointed Royal Botanist, John Bartrum and early naturist John Audubon. Many of Audubon's bird and animal paintings came from this waterway. At the mouth of the Wissahickon resides the hundred year old Philadelphia Canoe Club house. This organization does more than race rowing boats up and down the Fairmount Park water front but has promoted the recreational use of the natural waterways of the Valley.

The Schuylkill River history parallels that of the Lehigh. It comes from the hard coal country in the West. The Schuylkill River was a more direct and shorter route to Philadelphia than the Lehigh. In 1815, the Schuylkill Navigation Company (SNC) was chartered to build a canal system to reach the coalfields of Schuylkill County. This was a fast track system designed and engineered by Thomas Oakes to construct a 108-mile waterway from Port Carbon to Philadelphia. Instead of a single canal channel cut along the bank of the river, this used a series of lakes, locks and channels to move boats up and down the river [92]. The River still has the 12 low-canal built dams on the river between Philadelphia and Port Clinton. The canal had one tunnel with no incline planes to haul boats over dry land, thus making it a very efficient operation. It was completed in 1827 [87] making it the winner in the race to the black gold. The system continued to operate until early 1900's, with its peak hauling rate of 1,700,000 tons of coal in 1859. It competed with the Philadelphia and Reading Railroad, which could haul twice the amount in a quarter of the time. Both parties, in order to maximize profits, learned to fix prices. In 1870, the Philadelphia and Reading "Reading" bought the system on a 979 year lease. The Pennsylvania RR, which owned the Delaware and Raritan Canal, later refused to take shipments from the SNC for that reason. The SNC carried so much coal that in its upper limits, boats would become grounded in the black slurry. The amount of coal sludge in the upper sections of the canal would lead to problems that we are still dealing with today [88] [87] [92]. The Reading Railroad released its 979 year lease with the SNC [72], forcing the Commonwealth of Pennsylvania to clean up the mess. Today the mining companies pay a per ton tax on coal for clean up. Unlike other anthracite continuous canals in the valley, the Schuylkill Canal was fragmented from the start. Today it is part of the John Bartrum trail that is made up of sections of the old canal tow paths and of

abandoned rail beds between Philadelphia and Port Clinton. Unfortunately the path is still not continuous. Today, in Norristown one can still see chucks of coal on the River's bottom.

The Schuylkill River begins its 125 miles journey in the coal field of Pennsylvania. The east branch starts in the middle of the old coalfields between the towns of Tamaqua and Pottsville. This valley is a wasteland of cliff and hills of blue grey slate from the mines that operated there. At Schuylkill Haven, it meets the West Branch, which shares the same mining landscape as its sister. The East and West branch is still under the affect of Acid Mine Drainage and runoff. The Little Schuylkill starts from the same origin but moves out of the coal fields and as a fast moving cleaner mountain stream. This streams starts near Tamaqua and flows through steep mountain gaps before it merges its flow with the Schuylkill at Port Clinton. This should be the most scenic portion of the Schuylkill tributaries system for it avoids the scarring of the coal regions. At the town of Port Clinton, the Schuylkill enters the piedmont agricultural plain and farmland of Berks County. It is also in a limestone geological region for much of its length from Port Clinton to Norristown. Once out of the mountains, it takes a gentle southeastward journey through small industrial cities line Reading, Pottstown, Norristown and Conshocken before entering Philadelphia. In each of these towns, like a border around a picture, its bank are surrounded by railroad yards, old industrial factories, inactive smoke stacks towers and collections of old row homes. As it enters the City of Philadelphia the river squeezes through the last steep gorge at Manayunk before entering Fairmount Park. Here, the Schuylkill is known for skulking, hundred year old boathouses, the Philadelphia Art museum, and countless miles of walking trails under the watchful eyes of numerous bronze statues in the largest city park in the Untied States. Recreational power boating is discouraged in the Fairmount section of the river. After the dam at Fairmount, the river starts to see a new industry living along its banks; the petrochemical refineries of South Philadelphia.

Sandwich between the refineries of South Philadelphia, rail yards, urban row-homes of West Philadelphia and the Schuylkill lays the John Bratram's botanic garden. In 1728, he began collecting trees from all over North American. The dissidences of what he collected and his home can still be seen today. What can't be seen today is Rambo's rock. In the Schuylkill River a large rock called Rambo's rock was said to exist [154]. Before the construction of the Fairmount Dam this was a major shad collection point due to the rock and a narrow channel. These rocks or rock near Grey Ferry may have been the first port on the Schuylkill. The rocks were removed to widen the channel for navigation reason.

Because its mouth was hidden in tall marsh grass, the first early Dutch explorers missed the Schuylkill River and later named it the "hidden river". It would be nice to think of the river as a hidden fishing treasure today but it problems are many. The East and West branch are still suffering from the damage of coal mining "Acid Drainage". The numerous low canal dams block the strong flow that small mouth bass love and restrict the migration of strip bass and shad. Flathead cat fish do well in such slow moving water

environment but their appetites for small fish only restricts the grows of other fish. The low flow rates also promote the YOY disease for small mouth bass. Like inventories done on the Delaware and Susquehanna Rivers by the Commonwealth, the surveys on the Schuylkill have showed the same decreasing small mouth bass populations in slow flow sections of the River.

The most obvious solution to increase fish population would be to remove all of the dams on the river, which would open flow rates, flush out river sediment, cleanse the water and permit unrestricted movement of migrating fish such as striped bass and shad. But such a task would destroy what the river is best known for Rowing or Scrolling. The compromised plan presently is to build fish latters on certain dams and remove others. The problem with fish latters is they really don't permit movement of large quantities of fish. Building fish latters on river is only a compromised option that produces little but satisfies many sides.

To be fair to the Schuylkill it has some positive attributes. The river has been overlooked by fishing articles and many anglers. This lack of strong fishing pressure will greatly improve your odds of small mouth bass that have not been fooled by countless lures. With the amount of money that has been spent on cleaning this river the last few decades, one would think that it could evolve into an excellent small mouth bass fishery. The river bottom is full of hellgrammites. It also has an increase population of freshwater clams and insect hatches that are being noticed by local fishermen. The shallow consistent depth and flow of the river through its middle section makes it an ideal river to wade for small mouth bass. Professional guide services that advertise float trips to catch bass and trout are now operating on the Little Schuylkill. The river has many low dams that can provide an excellent spot to fish downstream. Many of the retention ponds used for coal reclamation are open to the public for all types of recreation including duck hunting.

In the piedmont section of the watershed, the limestone tributaries provide many good trout streams. Berks County has the largest section of limestone trout streams in the region. Many of these are class one wild trout streams and are hidden on private property through out the county. Fortunately, several of these streams are located in French Creek State Park. Hot pockets of wild trout streams can be found in the northeastern section of Berks County, near Hamburg. Other noted trout streams that get stocked in Berks County is the Antietam, Manatawny, Tulpehocken and Kaercher Creek. Stoney Creek in Montgomery County as well as others not documented, curtsey of Trout Unlimited

In Philadelphia, below the Fairmount Dam, the water is tidal, and with its strong current, and rocky channel it has become a popular and productive spot for large cats including reports of flatheads, and migratory fish like stripers. A fish ladder was built here and shad and other migratory fish have been spotted getting through the ladder. In fact, there is a web site where you can view the fish going through it. Shad can be hooked from Fairmount dam but most are lost on the vertical haul up the wall.

Blue Marsh Lake

Blue March Lake is has 35 miles of shoreline, is 8 miles long, and covers 1,150 acres of water during normal level and 53 feet deep is an excellent lake for boaters. Blue Marsh permits unrestricted horse power but restricts speed in the upper half of the lake. In the middle of the lake is a 60 acre island called Quarry Island[9]. A total of five streams feed the lake: Tulehocken, Spring, Powder Mill, Northkill, and Licking Creek The Tulehocken Creek is stocked with trout and is also designated as a fly fishing or lure fishing trout stream. Beside stock trout and the normal bass and pan fish populations, the lake also has walleyes and tiger muskellunge. The lake has a boat marina for launching and boat rentals. The Lake is surrounded by state owned agricultural land which provides good bird hunting with dogs on the weekdays, on fall weekend it's like every place too crowded.

Lake Ontelaunee

Lake Ontelaunee is owned by the City of Reading for water consumption and is situated just north of the City. This 5.5 miles long, 1,080 acre lake is wider than the other two major reservoirs in the region. Its source is the Maiden Creek which flows from rural farm land and growing housing developments. In a state sponsored fish inventory of the lake in 2003, it was discovered to have a higher than average inventory of catfish. The Pennsylvania Fish and Game commission advertises that it has the usual mixed bag of fish including some members of the pike family. Because Lake Ontelaunee does not get the same attention as other lakes of its size, I believe it could be more productive than most people think.

Green Lane Reservoirs

The upper five-mile long Green Lane Reservoir may be the best lake in the Urban Delaware Valley for fishing. Green Lane Park actually has three lakes with a total of 870 acres of water [19]. The Lake is fed by the west branch of the Perkiomenville Creek, which is also a nice creek for small mouth bass below the dam. Its surrounded parkland is noted to contain the highest percentage on native plant life in the area. For that reason and fear of intrusive vegetation Green Lane quarantines boats in the upper lake. One must be prepared to use rentals or leave the boat in the quarantine lot. For this reason the upper lake is not that heavily used and may be the reason the why some consider it the most productive lake in the Urban Delaware Valley.

Marsh Creek Lake

Marsh Creek Lake, which is not in the Schuylkill watershed but within easy driving distance of the river and local area. It is a 550 acre lake with a good selection of coves to fish in. The lake is electric motors only.

What will be the fish of the future?

The fish of the future will most lightly be intrusive, be able to live in warm oxygen poor water and be ugly with teeth. Lung fish fit this description. Many people classify these creatures as nuisance fish. The real reason for our resentment of these fish is fear, real or imaged. They having a primitive lung that permits them to live on land for very short periods, are all aggressive, equip with teeth, and can instill nightmares to anyone that happens to catch one for the first time. Their aggressive nature and ability to live in warm shallow waters have permitted them to outlive the dinosaurs of the Jurassic and Mesozoic periods. They all prefer slow moving waters, with lots of vegetation, generally in shallow ponds and lakes. The ability to gulp air has allowed them to live in such an environment when water and dissolved oxygen levels drop. Their lung can also act as a buoyancy devise. The two most common known lung type fish in the watershed today is the bowfin and northern snakehead [132], [1], [2], [3]. The North American alligator gar may have been present at one time in the State of Delaware. If by chance you catch one, notify the State Game Commission and be aware that roe gars are poisonous to eat.

Bowfins

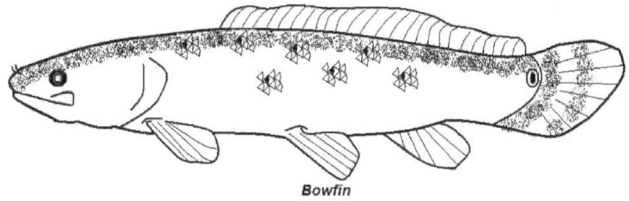

Names like dogfish, mudpuppies, grinners, mudcats, beaverfish, shoepike, buglemouth and lake lawyers are all appropriate names derived from the fish's canine sharp teeth, large size, and aggressive behavior [131]. They are native to North America but more common in the southern states, but can be found in northern New York and all through the Mississippi basin. In the south, they are known as dogfish. They have been introduced into the Delaware region by stocking experiments conducted by both New Jersey and New York and private individuals. Because of their aggressive nature and affects on the native fish, my research indicates the legal stocking ending some twenty year ago [132]. Still it's not uncommon to hear of catches of these fish the entire lengths of the Delaware River or in lakes where they may have been stocked. The most natural location that would match the fish's normal habit is in the shallow lily pad lagoons of the lower tidal fresh water section of the Delaware River. The average size in this area will fall between three to five pounds. The upstate New York record size bowfin, weigh in at twelve pounds thirteen ounce [2]. In New Jersey, a record dinosaur of eight pound four ounce was caught at a place called Tranquility Lake in Warren County in 1988[3]. Pennsylvania has listed them on the candidate for endanger fish and may not advertising

record large catches to encourage their return [1]. Like Catfish, it has small barbells, but unlike catfish, it has scales. The body is wide and heavy with a wide boney jaw and small eyes. The fish are dark on top with a light bottom. Males in the spawning phase will have a spots of bright green colors around it head and mouth. The males also have, a large dark spot near its rounded tail, while female lack the spot. They spawn in the spring and grow to a foot in size within a year. They are not fussy eaters, so there is no magic bait or lure needed to hook one, just strong line and some luck. Reports of catches all indicated they attack anything from fast moving lures to the smelliest of bait. The stories of catches all agree on one feature, they hit hard and will test your lines and skills quickly.

Bowfins appear to be related to the northern snakehead but are not. Marine biologist, state their close appearance is due to the term genetic evolution, which means they evolved separately but under similar conditions in eastern Asia. The easiest feature to distinguish between the northern snakehead and the bowfin is the anal fin. The anal fin travels the lengths of the snakehead's body while the bowfin is only a short fin.

Snakeheads

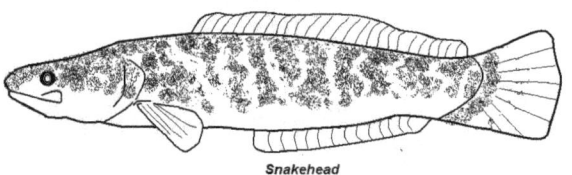
Snakehead

In 2004, the fish was been discovered in several urban pond within the lower Potomac, Hudson, and Delaware watersheds. The spread of this fish has game officials worried. In Asia, the fish is believed to have healing power, and is considered good eating. The fish is legal to sell in pet stores for private aquariums. The reason for this illegal introduction into our natural waterways is unclear. Two possible reasons for the deposit of these eating machines could be cultural and the fact that people might be getting tired of feeding them as pets and dump them in the local waters. As for a possible game fish, the stories are conflicting. Some sources indicated they hit anything with a preference for plastic type lures. A game warren once reported great frustration in trying to take a snakehead in a pond in Queens. Most caught are in the twelve to eighteen-inch size, meaning that the smaller snakehead is in the local water. The giant snakehead, can weigh five to eight pounds and inflict injuries to people, but are not in the local water yet. Because the snakehead is intrusive it should not be returned. Since the fish is an air breather like the bowfin and gar, simply depositing them on the bank to die might be a futile attempt to kill it.133][134] At first the fish was reported in a pond in South Philadelphia. Within a few the years the fish was documented as living the entire length of the fresh water tidal Delaware. With the increasing pressure on small mouth bass from the YOY disease the Snakehead may be a welcome new comer.

Saltwater

Saltwater is denser than fresh water so any line that is drawn to represent a salt-line or front will be vague. Like a weather front, the denser saltwater wedge moves up and down the main shipping channel created by the tidal pressure in the bay and the freshwater flow from the river. The denser wedge or tongue of saltwater forces the lighter freshwater to the surface and retards its flow all the way back to Trenton creating the tidal water elevation changes. This osculating movement of fresh and salt will gradually mix into a uniform salinity. The mean freshwater discharge of the Delaware River into the estuary here is 11,550 cubic feet per second [4]. The Delaware River Basin Commission monitors this movement closely, trying to keep a salinity level of about 25ppt (parts per thousand) near Chester[4]. Brackish water is defined at a level of .05 to 30 ppt while saltwater is between 30ppt to 50ppt. It is in this zone of brackish water that migratory fish like to congregate into schools before moving. It is also a place to adjust to the changing environment of salinity. These estuaries are also the nursery ground for anadromous and catadromous fish. This is also the zone of the highest pollution and lowest oxygen levels of the river. Catfish and carp can handle higher levels of salt while both fresh water bass cannot handle it at all. True trout, being members in the same family as salmon and chad can travel through this brackish environment but the lower Delaware warm water temperatures may not permit good survival rates. The most common fresh water fish found in the brackish water are catfish and carp, with some large mouth bass near the mouth of fresh water inlets that empty into the lower river. Common salt water fish that can be found in the lower river as far north as Wilmington are an occasional Atlantic croaker and some small snapper blues. Between Philadelphia and Delaware City, you can expect to catch a variety of fish that can handle brackish water conditions but the common ones here are striped bass, catfish, carp and perch. The quantities, location, and type of fish will be based on the salinity of the water which is a function of the fresh water outflow. Local fishermen report the salinity of the water will not reach the optimum saltwater salinity for all saltwater fish until it passes Ship John Light House.

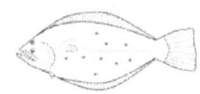

Striped Bass
Roccus *saxatihs*

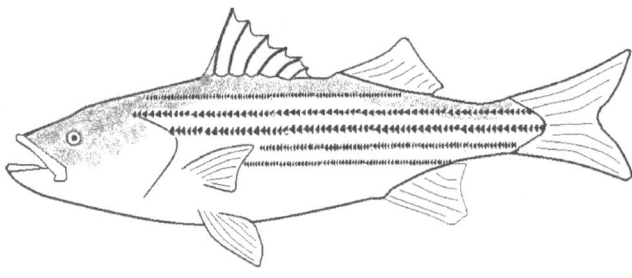

Its emerging crown spiny dorsal fish will be the first clue of what is on your line when you hook the King of Coastal Water Game Fish- The Striped Bass

From Bull Island to south of the Capes, from the end of March to the beginning of June, internet chat lines are alive with the talk of striped bass takings on the Delaware. The condition of the Delaware estuary can be measured by the amount of striped bass that makes it back to their spring birthplace every year. In fact, it's believed by some marine biologist that the fish are more plentiful today then when our early forefathers entered this land. In order to catch food and handle surf, the fish has developed into a strong and fast swimmer making it an ideal game fish for coastal and inland waterways. Unlike, freshwater black bass and trout this fish is not known for dancing on the surface, but with its strength, speed and beauty, no one is complaining.

No other fish in the region comes close to the striped bass visible appeal, strong fighting spirit, variety of sizes and ease of capture, once you know where and when to fish for them. The large legal keepers will be quick to test your knot tying skills and the condition of your fish equipment. The black lateral lines on the side are the calling card of the fish. The fish comes close in appearance to the white perch, fresh water white bass, and the fresh water hybrid bass which are all related. The best way to tell the marine apart from the others is the location of capture. If the waterway connects to the ocean, you have most likely caught a marine strip bass. If you caught one in a lake it's mostly a Hybrid Bass which are stocker than the marine strip bass members, lighter in color with fewer and less distinct strips. Off course, you can count the eleven soft rays on the marine's anal fin, its fresh water cousins normally have more and softer rays. Record fish of a 100 plus pound have been recorded but most mature fish will weigh in from three to fifteen pounds, with prize catches of 35 to 40 ponders are common. The weight/size relationship for a 20 inch fish is 3 pounds, for a 24-inch – 5 pounds, for a 30 inch – 10 pounds and for a 36 inch fish 20 pounds. The largest striper caught in the bay measured 62 ½ pounds in November 2000 by Jodi Clarkson. Al McReynolds caught the world record recreational fish at 78 ½ pounds in Atlantic City in September 1982. Scientists estimated today the

overall Atlantic Coast population of three to fifteen year old striped bass to be approximately 40 million [32]. The females, like most fish, are bigger and heavier than the males. Large females are called cows because of their wide girth and heavy weight. The males are term bulls.

Reading about the migration patterns of striped bass or rockfish (as they call them in Maryland and Virginia) is like reading about the migration habits of Canadian Geese. Each regional estuary group has a pattern that differs from the next estuary group and inside these regions are sub-groups and like geese, some subgroups are residents that migrate very little. Generally mature fish from the Chesapeake and Delaware will move into the waters around Long Island in the summer and early fall months. Some have been tracked as far north as Maine [32]. The basic pattern of movement for mature striped bass is after breeding the mature fish move back out into the open ocean, remaining close to shore and traveling northeastward in late spring thru early summer. While in the ocean, these fish follow the combination of water temperature and food. To locate the schools in the summer months takes skill, knowledge and a little luck. Once the water temperature starts to cool in September, they will begin a southwestern migration back to the shorelines of South Jersey and Delaware. In the months of November, and December, reports of big catches on the surf and at openings of inlets starts. There may be more in the non-tidal river during fall and winter than most would believe since the fishing pressure is lighter. Fall and winter reports of large fish, taken from the fresh water section of the river, will always lead to lots of controversy among fishermen as to whether it was a resident or migration fish. It has been well documented in some fresh water rivers that stripers do winter over in non-tidal fresh water sections [32]. The larger fish or cow "20 pound plus fish" tend to migrate slower than the medium size fish resulting in a duel migration pattern. The larger fish show up in the Bay by early December and leave by late May.

In early springtime, many will gather, in the brackish back-bay pools before beginning their journey up into the freshwater channels. In the Delaware, the salt-front at Chester is the gate where the fresh water migration starts in mid April. Even though reports of large stripers north of Chester will be announced before mid April, the main run of striped bass follows the blue back herring migration that will begin late April in the fresh water river. Besides herring, the bass will also follow the young eel spring run that begins about this time. It is always said that if you can find the main herring run, you will find the large stripers. When the herring are running up river, reports of other marine life such as whales and seals are commonly sighted. Once, a whale was reported as far north as Trenton Falls.

Daytime hot spots en-route up the river and in deep narrow channels (generally under highway bridges) and during low tides at the mouth of inlet streams that empty into the river. At high tides look for them up in the creeks and on covered mudflats. At night, deep holes along the bank and at the mouth of a stream are good places for the shore fisherman. The best time for fishing appears to be on outgoing tides. There are many

The Delaware Bay

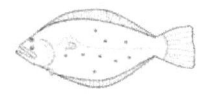

locations along the tidal limits of the river in the months of April to June for the striper run. Some comment that the main run stops at Bull Island. I have caught many juvenile bass there, indicating that large quantities of bass get further upstream. The limits of the migration seem based more on food source, and water conditions than a fixed location with a name. Striped Bass have been recorded all the way north into the State of New York with a record catch in Walton State Park NJ.

Typically, the fish like to lay their eggs above the tidal limits of the river in water that has a gentle flow with a stone or gravel bottom when the river water is in the upper fifty degrees. The eggs must stay afloat if they are left to settle on the bottom and become covered in silt, they will die. For that reason, the further up-stream the mature fish get, the better the odds of survival. The warmer the water, the faster the eggs will hatch with the average at 70 to 74 hours in 60 degree water.

Once the eggs hatch, the juvenile remains in the river for two year. The new fish will slowly work their way downstream to the brackish water estuary at the end of the second season. They will stay there until they hook up with the departing spring fish and head out to sea.

Tactics for these fish in the river depends on the time of year and temperature of water. In the early spring coldwater times, live or cut bait are normally the best because the fish are still sluggish and tend to feed off the bottom, while lures are good in the warmer late spring and early fall waters. When the water temperature drops below the mid 40's in January, the feeding stops. I judge the bait type, live bait or lures, by the water temperature of mid 50s degrees.

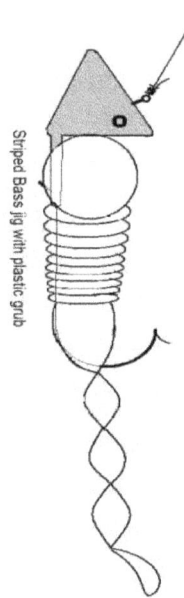

The most popular live fresh water river bait for the spring run was live herring and but now blood worms. Second and third choice bait, is eels if you can get them, and fresh clams. Good standby choices is cut herring, chicken liver, earthworms and large minnows or legal bait fish. Live herring is now illegal but was the most popular for people in the fresh water sections in boats. You tend to catch the bass in the same place you catch the herring. When fishing with hearing was legal and in great quantities, it was a family fishing trip. The kids would catch the herring, while dad fished for the big one. The herring would only live for a short time so many had to be caught.

Map 27:
River access is still difficult to find. On the DE side the Amtrak Rail Line and I-95 restricts people from the river. Even the small State Park along the River restricts fishing. Better luck may be found on the NJ side of the River in the soil mounds.

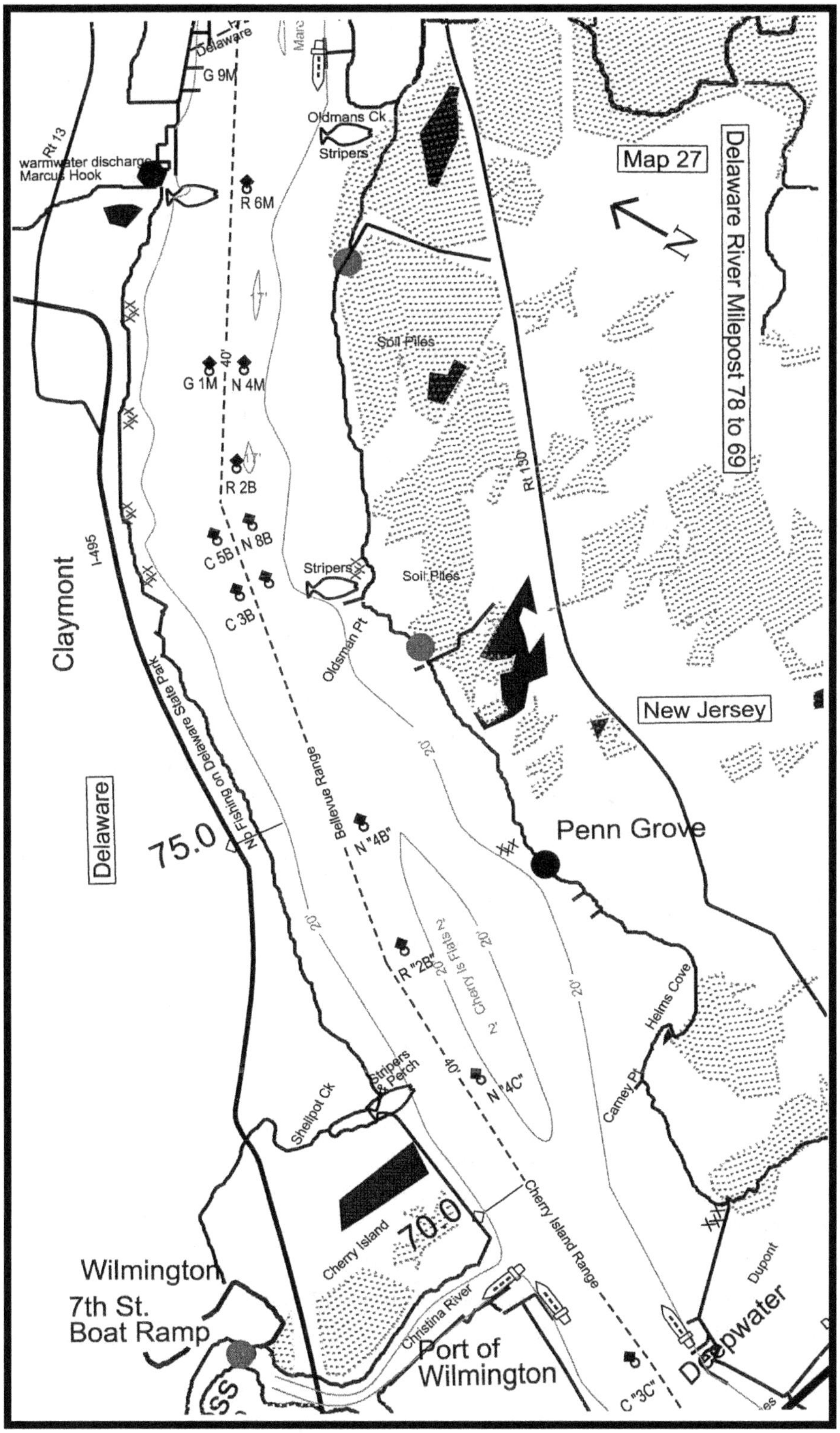
Map 27
Delaware River Milepost 78 to 69
Claymont
Delaware
New Jersey
Penn Grove
Wilmington
7th St.
Boat Ramp
Port of
Wilmington
Oldmans Ck
Stripers
warmwater discharge
Marcus Hook
Soil Piles
Oldsman Pt
Bellevue Range
Cherry Island Range
Cherry Island
Christina River
Shellpot Ck
Stripers & Perch
Helms Cove
Carney Pt
Dupont
Deepwater
No Fishing on Delaware State Park
I-495
Rt 13
Rt 130
75.0
70.0
G 9M
R 6M
G 1M
N 4M
R 2B
C 5B
N 8B
C 3B
N "4B"
R "2B"
N "4C"
C "3C"
Cherry Is Flats

Once the herrings are located in the main channel, the action starts. Because of the size, depth and shipping traffic, the most popular spot for fishing with herring is between Bristol and Trenton. Some people use perch today. When fishing with bait fish, you will most likely catch the larger cows of 15 to 30 pounds, so heavy tackle is a must. The legal bait fish is hook through the mouth and place back into the channel. Try to keep the fish suspended in the water near the bottom. One technique is to place the bait fish on downrigger setups with the fish placed close to the bottom while anchored in the channel. Always check the condition of the fish. If it looks dead, replace it with a fresh one. Blood worms are popular bait, unlike live bait fish, you can buy these but supplies are limited and prices are high. Channel cats are starting to get hungry this time and will eat up your $12.00 a doz. supply quickly. Most people on the banks resort to claims and frozen cut herring, which work well at night. Baby foot long eels are on the move in the river and as such are another favorite food. Few places sell eels in this section of the river. Eels are tough and on slow fishing trip, you can fish with one all day if you don't lose it to snags. Always have a cheap pair of cloth gloves on hand to handle these slippery creatures. Some people place them on ice to slow them down before hooking them. Set the hook up through the lower jaw and some like to have it protrude out through the eye. Some people will cut the eels with small scratches so to bleed it. A good place to set eels is just outside of large rocks piles where bass will be looking for them. If fishing from a boat, set the eel close too the bottom in the current of the channel but try to keep it suspended in the water. Don't let them lay on the bottom to long, try to keep them moving. In the open bay, most fishermen will draft eels through rips. Another, popular live bait are called spots. These 4-inch long small croakers come from Virginia in the fall. The technique for fishing with them is the same as eels. The spot bait is hook through the jaw and drafted across the bottom of rips or shoals when the tide is moving. When using eels, spots, and herring it's important to let the bass run with the bait for three or four seconds before setting the hook. Some fishermen will chum for striped bass in the spring. They seem to anchor in groups away from the shoals where other boats are drifting and set slicks.

Map 28:
River access starts to become plentiful around New Castle DE and Penn Grove NJ. This is the juvenile nursery of striped bass. Increasing numbers of white perches and dwindling numbers of Catfish mean increasing salt levels.

Know the season, size limits, the required hook type, and the geography of the region before going out. No one, rulebook covers them all. The rules change from year to year. In the river above Trenton, the rules are more generous while below, it becomes more restrictive in size and season. Saltwater rules are different as well with different restrictions in the open ocean. The types of hooks are controlled and should be followed when fishing live or cut bait in the river. A good safe rule to follow when you catch one of these magnificent fish is, take a picture and return it. The trouble is once you have eaten one, you will never want to throw it back.

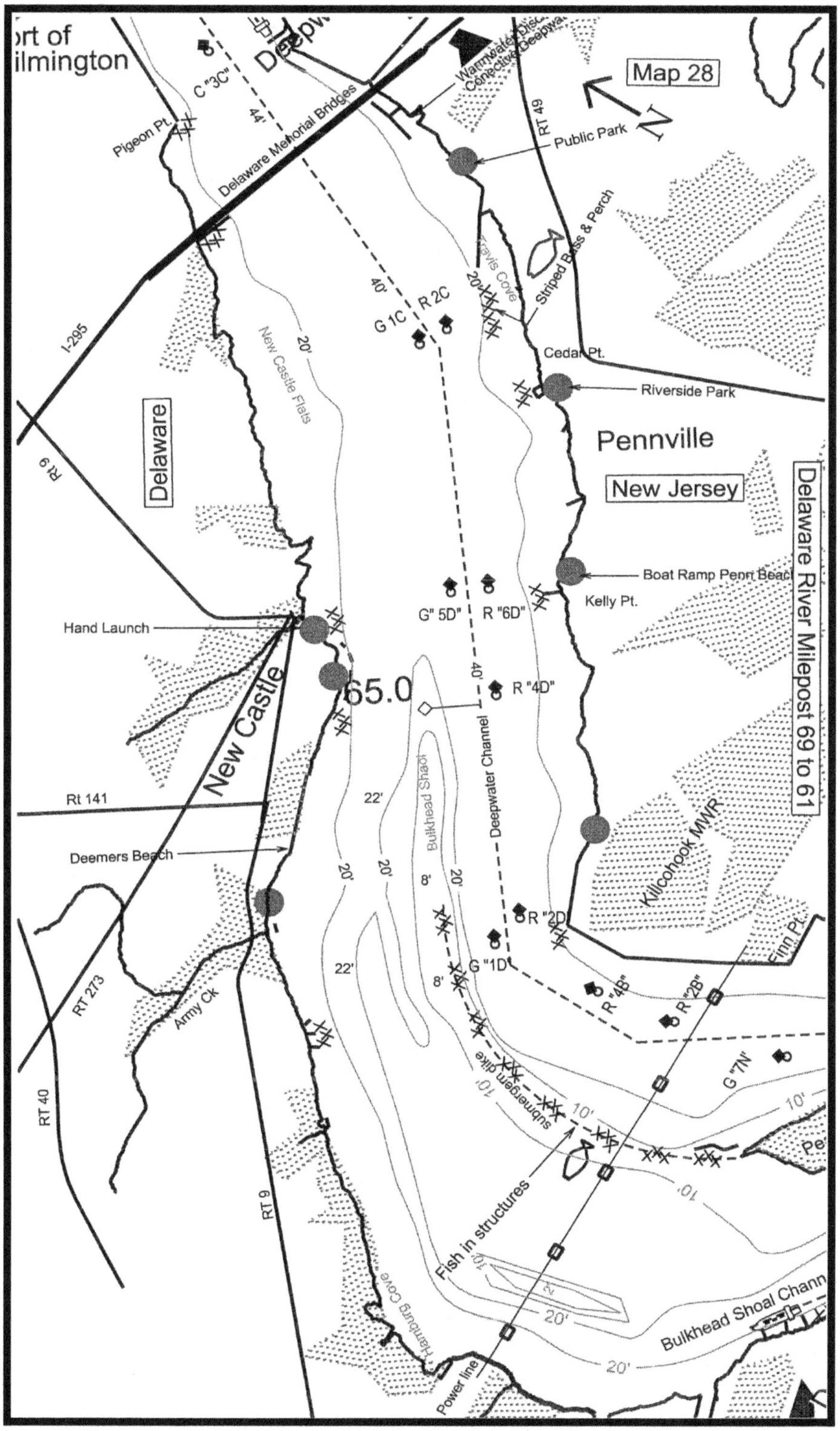
Map 28
Delaware River Milepost 69 to 61
Delaware
New Jersey
Pennville
New Castle
Delaware Memorial Bridges
Pigeon Pt.
C "3C"
44'
40'
G 1C
R 2C
20'
New Castle Flats
I-295
Rt 9
RT 49
Public Park
Travis Cove
Striped Bass & Perch
Cedar Pt.
Riverside Park
Boat Ramp Penn Beach
Kelly Pt.
G" 5D"
R "6D"
R "4D"
Hand Launch
65.0
Deepwater Channel
Bulkhead Shoal
22'
8'
Rt 141
Deemers Beach
Killcohook MWR
R "2D"
G "1D"
R "4B"
R "2B"
G "7N"
Finn Pt.
RT 273
Army Ck
RT 40
RT 9
submergen dike
10'
Fish in structures
Hamburg Cove
Power line
Bulkhead Shoal Chann

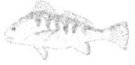

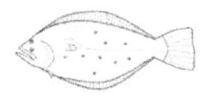

Fresh clams are good bait for both fall and spring for this type of fishing. The clam must be fresh. When using clams, it's best to tie string or a rubber band to hold the clam to the hook. Fall fishing in the bay is successful with both lures and bait. Don't just stick to the standard chosen color of white for both plastic and crank bait but try different color. The local favorite is 6 to 10 inch long, diving crank bait or what some call stick bait. This appears to be the bread and butter of artificial lures used here, with no particular choice of colors on top as long as the bottom is white. Most experts believe the shallow diving ones, are more successful than deep diving plugs. One interesting fact about striped bass taking lures is that sometime before striking the bait they circle the fish bait to confuse it, so snags fish are a common problem with crank bait. Some fishermen like to remove the center trivial hook on these large lures so not to overstress the fish with multiple snags when caught. I have found that plastic lures are the most effective means for the more plentiful smaller striped bass of the 18-25 inch size. For plastic bait, use long white twister tails weighted by a jig sinker. Surface plugs at night have been noted to be good also. These fish lack the cutting teeth of blues. They are also line sight sensitive meaning that they can see and detect steel leaders. When fishing for striped bass, keep this in mind when setting rigs or attaching lures. A clear monofilament line is the recommended leader for them.

- In the spring expect the warmer out going tide to be productive.
- In the fall expect the cooler incoming tide to be productive
- Plan your trips when the tide is moving, moving tides produce hits.
- Lower bay is more productive in the fall while the Upper Bay may is more productive in the spring.

Map 29:

Good places to fish from the bank can be found on the ground of the ancient military complex on the river, the C and D Canal and Port Penn. Many of the bridges on the Delaware side of the River have fishing walkways to fish from. During the low flow times of summer and fall the water can become full of snapper blues and croakers. The warm water discharge at the nuclear power plants is off limits. Below the plant marks the official end of the River.

White Perch

This is the most prevalent fish in the lower brackish waters of the Delaware River and Upper Bay area. This semi-anadromous fish is not related to the upper river yellow perch but is a member of the striped bass family. It has many of the same features and fin configurations of the striped bass but the stripes are lighter and less obvious than its bigger cousin. Like striped bass, these fish can live their entire life and reproduce in fresh water but prefer the brackish conditions of inland estuaries. They are smaller than striped bass with a mature two year old, fish reaching under a foot and weighing in just less than one pound. The female will be slightly larger and will need three years to reach maturity. caught commercially. The fish spawn April through June in fresh water with gravel bottoms in rivers. The juveniles will remain in the upper fresh water until fall and then

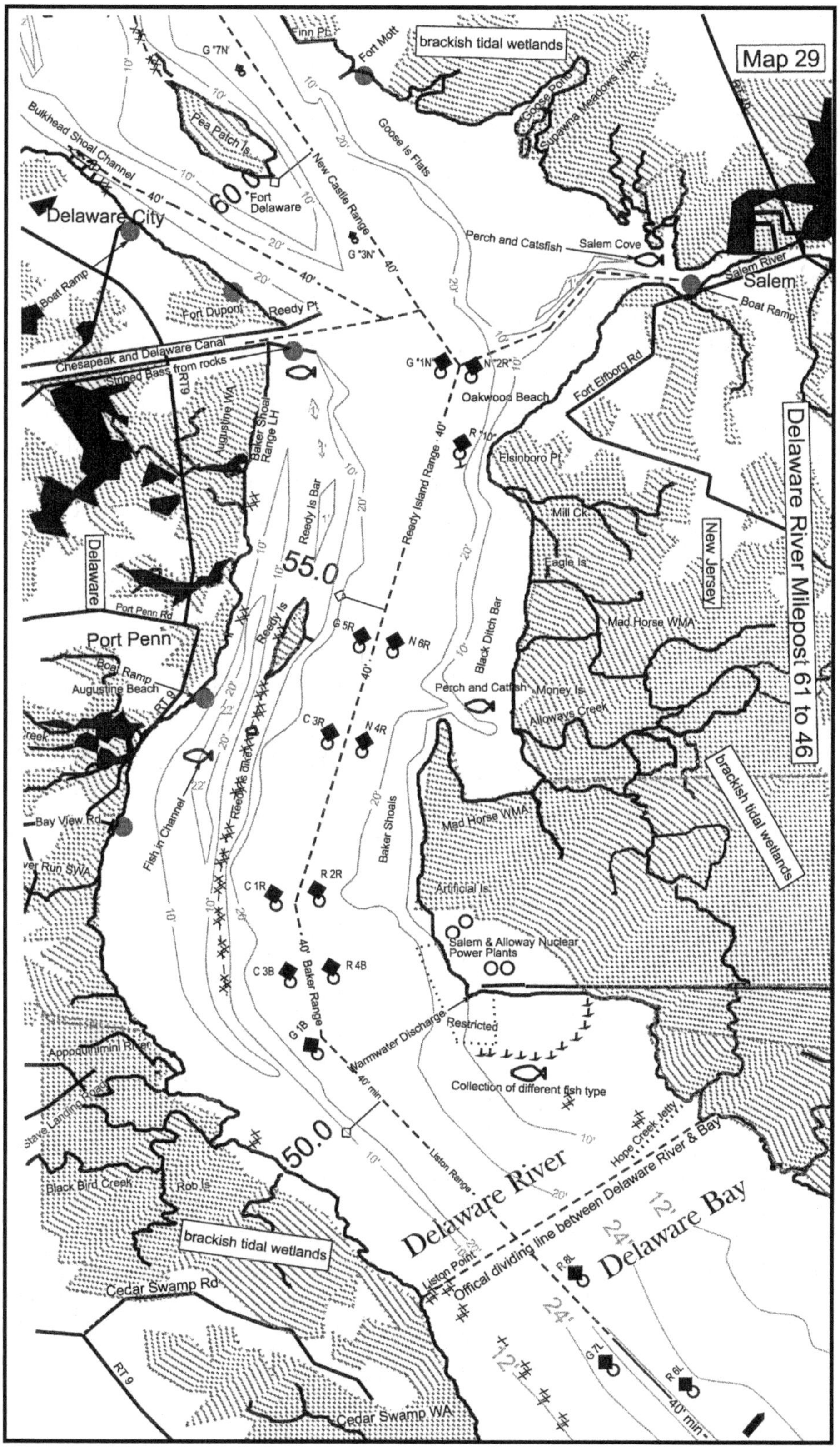
Map 29
Delaware River Milepost 61 to 46
brackish tidal wetlands
Fort Mott
Finn Pt.
Goose Pond
Supawna Meadows NWR
Pea Patch Is.
Bulkhead Shoal Channel
Fort Delaware
New Castle Range
Goose Is Flats
Delaware City
60.0
Perch and Catfish
Salem Cove
Salem River
Salem
Boat Ramp
Fort Dupont
Reedy Pt
Chesapeake and Delaware Canal
Striped Bass from rocks
RT9
Augustine WA
Baker Shoal Range LH
Oakwood Beach
Fort Elfsboro Rd
Elsinboro Pt
Reedy Island Range
Reedy Is Bar
Mill Ck.
New Jersey
Delaware
55.0
Eagle Is.
Port Penn Rd
Port Penn
Reedy Is
Black Ditch Bar
Mad Horse WMA
Boat Ramp
Augustine Beach
RT 9
Perch and Catfish
Money Is.
Alloways Creek
Reedy Is Dike
Fish in Channel
Baker Shoals
Bay View Rd
Artificial Is.
Salem & Alloway Nuclear Power Plants
Baker Range
Appoquinimink River
Warmwater Discharge
Restricted
Collection of different fish type
Stave Landing Rd
50.0
Liston Range
Hope Creek Jetty
Delaware River
Offical dividing line between Delaware River & Bay
Delaware Bay
Black Bird Creek
Rob Is
brackish tidal wetlands
Liston Point
Cedar Swamp Rd
RT 9
Cedar Swamp WA
40' min

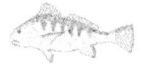

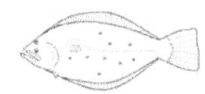

venture to deeper, higher salinity water in the winter. The adult fish tend to move often between fresh, brackish and saltwater. Their basic pattern is to spawn by early summer in near fresh water conditions then move to higher salinity water in bays and inshore saltwater environments by fall and winter. Talking to people who fish the upper bay and lower river, they comment that the fish can be caught just about anytime of the year with springtime being the most productive. These live in schools so if you locate them you will most likely catch many.

Hybrid Striped Bass

State fishing agencies prefer stocking hybrid in waterways because it enables them to control the population. The hybrid striped bass is a mix between the marine striped bass and the fresh water white bass. These fish are a little stockier than the marine striped bass and are normally half the size. The stripes are not as distinct as the marine striped bass. As for the difference between hybrids striped bass and white bass look at the tongue. If the tongue has two patches it's a marine or hybrid, one patch, it's a white bass. The hybrids are a fast growing fish and because of their larger size, they can provide an angler with an unexpected surprise if his rod and reel can handle these 10 to 20 pound aggressive fish. They bite on all of the usual lures thrown that a marine bass might hit and can be expect to school and feed at night.

The most interesting feature of the Moronidae temperate bass family, which includes white perch, white bass and striped bass, is that we don't understand the whole story of these fish. Like eels, they break or change the rules when they want to. There are reports of land-lock marine striped bass in the waterway, as well as "sterile?" hybrid bass that have bred with white bass and even themselves. If you catch a big one in the river in the fall or summer, post the picture on the internet fish chat line and no-one can agree on rather it is was a land-lock, marine or hybrid striped bass. [59]

Sturgeons

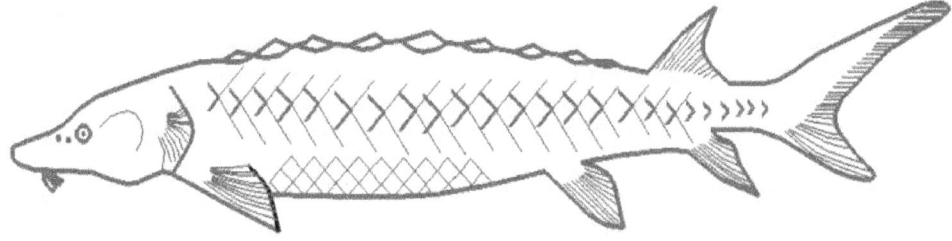

Sturgeons are not considered game fish but the history of them needs to be told. Fossil of sturgeon like fish litter the bedrocks of the world. So old are these fish that some sturgeons become landlocked. Today, large varieties of Sturgeons are found in North American, Europe and Asia, but for some reason none south of the Equator. Many debate if the different types of sturgeon came from a single fish or evolved separately. They are distingue by having bony plates called scutes instead of scales, cartiligens skeleton,

elongated bodies, barbells for bottom feeding, obtaining large size and old age. These bottom feeders may have been the most prevalent fish in the lower Delaware when Europeans arrived. Sturgeons were an evolutional success story before we started harvesting them for eggs. They are not game fish but they have a role bigger than any other fish in the River.

During times of dwindling supplies man has always been resourcefully in discovering new resources to withdraw from the water. At one time both the short nose and Atlantic sturgeon fit perfectly in the lower river. The stony bottoms of the upper tidal river were an excellent place to lay eggs. The lower river's and bay's muddy bottom were perfect for feeding. The Delaware permitted the Atlantic Sturgeon to grow to a length of 14 feet, weight as much and live as long as you or I. When Europeans fishermen started fishing the Delaware, the plentifully sturgeons were considered nuisance fish that destroyed nets and generated little in monetary returns. The meat was considered bad and only slaves, Indians and newly arrived immigrants with little money would eat them. The flesh of the fish must have had a strange taste to it because it was sold under the name of Albany Beef.

By mid 1800's the Delaware fishery was going into a decline and fishermen were looking for anything to increase revenue. A Philadelphia German immigrant by the name of Henry Schacht, is credited for the development of the North American caviar boom of the late nineteen century when he introduced a salty brim to preserve the eggs [151]. Between the years of 1888 to 1899 the Delaware would produce 80 percent of the total caviar produced in the Untied States. A popular South Jersey made fishing boat was called a Delaware Sturgeon Skip. At the heights of the Delaware boom the river exported 3,000 ton of sturgeon in 1888 [153]. How much of that was eggs, meat or both is not clear. The locally made caviar was even shipped to Europe and Russia. It becomes so prevalent that upscale restaurants and bars would serve salty eggs for free to increase the thirst of paying customers. So efficient were we at extracting this frivolous product that by 1901, the short lived Delaware caviar business was busted. Today most caviar comes from farm raised fish. What happen to the largest fish in the river, was it over-fished, competition of non-native fish, dredging, poisoned from sediments, diseases, or the lack of concerned for this non-game bottom feeder that caused such a profound drop in population. Clearly over-fishing was the chief cause of the drop in population at the start of the 20th century. Regardless of fishing pressure the pollution and oxygen levels of the lower river would have caused the same result anyway. To understand what happen to the fish in such a short time one needs to understand the fish.

There are two primary sturgeon on the river, short nose and Atlantic sturgeon.
Short nose sturgeons are smaller, growing to an average length of three feet. These fish can be found year around in both the river and bay. They spend their life in brackish water of the estuary and migrate up into fresh water with the Atlantic sturgeon to spawn in the spring. The monster size Atlantic sturgeon on the other hand does migrate out of the estuary and into the inshore ocean with tag Delaware fish being caught as far north as

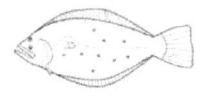

New York. Telling the two types apart is hard, for a juvenile Atlantic sturgeon is only lighter in color than the darker short noise. Both will inhabit the river before they reach maturity. Both sturgeon have been netted in surveys as far north as Trenton and I have seen one snag at the New Hope wing dam one spring Depending on sturgeons species, where, and who writes the report they typical take 6 to 10 years to reach maturity, with some reports as much as 20 years. Once maturity is reach they spawn only on selected years ranging from 2 to 10 year intervals, once again this time frame is not consistence with different sources. With this long maturity age and spawning cycle over-fishing is devastating to the species. These fish are the classic bottom feeders. In one report the stomachs were open up to revel a tremendous amount of sediment inside making them very susceptible to poisons from the bottom. When rivers are dredged the bottom changes and so does the current and bottom soil type Even thought these fish lay a tremendous amount of eggs the eggs are very sensitive to oxygen levels and the prime spawning grounds are in the middle of the highest pollution and lowest oxygen levels sections of the river, between Philadelphia and Wilmington.

The lack of concern for the fish cannot be overlooked either. The short nose is on the Federal as well of adjoining States endanger species list. The Atlantic sturgeon is not on the Federal endangered list but both fish are ban on harvesting. The problem arises with funding. A fish that misses the boat on the Federal endanger list will not get as much funding as a fish that is on the list. Since sturgeons are not considered game fish little money is availability for studies and stocking. The lack of interest in the fish leads to a lack of knowledge of the same. To study the effects of dredging, The Army Corp of Engineers along with local State biologist may have been the first to begin surveying sturgeon populations. In these early surveys the team of John O'Herron and Hal Burndage estimated that the Delaware both river and bay had a population between 6,000 and 14,000 short nose sturgeon indicating the river was healthier than most watersheds [153]. In fact, short nose sturgeon was moving from the Delaware to the Chesapeake by the C&D Canal. Survey for Atlantic sturgeon by both Delaware State and Federal biologist in 1994 caught 500 young Atlantic sturgeons, but by 1998 they only caught 20 as reported by Delaware agent Craig Shirey. In 2005 Phil Simpson for the State of Delaware planted transmitter on the fish to determine movement and location preferences [149]. On his maps he showed pockets of sturgeon concentrations from Port Penn to Trenton. To get an accurate picture of the state of the fish the surveys should be consistently done over many years with identical nets, places and time. Today there is pressure to get the Atlantic Sturgeon on the endanger list to haut dredging activities.

Still the largest fish of the Delaware remains a mystery to most people and when a smaller short nose is caught most think it is some strange shark or skate and it might get uses for bait. I was surprised to hear on the intra net how many were snagged by accident in the spring by shad or striper fishermen. Fortunately the large ones will destroy the tension strength of common fresh water fishing line.

Chapter V
THE DELAWARE BAY

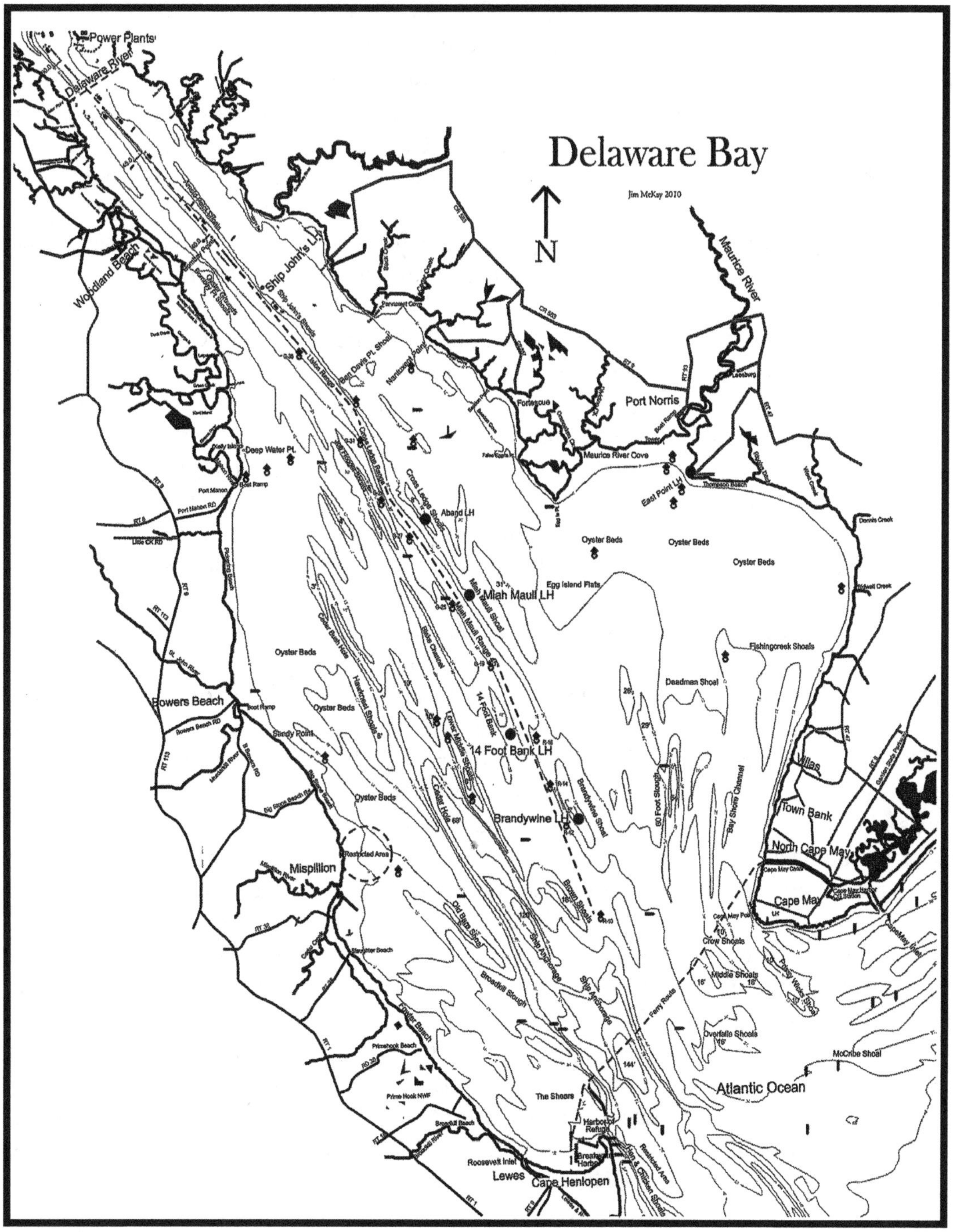

The Delaware Bay

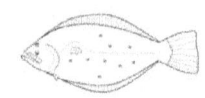

Where does the Delaware River end and the Delaware Bay begin? One will get a different answer for this same question from different people. One starting point for the Bay, are the Twin Delaware Memorial Bridges. This represents a gate between the river and bay. It also here that one can start to taste the salt in the water. The bridge, to some fishermen, marks the far upper limits of saltwater snapper blues and croakers seen in late summer and fall during low flows. A set of obscured monuments agreed by both The States of New Jersey and Delaware in 1906 in Liston Point, Delaware and at Hope Creek, New Jersey, (south of Salem in the Mad Horse Creek WMA) mark the official division between Bay and River. But, another more common location that can mark the line between River and Bay is at Ship John's Light House that sits off Bombay Point Delaware. The water body widens south of Ship John's Light House and the salinity of the water reaches a point where it becomes acceptable to all saltwater fish.

The estuary, from the twin Memorial bridges to the Capes is 65 miles. Approximately 170 miles of shoreline surround the bay not including the many maundering channels and islands. Width ranges from 12 miles at the Capes to 37 miles at the widest. The main shipping channel today follows the center of the bay at the state dividing line between New Jersey and Delaware. The channels length is measured by a mileage system set by the Delaware River Basin Commission [31]. The milepost system begins at a point between the Capes at milepost 0 and follows the main channel to the junction of the East and West branch in New York at Milepost 330.7 A secondary shipping channel in the Lower River, west of Pea Patch Island handles traffic to and from the piers at Delaware City and Chesapeake & Delaware Canal. A series of shoals or shallow water sand bars in the Bay parallel the main shipping channel. Besides the main shipping channel, two natural channels parallel the main shipping route on either side of the bay. These natural channels are less defined, with average depth of 20 feet increasing to 80 feet between the Capes. The deepest part of the bay is on the Delaware side called Cedarbush hole on the Delaware side. This may have been the original channel of the Bay but was closed off to the ocean by shifting sand bars at the mouth. In between the Capes, pockets of shoals can cause hazards conditions called "rips" during periods of strong tides currents and apposing wind. The underwater topography near the marshes is basically a flat shallow plane of 6 to 12 feet depth until it reaches the beginning of the natural channels, where it drops off rapidly on both northeast and southwest side of the inter bay. The Delaware Bay enjoys a continual exchange of water from the ocean and fresh water tributaries. Its neighbor, the longer and larger Chesapeake Bay has had more problems with aquatic disease and agriculture runoff; due to the poorer water circulation and larger watershed coverage, and of course gets many times more money than the Delaware for cleanup. The Delaware Bay has a greater bottom relief than the Chesapeake making it a more desirable place to predict fish location. On the charts through out the Bay are areas of restricted fishing, like main shipping channels as will as old ordinance fields that populate the upper bay and lower river.

Fishing The Big D

Every year on the news, there are sad stories of pleasure boater who get tangled in the tow line between the tugs and barge or get swamped in the wake of a freighter. Safely navigating between the shipping and strong current in the Lower River and Bay requires knowledge and common sense. Maritime regulations require a qualified pilot to navigate ships through the bay. At Cape Hemlopen ship pilots are transferred, onto arriving and departing ships. The pilots will guide the ship to its port of call or through the Chesapeake and Delaware Canal. Like airport traffic controllers the Delaware Port Commission controls the movement of ships through the waterway with rules for designated anchorage locations, speed and route [103]. Since the 1970s, traffic on the Delaware has increased with improvements in the Chesapeake and Delaware Canal. Today, 40 percent of the Port of Baltimore ship traffic transit through the 14 mile canal to save a 300 mile trip around the lower Chesapeake [103].

The Bay and lower River tends to be a forgotten entity, in our world for it has few news worthy stories. The bay's only reminder of its presence is the pear shaped outline seen on the daily weather maps. In fact, a car driving along the bay yields only a few points where one can actually see water. Most roads end at isolated small marinas or observation platforms where the view is not of water but a horizon of endless green mashland grasses.

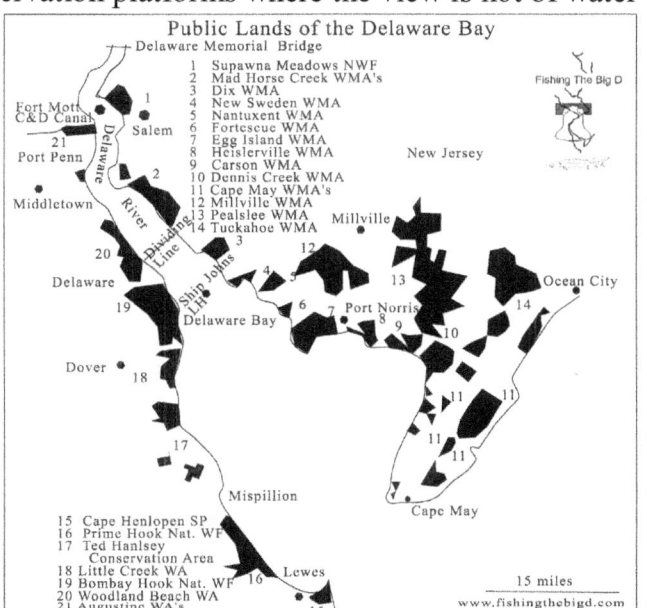

When you look at a nighttime satellite photo of the northeastern United States the coastlines are clearly highlighted except for the shores of the Delaware Bay, which fade and disappears into a dark hole.

The forgotten shoreline gave us one major gift; it bought time for government agencies to recognize the importance of the marshlands and permitted an opportunity to begin property accusations of land that had not yet been developed. Within the bay about 50 percent of the inter coastline is under protection of State and Federal control [62]. It is estimated that there is 350 square miles of salt marshes in the Delaware Bay area [126]. Today New Jersey has 51,910 acres and Delaware has 51,054 acres of wetland preserves [62]. The reserves

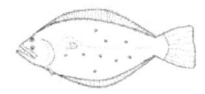

along the bay, all share one common attribute; isolation. Boat travel remains the best way to see the natural beauty of these water and land interfaces. On the New Jersey side of the Bay there are a series of reserves called Wildlife, Management Areas (WMAs). These marshes were first bought with hunting and fishing license fees but later New Jersey voters passed laws for the Green Acre Act which authorities bonds for more acquisitions of WMAs. Today both states have strict laws on wet land usages with New Jersey being one of the most restrictive. There are over a dozen of these WMA along the New Jersey shore that provides access for fishermen, hunters and bird watchers. These New Jersey's WMAs are famous among groups who follow the migration patterns of geese, most notability the snow goose. It is a win-win situation for all parties involved, including wildlife. On the Delaware side, there are two national Parks, Prime Hook National Park and Bombay Hook as well as several state parks. Besides the benefit to wildlife, the open public land provides a source for the recreational industries to service the fishing, hunting and bird watching enthuses.

In the Delaware Bay and Lower River, one early human activity would play havoc on the fishery. The success of the any saltwater fishery comes from the estuary. The glaciers never got down to South Jersey but the sediment they produced did. During this span of time, repeated seasons of vegetation growth laid a thick layer of peat. When the early Dutch settler visited this world, they found the land very similar to their native Netherlands where the land was routinely reclaimed from the sea. The Delaware Bay coastline would be ideal for this transformation from wet to dry. It was far enough from growing urban centers to be low in price and yet close enough to have a market for their products. This process was encouraged by the New Jersey State Legislation. In 1788, the State of New Jersey, enacted legislation that would control and allowed owners of tidal marshes to reclaim and maintain such land in organized companies or corporations called meadow companies [126]. This 1788 law would be the first of many in the Garden State governing the use of wet lands. This first act was done more inline with encouraging the development than restricting it. One of the first land inventories in Cape May County, conducted by the State Geologist, appeared in 1857 which stated that the county had 58,824 acres of marshland out of which 1,918 had been improved and 17,223 acres were used as meadows [126]. Later in 1866, the same state agency reported that New Jersey had a total of 274,000 acres of wetland out of which 20,000 acres had been reclaimed, with Cumberland and Salem counties taking the most reclaimed land. The State geologist later determined that half of the original 30,000 acres in Salem County had been reclaimed before the end of the 19th century [126]. By 1885 in Delaware, 10,000 acres out of 15,000 acres of wetland in New Castle County would be lost. Kent and Sussex County Delaware would lose 8,000 acres by the same process. Some of the reclaimed land was used for production of general garden type vegetables but the two largest usages for reclaimed land were cranberries and salt hay production. Most of the cranberry production took place in manufactured bogs in the pinelands of central New Jersey and not the regions near the bay. At the height of cranberry production at the start of the twentieth century, 9,000 acres were in cultivation [126]. By far, the unique product from the bay was salt hay that came from its 350 square miles of marshlands. In order to harvest it, channels and dikes were built to control the water levels and gain access to the meadows. The demand for this hay came from sources like the need to feed livestock, rope making, foundry uses, landscaping mulch, packing and installation material for ice boxes. Due to the heavy weight of early tractors on the marshland, horses were employed until 1950's. Because of the large green head flies and mosquitoes population, the horses needed to be covered or dressed from head to hoof. The horse also had to wear special wide shoes to keep from sinking in the mud. The practice of salt hay farming is a Delaware Bay tradition that continues on today but at a smaller limited level.

Milutin Milankovic VS Al Gore
Global Warming and New Flood Maps

In the 1920's, a scientist by the name of Milutin Milankovic calculated the earth natural wobble, rotation and distance from the sun, which provided a relationship between globe cold and warm cycles we called "Ice Ages" In other word the North Star has not always been true north and every 100,000 years we go through cycles of ice and no ice on the earth land surface. Because we still have land ice in Greenland and Antarctica, we are still in this 100,000 year ice age cycle. Within this 100,000 year cycle are smaller twenty-one thousand year hot or interglacial periods and cold or glacial periods. His theory was not taken serious until the 1980's when other scientist began study deep sea sediment and old glacial ice bores. At that time, most people were trying to prove that the temperatures were increases due to man's present. Where it gets interesting is that the boring samples contained high levels of CO_2 and dust at the end of the warmer or interglacial periods. Did this indicate that warm season produced high levels of CO_2 and dust without man's help???

Today we ripe our bodies and center our lives on some form of carbon type compound. The oil and coal that drives our world had it origin in water. 300 million years ago our atmosphere and oceans where influence by geological forces more than what it is today. The movement of continual landmasses was in high gear. These active geological forces contributed a high degree of volcanism, which flooded the atmosphere with CO_2 and dust during the warmer Milankovic's cycles. The fossil fuels we burn today came from shallow seas and swamps with low oxygen levels. As water warms, its oxygen levels decrees. This could have been the reason early fish developed lungs. As we burn carbon today are we transferring our world to what it was 300 million years ago?

The problem with the Milankovic theory is we have no fix date to predict the next turn over. The height of the last 21,000 glacial year period ended some 12,000 years ago:

you do the math. Has our carbon output prolonged the start of the next glacial period or has the earth axle not reached its maximum angle to trigger cooling.

Are the marshlands getting bigger or smaller?

With the drop in demand for salt-hay, many of the dike and channel systems fell into disrepair. The dikes were normally maintained by dredging sand from the channel and depositing it on the dike. Much of the reclaimed land started to disappear in the mid twentieth century. By 1972, New Jersey legislation had claimed ownership of all waterways and the dirt under them. Dredging channels for soil soon became unlawful. With the lengthy permit process of dredging and the economics of farming, reclaimed land became even more unprofitable. Traveling through the bay regions one would guess, on the New Jersey side that most of the "reclaim land" had reverted back to its normal state within the 51,000 acres of the WMA's land. Without the dike system in place, salt water gets further inland [126]. The results of this saltwater influx can be seen in the line of dead trees that border the edges of these Delaware saltwater meadows lands. This influx of saltwater also creeps into fresh water wells of nearby homes. Environmental reports by the State of Delaware, other agencies and environmentalist, provides evidences that brackish wetlands are decreasing, due to rising sea levels, about 1mm per year. On the New Jersey side of the Bay wet lands appear to be creeping inland and growing in size. The truth, to the argument of growing or decreasing wet lands, needs to be monitored over a longer time frame, not a few years.

Like blood vessels, the slow maundering channels provide an avenue to create a water and nutrient exchange between land and water. The ground acts like kidneys, it filters the excess nutrients or pollution, storing it and later release it slowly. The grass is the skin that holds the system together. It catches silt when the water floods, and the collected silt and debris become the banks. Many types of marine life, such as oysters are the enzyme agents that convert nutrients to food and later back to soil. The force that drives the exchange is an object we see daily but never seem to recognize its importance. Like the heart, the moon's energy moves the blood of the estuary to and from the marshes and channels, flooding the land and carrying the food needed to sub stain the life of the marsh. Without this tidal force, our world saltwater fishery would be radically different. Without diversity, our ability to consistently withdraw a steady supply of food from the world's oceans would stop. Without a steady supply of food from the sea, our geopolitical world and population distribution would not be what it is today.

As one progresses seaward the vegetation of the marshes begins to change in appearance from the tall fresh and brackish water grass marshes parries to the short stubby flat grasses of salt water. This contrast in vegetation can be easily observed in the marsh land behind the barrier islands of the coast. After a mile from an open channel the grasses begin to get taller with a more ragged appearance. This type of vegetation diversity is

caused by different levels of salinity. Generally the first lines of trees are cedar trees that later blend into a mixture of hard and soft wood forest.

With all of the research about water quality and estuary preservation we often overlook the bottom environment. The Army Corp of Engineers is always researching the effects dredging has on the habitat of oysters and other shellfish with recommendations on correcting the problem [39]. As early as 1885, the United State Government funded the construction and maintenance of a 600 foot wide, 16 foot deep channel from Philadelphia to the Bay. In 1899, it was deepen to 30 feet and today the Army Corp of Engineers maintains a 40 feet deep channel [26]. With an average draft of a tanker at 25 – 30 foot, a ten-foot bottom clearance is not enough to prevent an oil spill from a ruptured haul hitting submerged items. Most of the oil spill on the river can be traced to striking submerged object. The channel width varies from 400 feet in the upper port to 1,000 feet in the lower bay. In 1992, Congress authorized 227 million dollars to be used to increase the depth another five feet and straighten out 12 of the 16 curves in the bay and river. The dredging would begin at Becketts Terminal and then proceed southward approximate 60 miles until the bay's depth reaches 45 feet at Bombay Point [26]. The amount of sediment is rich in Mercury, PCB's and pesticides which will be reintroduced back into the water. The increased amount of suspended sediment will cover the clams and oyster beds, and also disturb the winter breeding grounds of blue crabs. To achieve the desire depth in a river the dredging is continuous, thus added sediments will always be present. High sediment quantities in water disturb the gills of fish and most fish will avoid high sediment areas. Deepening the channels could also bring the salt line further up the river thus affecting the underground fresh water aquifers in New Jersey. Another major problem with dredging is what to do with the soil and sand. It was customary to fill in wet lands on the New Jersey side with the soil. One likely place is to haul it to the coal regions for strip mine reclamation rather then piling it on local wet lands. The Army Corp of Engineer had plans to ship the spoils by rail to old coal fields in Pennsylvania but with the airport expansion this might not happen.

The concept of dredging as with many projects of the Army Corp of Engineers is controversial with no easy answer. When the authorization to deepen the channel from 40 feet to 45 feet was granted by the federal government in the late 1980's, a battle, between boarding States developed. Pennsylvania was quick to approve and endorsed the dredging. New Jersey approved the dredging with the condition that the soil not be placed in their State. After twenty years of study the State of Delaware had yet to approve the project so in 2009 the Army announced that they were going to start dredging the extra five feet with or without the state's approval. The battle ground over the dredging will affect the unseen and forgotten sturgeons that live on the bottom. By far the most obvious activity affected by dredging will be the shellfish industry.

The Bay's largest oyster bed (30,000 acres of public ground) is on the New Jersey side, south of Port Norris and center in the area of Maurice Cove River. Today, it is only a shadow of what it once was, but its existence is a key indicator of the water quality of the estuary. At the turn of the century it employed 4,000 people and 500 boats in Cumberland County alone, with a recorded catch of 2.4 million bushels in 1890 [38]. Sail driven dredging schooners like those in the Chesapeake were common in the Delaware Bay at that time. Two remaining oyster schooners or "skipjack" still afloat in the Bay, A. J. Meerwald and Ara C. Lora both anchored in Port Norris NJ.

The town of Port Norris was the capitol of oyster harvesting with a massive infrastructure to support the oyster industry [38]. By 1960, the 1890 2.4 million bushel harvest had dropped to approximately 49,000 bushels. The Delaware oyster industry mirrored the Chesapeake, where over harvesting, bed destructions, pollution and diseases all contributed to the decline of the industry. The reasons for the death of this once profitable enterprise are many folds. In order for oyster to grow they need a bed to attach themselves to and this was generally the shells from pervious oysters. After harvesting the very early watermen found the lime in the shells had a value and the shells were sold to limekiln operators and never returned to the beds. One of the first fishing regulations enacted was to halt this practice of not returning the shells. Dredging the shells also damaged the beds. The Chesapeake's early regulation required the dredging to be done by sail power instead of power driven boats. Power driven boats were also banned in the Delaware but later were permitted in the Bay. It probably did not matter if the boats were powered by sail or gasoline the act of dragging a large steel bucket over the bed would still damage them. In reading about the Chesapeake oyster industry the watermen knew they were slowly destroying the beds but the attitude was if you did not take them, the next person would. Armed conflicts in the Chesapeake between fisherman and law enforcement, were common at the height of the oyster industry. The biggest enemy to the oyster industry came in the late 1950s as a disease known as MSX, which created a 90% to 95% mortality rate in planted beds and a 50% in seed beds. This disease was believed to be created from parasites carried in the ballast of ships that was dumped into the bay. To counter the MSX disease, the practice of planting spats or seed oysters in beds in the lower salinity water (5 to 20%), in the upper bay was put into practice. In the narrow upper portion of the bay there are about 20,000 acres of oyster seed ground [130]. The disease could not grow well in the lower salinity water giving the young oysters a better start. Later the spats are transplanted in the lower bay water with higher salinity (20% to 26%) to reach a mature harvest size. With improvements in management, the oyster industry was looking to make a comeback by the late 1990s but another disease, Dermo created setbacks [38].

Why do we care about oysters today? An oyster is a filtering machine that can remove algae and detritus matter from the water. A healthy 3-inch oyster can filter 50

gallons of water a day. At the height of the oyster occupation, the bay could be filtered in less then a week. Today that is not possible. The oyster beds are akin to the tropical coral reefs of warm water oceans where they provide food, shelter and a unique ecosystem of its own. Without the oyster beds, much of the bottom is just a sterile mud flat. Some of the best fishing is near the remaining operating beds. Today, the Army Corp of Engineers has oyster bed programs and monitors the situation [38]. We can easily blame navigational required dredging as the major source of silting the oyster bed, but it is our needs and wants that drive the machines to dredge the River and Bays of our nation.

The State of Delaware has recently built 11 artificial reef sites, all on the Delaware side of the Bay and south of the Ship John's lighthouse to the Indian River outlet [109]. The State of New Jersey has built more artificial reefs but on the ocean side of their state with a total of 25 square nautical miles of underwater reef structures [111]. The importance of underwater structures for fish habitat has been known for a long time. The history of the oyster industry is a perfect example of the need to monitor and control the bottom environment. Not only are these structures good for summertime fishermen to pull sea bass from the bottom but they provide many other benefits as well. The structures provide a home for barnacles and oysters which help clean and filter the water. They also provide refuge, hiding, and nesting spots, for the diverse fish life, thus providing a better commercial fishing industry. The sites are also a benefit for the recreational diving industry. Man has been using the ocean as a landfill for thousands of years. The corrosive properties of saltwater and the bacteria in which it lives, eats many of the materials we have dumped and what it cannot eat, it will eventually be cover over with sediment. It is said that in corrosion prevention on boats and ships the sea will eventually win the battle. Today there are over 3,000 [111] shipwrecks off the New Jersey Coast that is slowing being dissolved and covered.

Decades after the passage of 1972 Clean Water Act, water testing revealed that the dissolved oxygen counts were on the rise while nutrient levels continued to drop within the freshwater waterways. But on the other hand, Northeast Fishermen in the brackish estuaries have been experiencing dwindling catches of weakfish, shad, crab and oysters. The Chesapeake, the largest estuary in North America is also the most studied waterway in the States. NOAA reported that the Chesapeake lost 4,500 crab-related fishing jobs between the years of 1998 to 2006 [156]. For this reason most crab meat is imported today. The only fish that showed any strength of remaining strong in the estuaries were striped bass. Research also revealed that more and more striped bass in the Chesapeake were infected with mycobacterious, a fatal disease thought to be caused from poor nutrition and water quality. The chief cause of the Chesapeake's problems was obvious, the increasing amounts of nitrogen and phosphorus used in fertilizer had created dead zones, areas free of algae blooms and oxygen. An easy indicator of dead zones is the absence of sea grass on the bottom, which the Chesapeake has plenty of barren spots. The

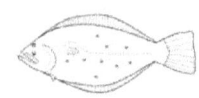

Chesapeake's new title was term the "phosphorus sink" because it collected runoff from a vast amount of sources and was slow to drain into the sea. In 1998, The Chesapeake Foundation gave its Bay a D minis regarding to its health [157].

In 1999, Washington Post investigative reporter Peter S. Goodman exposed the practices of the Delmarva Chicken industry in an article called "Poultry's Price." The chicken industry of Delmarva, once a small cottage industry, was now a $500 million plus enterprise [158] [156]. The industry is centered in Salisbury, Maryland and extends north into Sussex County, Delaware and south into Virginia. Here, the agricultural landscape is dotted with grain towers and long white buildings. Approximately 40,000 chicken can live in each single 500 foot long building. Today, 600 million birds a year are produced on the peninsula, which equates to 750,000 tons of manure that will be deposited on local farm fields as fertilizer [156]. This matches the waste from a city of 4 million people. Bird manure is richer in nitrogen and phosphorus than livestock waste. At one time bird manure was used in explosives. The problem arises when crops cannot process this high amount of fertilizer and then once the ground is saturated, the chemicals will leach into the water table or runoff into local streams. As the amount of farmland decreases due to new home construction and golf courses, the concentration of fertilizer increases per farm acre. Over the years the demand for chicken feed has outstripped the local feed supply so daily shipments of grain are brought in by rail. According to a U.S. Department of Agriculture survey the Delmarva Peninsula lost 15 percent of its farmland between 1982 and 1997 but the chicken industry grew by a third [158] [156]. Today, from a USGS survey, one third of the ground water in Delmarva is unfit to drink by EPA standards [156]. Not just the waste from live chickens but the processing of them has become a problem. In the final processing of the birds a tremendous amount of water is required to wash the blood and other waste from the chicken. The success of these private treatment facilities in removing waste becomes debatable when the water is tested downstream from the plants. In the end, a thick black residue tar is left and must be disposed of by other means. The solution thus far has been to inject the black residue back into the farm field; however this is permitted in Maryland but not Delaware.

Three companies monopolize the industry: Perdue Farms, Townsend, Inc and Tyson Foods. The three big chicken companies may be the biggest employer in the Delmarva economy. Anytime proposed state legislation to regulate the poultry business is brought to the table an army of lawyers and lobbyists come forward to fight the controls. Even Frank Perdue Sr. was caught on camera at Annapolis defending his company's repetition. EPA and USGS has clearly demonstrated the damage done to the waterways but has done little in proposing a solution to this dilemma. Instead the EPA has left the individual states to enforce the compliances of the agriculture industry. To be fair, the poultry industry of the Delmarva is not the only ones filling the Bay with fertilizer. It also comes from the farm lands of Pennsylvania, the rich green suburban yards of Maryland, Northern Virginia and the water treatment plants of the same. Water quality has improved

little in Chesapeake over the last ten years. The Delaware Foundation has upgraded its score of the Chesapeake from a D minus to a D in 2008 [157]. As per The Chesapeake Foundation, "until the Federal Government steps in with a workable solution little will change". The response from the Big Chicken lobbyists when questioned about what to do, is best described in a comment from one of them "where do you want us to place it: in the air, in the water or in the ground" [156]. The solution to the Chesapeake problem can only be found in a uniform tri-state or under federal control regulations resulting in a slightly higher priced to be paid by the consumer for each bird.

Fortunately for the Delaware Bay and River, between Route 13 and 113 a small ridge separates three watersheds. The Big Chicken Industry watershed drains most of the State of Delaware's either into the Chesapeake Bay through Maryland or the Atlantic Ocean by the Indian River.

In Salem and Cumberland Counties of the Garden State another growing agro business is quietly blooming green water. The agriculture business in these two garden state counties has always been strong. According to the U.S. Agriculture 2007 census survey, the area has been increasing its dollar value of agriculture products with little change in farmland within the last 5 years [158]. The labor required to work the farms has meant a cultural change in the make up of population. The US 2000 census showed that 19% of the population of Cumberland County is Latino but the number may be higher due to the transience nature of farm labor. Unlike the chicken industry to the south and the traditional local vegetable output, this new product has no food value. The number one crop measured in dollars from a 2007 census survey by the US Agriculture in Cumberland and 2nd in Salem, are the nursery or landscape produces like sod, trees and shrubbery [158]. To place fertilizer on our fields for non-food products might be akin to over harvesting our fishery for fish eggs. A study is needed to evaluate the impact of this new agriculture produce on our waterways.

As commercial fishing decreases, blame is placed on many corporate entities, one being the Salem Nuclear Power Plants, owned by PSE&G. The reactors operate on both an open and a closed circulation. The first two reactors completed in the 1970's, known as the Salem Power Plant, still uses an open circulation system. An open circulation system draws and returns the water directly to and from the river. The third reactor on the island, known as Hope Creek, uses a closed circulation system and was completed in the 1980's. A closed circulation system utilizes a cooling tower to cool its water before recycling the water. Periodically, nuclear power plants are scheduled to renew its operating license. This renewal is met with protest, frequently from neighboring communities and environmental action groups with the hope of "unplugging the power plant'. This author would assume that the number one issue would be the death and destruction from a

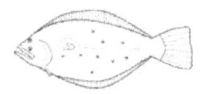

nuclear meltdown but instead the protests are usually surrounding more on emotional issues, such as fish kills or how PSE&G handles its weed problem.

As with many nuclear power plants, the Salem Power Plant and Hope Creek are located on an island. The Island is covered with an intrusive marsh weed. After flooding or high tides, the dead weed grass floats into the river and collects at the reactor intake pipes. By design, large rotating 3/8-inch filters are used to trap all water debris, including weeds and fish thus preventing them from entry into the pumps. Clogs from the weed grass, has been an ongoing problem for the plant, causing the plant to cut back on power output. PSE&G could control the weeds by herbicides or controlled burns, but both options bring controversy.

The fish kill story is another tool environmental groups use to unplug the plants. Various environmental groups publicize that anywhere from 845 million [160] to a billion fish a year are killed due to the Salem's open circulation system. The stories imply to the reader, that thousands of fish are sucked into the intake pipes where they are crushed to death from an intake pump, cooked at the discharge outlet or die of radiation poison every day. It is true that bay weakfish catches were at all time high at the time of the Salem Power Plant start up and soon after the weakfish population decreased, with little rebound The obvious flaw in the relationship between the decreased weakfish numbers and power plants is location. The limit of weakfish migration is located at Ship John's Shoals, about 20 miles down river. Due to a decline in salinity levels, few weakfish continue past Ship John's Shoal. Contrary to the weakfish, striped bass, which swim by the plant, has not shown a population decrease. Before September 11, 2001 and the heightened security, the discharge point of the Salem units were once a favorite spot for early spring and late winter fishermen with no one complaining of thousands of belly up fish in the water. The billion dead fish kill story becomes murky when one of the sources, was named in a NOAA October 25 press release [159] for falsifying fish reports and embezzling funds on an unrelated incident. Another source, the Delaware Keeper Network states the numbers come from the PSE&G application license.

To be fair to the activist and the so called scientist, there is some truth in their statements, but not as a fish-kill with glowing bodies of dead fish floating on the waters of the lower Delaware River. Their point brings up a good question that we seem to forget when talking about water quality for an aquatic life chain. A gallon of unfiltered river water is full of microscopic life that begins the food chain. After boiling the water to generate steam it becomes devoid of the phyto-zooplankton that creates the chain we need for mature fish. A 2005 survey of water usage for power generation by DRBC, estimates that the two Salem stations boil 1,300,000 billion gallons of water each year, thus making the Salem Station the largest consumer of water along the river. Exelon Plants follow up as the second largest user of water, boiling about 320,000 billions of gallons per year. About 98 percent of this now clean water is returned to our estuaries devoid of any life. DRBC states that 66 percent of the total amount of water taken form the river is used for energy production; the rest is used for portable water, industrial and agriculture usage.

The same alteration of our water supply can be said about water treatment plants that returned water with chlorine injected into it. In a 2001 slide presentation by DRBC the consumption of water for portable drinking water will remain consistent through the year 2040 but the demand of water for energy will continue to increase.

When the combine water flow at Trenton and Fairmount dam is 19,000 cubic feet per day, the Delaware River will push approximately 10,017 million gallons of water a day past Philadelphia. The total daily usage in the watershed from a 1996 survey by DRBC states that we use 8,530 million gallons of water a day from both surface and ground water per day. **That means that eight out of ten gallons of water are altered and returned within the Delaware Watershed.** Out of this, a billion gallons a day are exported to other watersheds such as New York City and Northern New Jersey. These numbers do not cover the tons of rainwater that fall on fields and pavements where it absorbs fertilizer or road salt. Droughts and floods will alter the ratio. It is amazing we can catch a fish at all.

PSE&G admits its open system is hurting the aquatic environment and developed a program of reclaiming 20,000 acres or about 3% percent of the total estuary into wetlands northwest of Port Norris. PSE&G commission a study for program models to predict aquatic biomass results from the wetlands reclaiming program. By 2001, the ecological models did verify an increase in fish biomass within the Bay and the importance of the wetlands to the overall aquatic environment [167]. Unfortunately with the increase in water usage any gain from the new 20,000 acre wets will be lost.

Talk to anyone that has lived by the bay and a recurring comments will come from the old timers. The water is cleaner than what it use to be but not in a good-way. Years ago the water under the docks were full of life, with minnow, crabs and invertebrates which would hide for cover under the grass when one walked across the wooden planks. Today the view of the bottom from the wooden piers shows a landscape of mud at low tide.

Lighthouses

At the time of the American Revolution shipping traffic on the Delaware was greater than the Hudson. Local maritime historian, author and artist Ellen Rice listed over 2,000 shipwrecks on the floor of the Delaware Bay. She documented over 1,800 on the larger Chesapeake Bay. Clearly the Delaware was a hazardous bay to navigate. There are over 3,000 [111] shipwrecks off the New Jersey Coast. Recently on a sand replenishment project on a beach in Lewes, the contents of a pervious unknown late 18th Century British cargo ship was pump onto the beach. It's possible that the Bay could be a marine anthropologist gold mine.

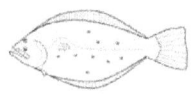

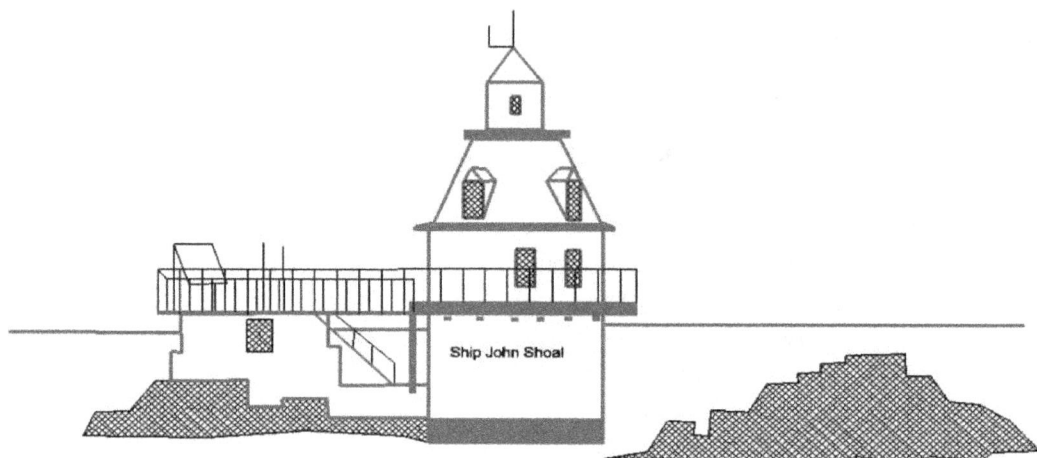

The first attempt to improve the navigation started at Cape Henlopen. Because the Delaware Bay sat in the middle of the nearby North-South shipping route along the East Coast a close safe harbor was needed. In 1826, construction of a long break wall was started at the west side of the Cape to create what is known as The Harbor of Refuge. When northeasterly storms came through as much as several hundreds ships might have

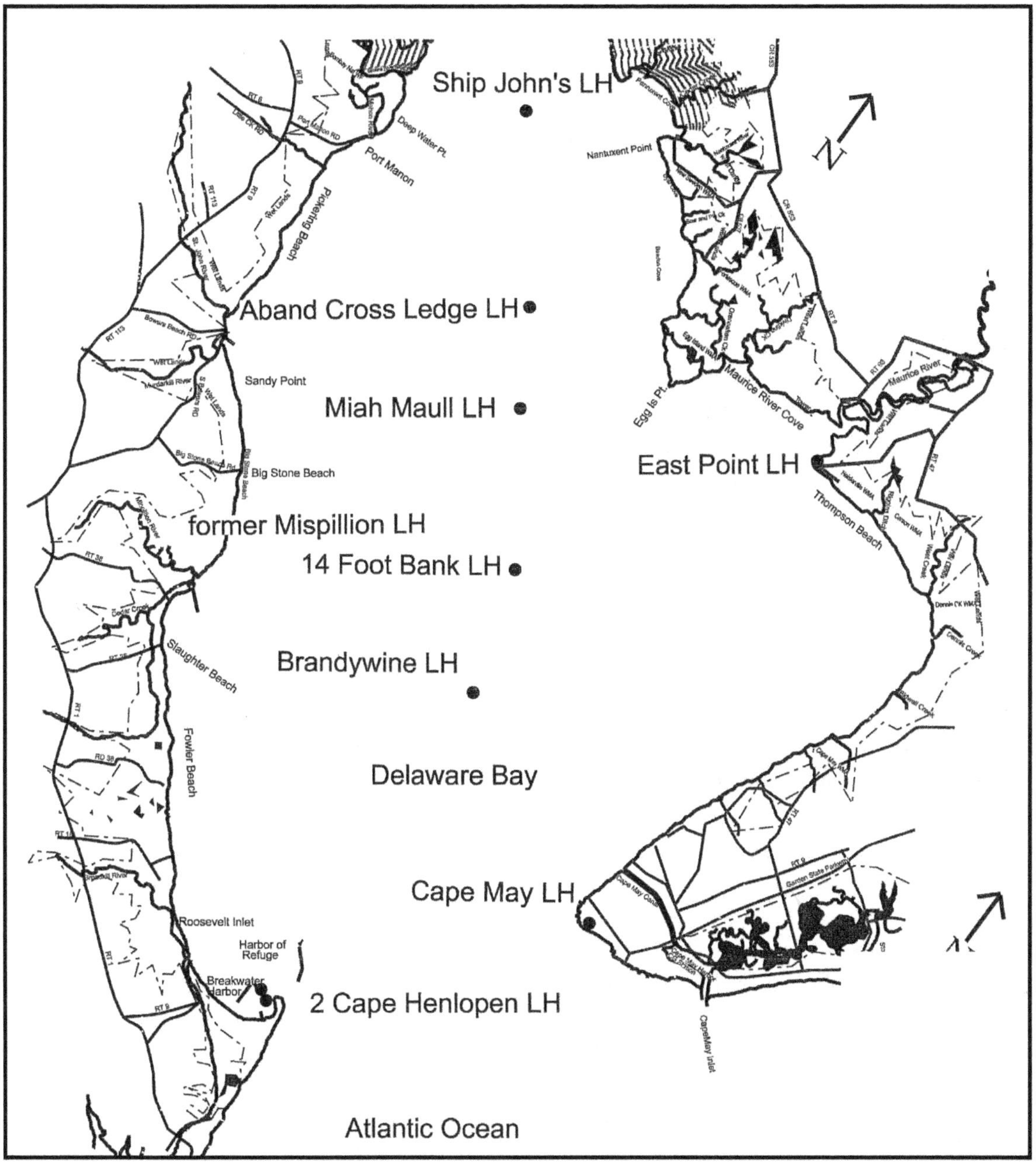
Ship John's LH
Aband Cross Ledge LH
Miah Maull LH
former Mispillion LH
14 Foot Bank LH
Brandywine LH
Delaware Bay
Cape May LH
2 Cape Henlopen LH
Atlantic Ocean
East Point LH
Port Mahon
Pickering Beach
Sandy Point
Big Stone Beach
Slaughter Beach
Fowler Beach
Roosevelt Inlet
Harbor of Refuge
Breakwater Harbor
Nantuxent Point
Egg Is Pt.
Maurice River Cove
Maurice River
Thompson Beach
Cape May Inlet
N

been in port. It was in this time frame that the Federal government started construction of the traditional high ocean beacon towers at Cape May and Fenwick Island. The first major light house at Cape Henlopen fell to erosion in 1924. Today the Lower Cape has two remaining lighthouses, the smaller Breakwater built in 1885 and the larger of the two with the white superstructure Harbor of Refuge built in 1902.

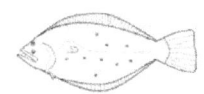

Every shoal has a story and name of shoals comes from such stories. Ship John Shoal is situated at a point where the bay narrows or some say the river ends. The shoals were named from the wreck of a German ship of the same name that grounded on Christmas Eve in 1797. The construction of the light house started in 1874 using a combination of screw steel pilings and a steel casing. The rock piling was added to help with stability during ice floats. The superstructure of Ship John Light House's first view of the Delaware's water was not on the Delaware Bay but the Schuylkill River in Fairmount Park at the 1876 World Exposition. It shared a stage with many new developments of the age including parts of the Statue of Liberty. The superstructure was moved the next year to its present location. So important to navigation that the facility remained manned until 1973. Ship John is still owned by the Government as an operating light house and is the oldest structure on the Bay [151]. The next major set of shoals on the Bay is Cross Ledge and the Miah Maull Shoals. The shoals run parallel to the main shipping channel on the New Jersey side and are considered one of the most hazardous in the bay. The Miah Maull shoals got its name from a skilled Delaware River pilot who perished there in 1780 from grounding. At the time Mr. Maull was a passenger on his way to England. Cross Ledge shoals has never been a friendly place for light houses and light ships. The first Cross Ledge Lighthouse built just before Ship John using steel screwing pilings was destroyed by ice. The second structure was abandoned after the completion of the larger caisson Miah Maull Light house in 1902. Miah Mull is unmanned today but is still owned by the government as an active operating lighthouse. The abandoned Cross Ledge Lighthouse was used for target practice during WWII. The only remaining feature of the Cross ledge lighthouse is the stone base that is un-lighted and a now a shipping hazard sometimes called "Flat Top". The next is Fourteen Foot Bank Lighthouse which resides on the Delaware side of the channel. This is an attractive caisson type house built in 1888. The lighthouse was sold to a private owner in 2007 but still has it's operating navigational lights on it. At the entrance of the channel is Brandywine shoals. Like the other shoals this location started as a lighthouse boat station then became the first steel screw piling lighthouse built in the country. The Chief Engineer, George Meade build the first Brandywine lighthouse using screw pilings and also built others lighthouses in the area. Latter he would successfully command the Army of the Potomac at Gettysburg. The steel screw pilling light house was removed and replaced by a caisson type in 1914 which is still visible today.

In order to mark the river channel, tall black tripod wrought iron towers called range lights were constructed. Some would sit a mile from the river channel and generally at a bend in the river or channel. The main propose of these early oil fired range towers was to act as reference points for navigation. They work in pairs, with a short tower, sometimes on the caretaker's house, but always in front of the tall tower and inline with the shipping channel. These towers followed the river all the way into Philadelphia.

Navigational oil fired beacons were also placed on houses generally near rivers of small ports. Only a few of these beacon-houses still survive today. When the Coast

Guard sold these structures, the control of them passed into private ownership. The cost to maintain these facilities has always been an issue. The East Point House owned by The State of New Jersey was almost burned down from vandals. Vandals did succeed in burning the house at Reedy Point in 2002. The saddest story of the beacon homes was the Mispillion house, which after surviving 129 years of storms and broken promises of repair was destroyed for want of a functional lightning rod in 2002. What was left of the burnt structure was sold again and hauled away from the small tradition fishing village of Mispillion and built into a private upscale home in Lewes. Due to storms eroding its base the magnificent looking Harbor of Refuge lighthouse may be the next lighthouse to be lost on the Bay. Today the main visual navigation aid is the Alloway Creek nuclear reactor cooling tower. The tower and its cloud can be seen over much of the Bay and Lower River supplying a common reference point to all.

Commercial Fishing

Today 81% of the seafood consumed in the United States is imported and 40% of that is farmed [122]. In the Bay, large netting operations are now illegal. But sea bass, herring and other selected fish are taken by traps and gill nets are still permitted in the Bay. Still, commercial fishing on the Delaware Bay and inland waters is still alive today but on a much smaller scale. To keep the industry alive local fishermen had to learn to adapt to changing markets, environmental problems, keep operating costs to a minimum, practice seasonal diversity and create new markets for what they can still pull from the water. It cannot be money that draws commercial fishermen to the profession of taking crabs and fish from the waters of the Bay and Ocean. Many are small family operations which have been forced to operate part time relying on other incomes for part of the year. Watermen in the bay lease clamming and oysters sites from the state. In the Spring the same waterman will plant nets for striped bass and herring. The biggest income for many of the waterman are blue claw crab still provides employment. With the dwindling saltwater resources of today and the nearby domestic market, research is always looking for new sources of protein from dogfish, sea robins and other common fish of the water. Another product from the waters, which is used for medical research and cancer treatment, comes from the blood of horseshoe crabs. The living fossil shellfish blood provides endotoxins substance, which can fight cancer cells. Today the harvesting of horseshoe crabs is regulated and highly contested.

The regulations, limits and sizes for commercial fish are hotly contested each year by local fishermen and three government agencies: Atlantic States Marine Fisheries Commission, The Mid-Atlantic Management Council, and the National Marine Fisheries Services [107]. The agency decisions are based on progress toward a target goals for fish levels or, as they call "biomass weight". The fish that seem to generate the most controversy in the biomass topic is the Summer Flounder. This highly sought after fish generates millions in both commercial and recreation revenue. In 1993, the National

The Delaware Bay

Marine Fishery Service (NMFS) placed local flounders at a biomass level of 46.9 million pounds. With increased restrictions on both recreation and commercial catches, the biomass level increased to 61.4 million by 2000. Environmental watch groups with money brought a law suite against the NMFS at that time forcing the target biomass for flounder to 200 million by the year 2010 [135]. With the higher restrictions, many fear commercial flounder watermen will go out of business and require all recreational caught flounders be returned. The net result of the conflicting biomass numbers has resulted in larger minimums sizes, shorting seasons, and smaller quotes. What we can do is report catches through the new saltwater license that is required by all saltwater fishermen.

Inshore fish

Croakers

Croakers are a very abundant fish family found up and down the east coast. They may come in a variety of shapes and sizes but they all share a feature that distinguishes them from other fish families, the vibrating sound they make. The sound is produced, by vibrating a muscle next to the swim bladders. Another common feature is the small chin barbells. The bottom feeding habits of croakers make them an ideal target for party boats captains. Although they are many different types of croakers the primary one founds in the Delaware are weak fish, king fish, Atlantic croaker, and the black drum. The red drum is usually found in southerly waters but at times they can be in the Delaware. Spot croakers are small fish that are used for bait: when you see this small hand-size fish with a black dot, expect larger fish in the area.

Weakfish

Once you eat your first weak fish, you will never throw another legal one back.

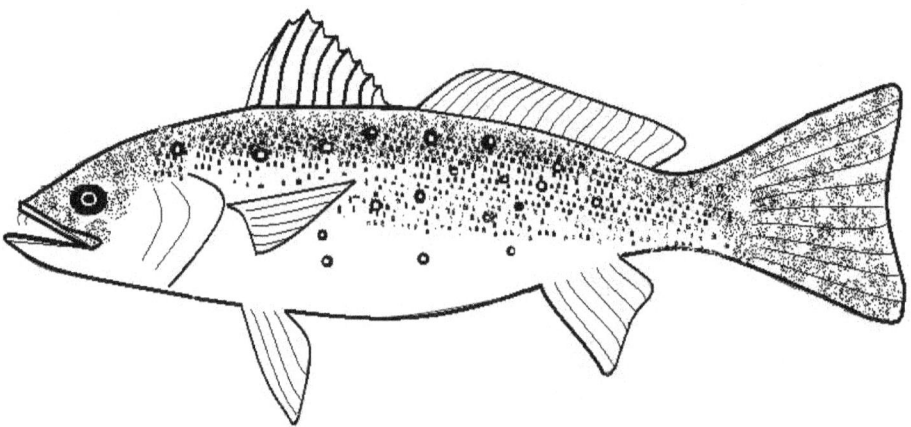

Weak Fish or Sea Trout

Fishing The Big D

The Official Fish of The State of Delaware was once the most popular game fish in the bay and estuary of New Jersey and Delaware, the weak fish. The Delaware Bay held the World Record set in 1944 at Brandywine shoals for a 17 pound fish. Than in 1989 a 19 pound 2 oz fish was caught in the bay which tied with an early catch at Long Beach Island NY. Today the limit is one fish with a possible close season.

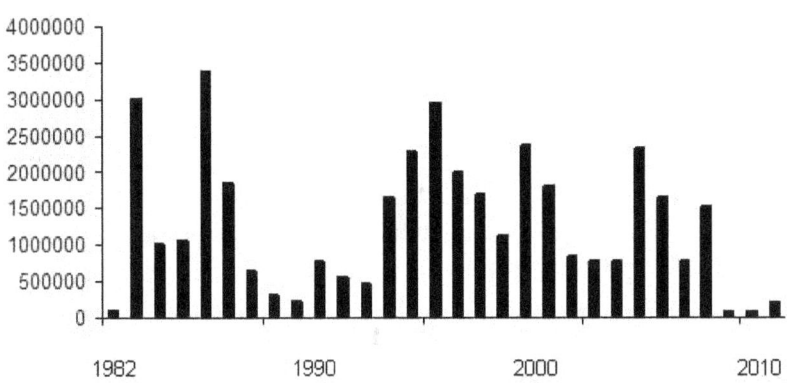

They are called weakfish here because of the weak lower jaw that protrudes beyond upper. Because of their fresh water trout like appearance in Maryland and Virginia, they are called sea trout but should not be confused with steelheads and brown sea trout. The males make the croaking sound while the females remain silent. The weakie is a slim looking croaker with a dark olive green color on the back with multiple colors of purple, green, lavender, gold and blue dots along it sides thus giving that trout like appearance. The biggest clue to a weak fish identity is the two long canine teeth that drop from the upper jaw. This vampire look will tell you it's a weak fish not a king or drum type croaker. The diets of these fish are crabs, shrimp, squid, worms and smaller fish and minnows. They are slow growing fish with many being barely legal one taken at age three. A NJ record weakfish of 18 pound 8 oz was taken by Karl Jones in 1986 in the bay [3]. A NJ Second place is held by Monica Oswald who also holds the unofficial world summer flounder record. Most fish caught will be at the legal limit of around 13 inches but that could change from year to year. Fish in the size range of 12 to 14 inches will weight about one pound and could be 2 to 3 years old. A two-pound fish will be about 18 inches long and between 4 to 5 years old. A 30-inch weakfish, could weight about 11 pounds and may be as 12 years old. Weakfish reach maturity between two to three years [37]. The population number varies but not just from season to season but from decade to decade. It might be due to the slow growth and reproduction cycle of the fish and the commercial pressure placed on them. Other people say it's the present of large blue fish populations that produce this cycle, or it could be a combination of all of the above. Generally, weakfish will be good for several years in a row with each

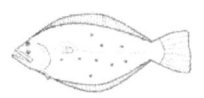

consecutive year bring bigger fish until the quantities caught drop off and the estuary will see another 5 to 10 year cycle of poor weakie population. During those times of large weak fish taking, more weak fish were caught than stripers. In 1979 the Milford Chamber of Commerce and Cumberland County started tournaments for weakfish/sea trout, in May. The record fish started around 10 pound but after several years the amount of weakfish dropped off and with third and forth place only around one pound range. The weakfish catches has not recovered from the mid 1970/1980 high reports [40]. Some believe that a genetically different and larger croaker may have been invading our waters in the 70/80 booms. Maybe some day we can experience a cycle where, stripers, blues and weakfish can share the water with an equally high population.

Weakfish enter the bay in two waves, the first are the larger older breeding fish that enter in late May. The smaller one-pound fish enter in early July and remain through the fall leaving around late October. The smaller weakfish will be the one the party boats will take you out to catch. Weakfish tend to feed off the bottom in bays. The best places for the fish are along reef and rock walls and near the edges of deep channels that go through out the bay. You can also expect to find them in inlet channels between the barrier Islands and river outlets in the bay. Some are caught along grass beds near the shores lines. The most noted location is Ship John's lighthouse at the upper limit's of the bay. In the center of the bay Buoy numbers 35, 32 34 are reported good places for weakfish. Along the Delaware side named locations are the walls at Lewis, Blake's channel, Coral Oyster Beds and Slaughter Beach. On New Jersey side look for jetties near Cape May and near the outlet of fresh water that empty into the bay Ocean.

Boats would generally drift through a feeding school on the bottom. One should learn to keep your line ready to hook the slightest tug. You cannot set the hook hard or you will rip the hook from its jaw. Use a meat strip about three inches long, triangle shaped and hooked through the wider end, leaving a trailing narrow edge. Do not ball the bait on the hook. If the bait gets dirty, replace it. Weakfish are very fickle eaters. If you think they might be out there, bring some peeler crabs with you. When fishing from a boat it's best to try to float the bait to the depth that the fish are at, generally near the bottom. As for live bait, squid, clams, bloodworms, grass shrimp are all good but the most popular are shedder crab or "peelers". Unfortunately, most fish caught today are the two-year-old fish that will be right on the edge of legal keepers. Keepers, make an excellent meal. Unfortunately, the limit is now one weakfish, hardly worth keeping.

If you want bigger weakfish, you will have to book a private charter or fish the inlets in mid May through June at night. Weakfish are attracted to light at night. Large one can be picked up under lighted bridges in the spring. Some fishermen will use strong lights to attract these fish to their boats.

King Fish
Menticirrhus *saxatilis*

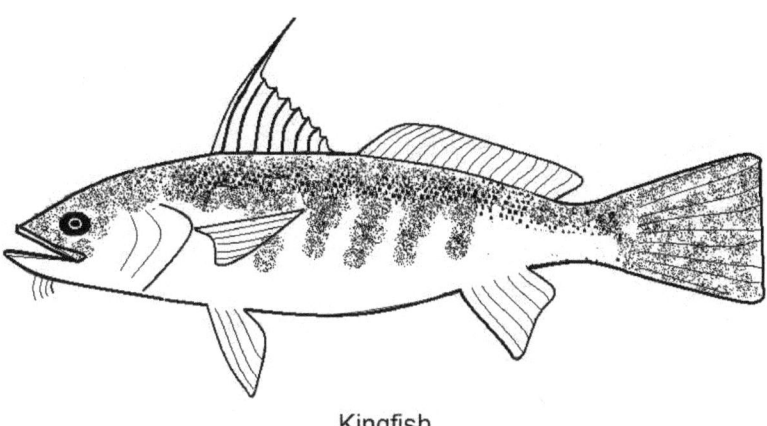

Kingfish

These fish are an all time favorite for surf fisherman in the summer mouths. They tend to congregate on the surf on sandy bottoms. The croaking sound of this croaker does not come from their swim bladder but from muscles in the jaw. Kingfish populations very from year to year and seem to be on opposite cycles of the weakfish. Because of the similar shape and croaking noise, many people confuse these fish with the smaller weakfish. The biggest different is that kingfish lack the canine teeth. The kingfish also is darker in color, with dark V-shaped vertical strips and has a pointed high dorsal fin on the back. The kingfish maximum size might get to 18 inches while the weakfish can grow to 30 inches. Most caught in the 10 to 14 inches size range [3]. Kingfish spawning begins as early April and can last to July when they come inshore to spawn in shallow water. During the winter months, they are believed to venture off shore in deeper water. They are fast growing but short-lived fish with a maximum life expectance of only three years. An eleven inch king fish caught in October could have been spawned in April of the same year, making the king fish an ideal game fish in the late summers early fall fishing season. There are several different types of king fish but the one that is very common to the Delaware and Chesapeake is the Northern kingfish, which has the more pronounced markings. For its small size, these fish can put up a nice fight when hooked. They also come in large numbers making than an ideal fish to go for when the schools are in. [36].

Small hooks with squid, bloodworms, or clams placed on the bottom is the easiest method to catch king fish. If fishing from a boat look for pockets of 8 to 15 feet water near shores lines with sandy bottoms.

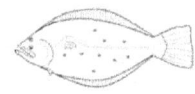

Atlantic Croaker

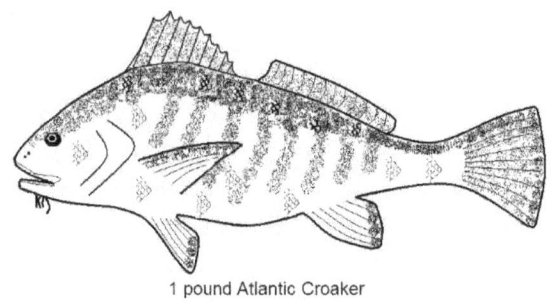
1 pound Atlantic Croaker

The Atlantic croaker is more abundant in the southern estuaries of the Chesapeake and Virginia with Northern New Jersey being considered their upper limits. At times of high population they will spill over from the south and enter the Bay and coastline of Southern New Jersey and Northern Delaware. When they show up it becomes a bonanza for the party boats owners. These are ideal fish for party boat anglers. They come in large numbers, easy to catch and arrive in the same time as the summertime migration of vacationing anglers.

The average size of these bottom type fish is between one-half to two pounds with a records size of 6.2 pound caught in the Chesapeake Bay [3]. They are identify by a bright silver background with a pinkest hue with black doted vertical strips running from it dorsal fin half way down its side. Older Atlantic croakers may have a brassy color with brown dotted strips, croaker style barbells, a down turn weak mouth, broad wide body. They will arrive in the shore area in May and slowly proceed up the bay channel as the season progress to September. By the time the water starts to cool, they start to move back toward the deeper ocean water for their fall spawning. Juvenile croaker will not returned to the ocean but prefer to winter over in the brackish and fresh waters of the lower Delaware River and upper bay region. The fish will reach maturity between two and three years of age [36]. They eat what it can find on the bottom.

These bottom dwelling fish are easy to catch in large quantities from party boats if they can get over them. Used a system with the sinker set on the bottom with several hooks set above. The first hook is placed several inches above the sinker and second hook a foot above the first with most of the strikes on the lower hook. The size of the hook and sinkers should be based on the recommendations of the mate. Bait for these fish might be base more on what the captain can find a deal on, but most of the time you will be given squid. Peeler crabs or bloodworms are a good choice to bring along on a head boat trip. Like all croakers, they have weak mouth and you can pull the hook from their jaw on a hard set. A croakers hit is very soft and you will have to feel the line for the slightest movement. Once you get that movement slowly raise the rod to see if something hangs on. These fish are caught commercially in large quantities in the open ocean. Most of the catch seems to be sold overseas. Much research is centered on Atlantic croakers because of their commercial value.

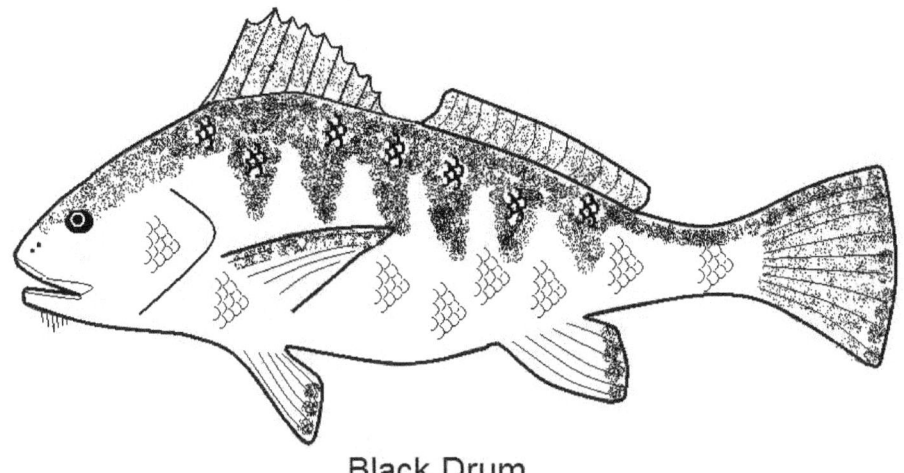

Black Drum

    This is the largest of the croakers. In fact, outside of sharks, the black drum is the largest of the inshore game fish. The size of fish may range from 20 pounds to 60 pounds but fish over a hundred plus pounds are out there with the largest on record in the bay at 109 pounds caught on the New Jersey side, Delaware and another at 113 pounds off the shore of Lewis Delaware which is the World Record. One catch on the New Jersey side was reported to be weight as much as 160 pounds but was disqualified by New Jersey official after discovering that the fish, was weighed on a truck scale in back of a pickup truck while still in its cooler.

    Biologists believe this fish can live up to forty years. The appearance and shape of the black drum is similar to the small Atlantic croaker. The black drum shares the bulky size, barbells, and silver color with black vertical strips of the croaker. The drum will differ, but not just in size but the vertical black strips will be wider and more solid in shade with few rows of 4 to 6 black strips. The drum mouth has cobblestone like teeth for cracking oysters. So of course, you might expect to find them in oyster beds. The Black drum can be found from Florida to Maine with the highest concentration in the Chesapeake Bay area. The black drum begins spawning when the water temperature reaches between 57 to 67 degrees in mid May and will last into early June [3]. The spawning locations are generally in the same places year after year in the lower bay during the spring. During the spring spawning congregation, their croaking mating call is also a magnet for fishermen. After the spring spawning ritual, the mature drums seem to disperse through out the bay and inshore ocean waters. The juveniles, called pups remain in the estuaries near their place of birth until three years of age. After that, some migrate to warmer waters in the winter and return in the spring just ahead of the adult drums for the spawning. Drum feed on crustaceans and mollusks, which are in great supply within the bay. They feed in shallow waters when the tides are moving spending the rest of the day in deeper water near channels. As might be expected, good locations for drums are

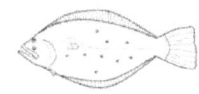

the boundary lines between oyster beds and channels.

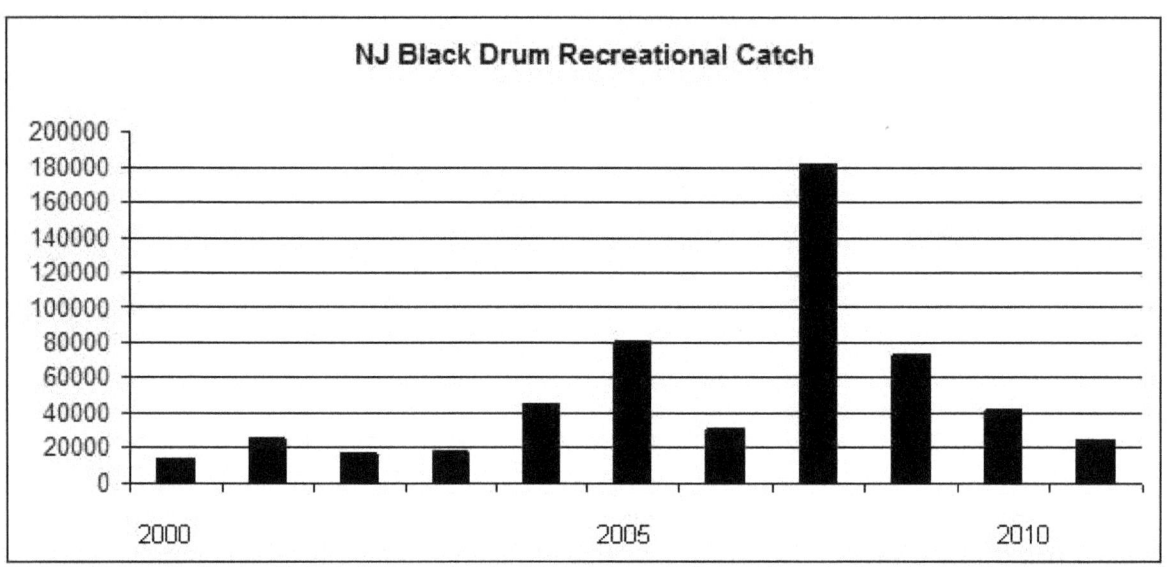

No other fish brings out the debate of moon phases and how it impacts fish behavior than the Black Drum. The first bite will begin for several days before and after the new moon phase. The strongest periods some argue is the full moon phase. On good years the bite will remain strong between the phases and well into June. Some believed that the moon emits a mysteries gravitational pull that excites the fish. A more realist explanation might be the tides are stronger on full and new moon phases and it's the movement of the water with the accompanied various temperatures and food that excite the fish.

Most of the enthusiasts do it at night. When the reports are good, the spawning beds are loaded with anchored lighted boats. The reel should have a good drag system and have the ability to hold lots of 40 to 50 pound braided line. The rod should be rated to handle 30 to 40 pounds of pull before breaking. These fish are not known for being great fighters, they will not jump around on the surface like blues, but they are strong and will test your equipment and knotting skills. A 60-pound drum can easy de-spool a reel or break a rod if the drag is not properly set. The bottom rig should have a 7/0 to a 10/0 hook secured with an improved clinch knot to an 80 pound 4 feet leader under a 100 pound test ball bearing barrel or swivel for the sinker. The sinker should be just heavy enough to hold bottom. If the current is too strong the downrigger ball should be used. The drum will suck the bait off the hook and spit it out like a crush oyster shell. The bait is always clam and should be tied to the hook with cotton thread so as not to be easily removed by a drum. The cobblestone like teeth mouth of the fish makes setting the hook difficult so first timers should be under the direction of a good guild. Use braided line so a hit can be felt. Chumming is used to attract the fish and hold them under the boat. Some people may just cut open the claims and dump the shells directly under the boat.

Fishing The Big D

The preferred chum mixture is of ground clams and crab, stored in a chum bag and placed deep under the boat and secured from the bow Anyway you fish for them; fresh clams are clearly the bait of chose by both drums and anglers. Because of the high demand for clams this time of year, one should plan on ordering a bushel several days before going out.

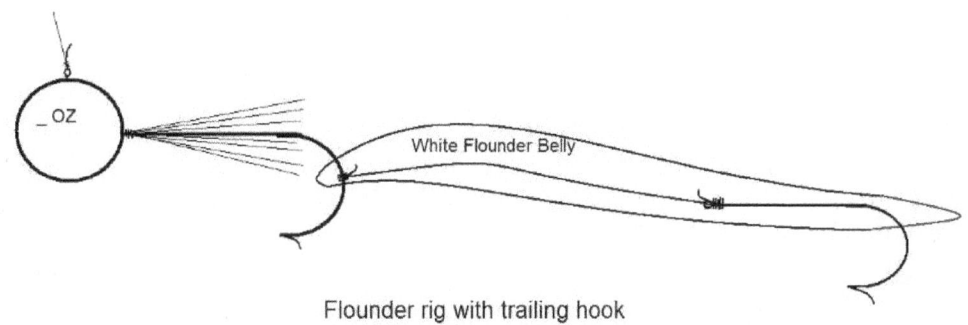

Flounder rig with trailing hook

Flat Fish

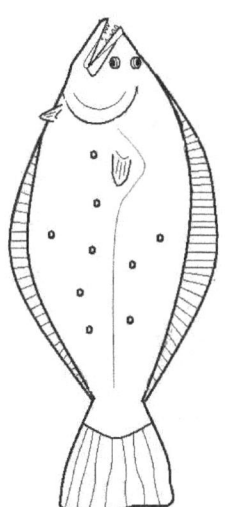

Flat fish can be left or right sided fish depending on which side their eyes are on. They all start in the normal fish development stage with both eyes on opposite side of the body. During the first year or the metamorphosis stage, one eye will migrate to the other side. Another common feature is they have the ability to match their color with the bottom. Of the many types of flat fish in the ocean, two common ones in these waters: summer fluke (left sided) and winter flounder (right sided). For this story, to make it easy for all call them flounders. Another important concept on flounders is that they are ambush-eating fish, meaning they like to bury them selves in sand and wait for food to swim by them. So, if you are going to throw your line out from a shore and place your rod in a rod holder it will remain in there a long time.

Summer Flounder (Flukes)
Paralichthys *dentatus*
These soles are the heart of any dinner plate

No other summer time fish attract more attention than the popular summer flounder. The average sizes of these fish will depend to a large degree on where you catch them. Bay flounders tend to be smaller than the deeper ocean flounders. A 17-inch flounder will weight about 2 pounds: 20-inch 3 pounds, and up to a 30-inch fish could weigh as much as 15 pounds. Most fish caught in the bay will be in the range of 15-20 inch size. The unofficial world record summer flounder caught by rod stands at 24.3-pounds taken by Monica Oswald in 2007 on the Jersey Shore. The night before the weigh in the fish was attached by a dog or a raccoon. She was denied the title not because of the condition of the fish seen in her catch photograph but she admitted that she had rested the rod on the rail of the boat while bringing it in. Large fish of plus 24 inches called door mats weighing about 5 to 8 pounds and should win you the pool on a head boat. The color of the summer flounder bottom is a uniform white with the top matching the color and patterns of the bottom. The flounder's common colors are brown or beige to black. The fish can copy the patterns of the ocean floor, an interesting feat when you realize that it is always looking up and not down. The mouth of a summer flounder is full of pointed teeth. The larger the fish the longer the teeth and they can inflect minor injury and infection. The teeth are there to hold the pray not rip it apart like blue fish. This fish is tolerant of the lower salinity waters of brackish bay and inlets. The smaller or young ones have been known to be caught in freshwater. Small flounders have being caught up to the beginning of the saltwater line near Chester, Pennsylvania but Ships John Light House is the accepted upper limits for good flounder fishing. The deeper and saltier the water the larger and more plentiful they become. The fish like to bury them selves in sand or mud bottoms with only their eyes exposed, in vicinities where small fish for food might float by. A good place that a flounder might be found in the bay are near piers, eel grass, rocks and any structures that would hold food and a near by sandy or soft muddy bottom for them hide in. When the fish is feeding it's not uncommon to find them within a few feet of the shore line, where they chase smaller minnow right up to the bank. They can bury them selves in seconds under the sand and quickly jump from the sand and attack or chase their prey. You can expect the bay and inshore ocean bottom to be full of summer flounders in the warmer months of June to September. In the bay, popular spots for flounders are known as the Eights, The Shears Haystacks, Prissy Wick Shoal and Overfalls Shoal just to name a few. In the colder month of the year from October to May they are deep in the ocean at depth between 25 to 60 fathoms. At this depth and during this time of year few pleasure boats will go on the search for these fish. Because of the high price these fish command on the market place the commercial fishing boats will make these winter time journeys. Flounder spawning habits are not well understood but it's believed they spawn in the deeper ocean in the

winter. When eggs hatch the juveniles will slowly work their way inshore by spring. By the time, the fish reaches three years of age they are generally of the legal keeper size [48] [3].

When fishing for summer flounders or even winter flounders one most always remember these are ambush hunting type fish. If you ask an experience boat fisherman what tide cycle is best for flounder fishing they will say it's when the tide (or current) is moving moderately. If you ask an experience bank fisherman the same question they will response when the tide (or current) is not moving, or an hour before and after high or low tide. They are both right because of the way they fish. At ebb tide, the water is still and clear, and at that time it makes it easier for the fish to distinguish floating food from floating trash. Also at ebb tide, the fish will come closer to shore, where more bait fish might be. When the tide starts moving again, the fish seem to retreat to deeper waters, the fishing lines from the shore or piers start to collect grass and the game is up for the bank fisherman. If there is no wind, fishing from the boat at ebb tide will leave the boat and your bait near motionless. To be successful at flounder fishing the bait has to moved slowly by the flounder, it as simple as that.

From the shore or pier, throw the bait or lure out and slowing work it back. At times, reel it in fast, other times it's a slow pull and stop process. When bring in the line always be prepared to take a strike right at the edge of the water, because at low tide or high tide they come in close. In fact, fly rods and light fresh water rods can be used very affectively during that time. The bait of chose is live minnows, if it dead feed it to the crabs. Other cut bait can work as well, like cut squid, peelers, slices of fresh caught blue fish and bloodworms. Some people will cut strips of chicken and marinade them in peeler crab juice or chicken liver for bait. The best seems to be strips of the white belly of another flounder. The sinker should be as light as possible to achieve the proper cast and to hold the bottom. You should always set your rig as to be able to quickly switch weights when conditions change. Because the fish has a large month, a wide variety of hook will work for catching summer flounder. Hooks in the size of 4/0 to a 6/0 are adequate, don't use smaller ones because you will catch smaller undersize fish and possible kill them. The gold color odd shape hook work well also. The fish will also hit small lures, good results can be achieved with a short scented plastic twister tails, much like what is used for striped bass and weak fish, but smaller. When fishing from the boat keep repeatedly raising your rod which will entice a hit or let you know you have a fish on line. Flounders are master bait thief and even a door mat size fish can take the bait from you without a tug. The trick here is having the ability to feel the line, by using the lightest sinkers possible to hold bottom and a long flexible pole with light 12 to 20 pound line. Since flounder like to grab the bait from the tailing edge, so add a second hook at the end of the bait to catch these thieves.

Another type of flounder fishing technique though not legal here but interesting is night gigging or trapping. On the Mississippi gulf coast where the bottom slope gradient is almost zero. You can walk for several hundred yards in the water seaward

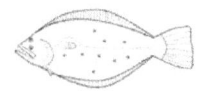

and it may never go over your waist, it is that flat. At night it's a common practice among the locals to go out with a high powered flash light and spot the fish as they rest on the bottom. Only the reflection from the fish's eyes from the light's ray will revile the hiding spot under the sand. Notice that the top eye is a different color than the bottom and the more experience people who do this can tell what direction the fish is resting from that observation. Once you see the two different colored reflectors glowing from the sand below you will know what to do with the gigging pole. Step on and grab the fish before raising the pole. Sometime they can swim off the pole before you can grab them.

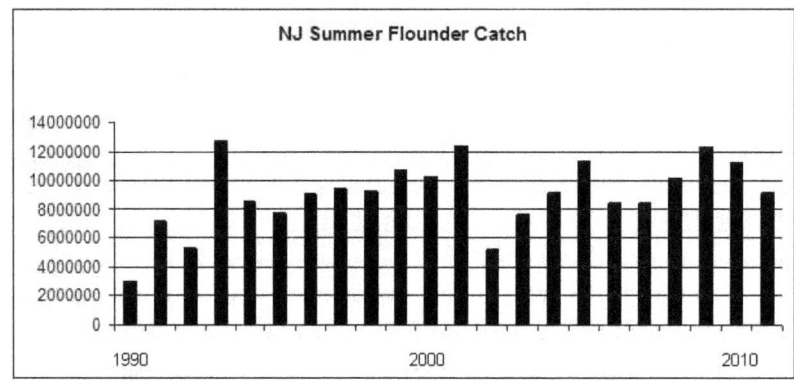

  Winter Flounders are right sided soles, just the opposite of the left sided summer flounders in both, spawning and regional movements [48]. They start to appear in the colder months starting in late November and leaving the Bays and inshore locations by June [3]. Because they spawn in the winter there is now a season for winter flounder that begins in March. These fish are smaller but still retain the same ability to match the bottom as its larger summer cousin. Most fish are dark in color due to the winter's darker bottom characteristics. They are small and have a smaller mouth than the summer fish but they hunt food much the same way. On the white under belly of the winter sole one can see a yellow hue to the lower half of the fish's tail. Because of the small size of the fish and colder weather, these fish are not heavily thought after. Because of the smaller month of the winter over the summer a long different hook is used. Winter flounder hooks have a long black shaft, small hook and a color bead attach to the leader. Favorite bait are small sections of blood worms.

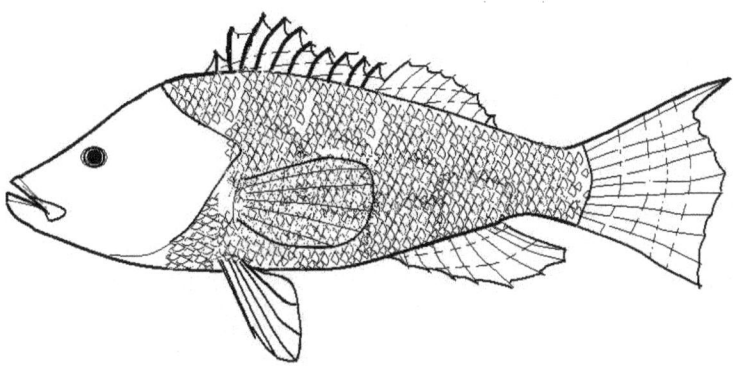

SALT WATER BLACK SEA BASS
Centropristis *strianta*

The Black Sea Bass is a favorite of head boat captains. They are plentifully, easily to predict, and are a good match at of the height of summer fishing pressure. These fish weight between 1 to 3 pounds, with a NJ record set at 9 pounds 8 oz. but the average caught in the bay and inshore waters will be 1 ½ pound [3]. This fish are the classic structure fish. They can be found near piers, bridges, rock walls, reefs, and any natural or manmade structures. These fish, although ugly at first glance have an amazing set of colors that match well with it various shades of black. Like flounder, they can adjust to the natural colors of the bottom. The first feature of this fish you will experience is the sharp cutting spinning dorsal fin. Inform your youngster about this feature before they handle the fish. The fish is sometimes confused with the Black fish or Tautog. You can tell the different by comparing the mouth, sea bass has a bigger mouth, and no teeth, Tautog have blunt teeth. The black sea bass will spend the winter in the deep ocean at 25 to 60 fathoms and go shallow and inshore as early as May to begin spawning. The fish will remain in the inshore and bay area until October or November. They are not very tolerable of lower salinity levels so do not expect to find many in the northern narrow portion of bay north of Ship John lighthouse. Several popular places the captains might take you are Brandywine Shoal, the artificial reefs at Flounder Alley, and the wreaks at Cape Hemlopen.

Black sea bass are protogynous hermaphrodites, meaning that they change sex from female to male. Born as females, most bass will change sex to males between ages 2 to 5 years. This gender transformation has lead to problems with commercial farming attempts, for the bass has tenancy to change sex sooner in captivity. This Gender transformation is common among certain bass fish. Studies done in the south branch of the Potomac showed freshwater small mouth bass have been observed to be change sex. But there their transfer from male to female with population drops. The reason for this is unclear and further studies need to be conducted to determine if this is generic, social or chemical driven event among all bass type fish.

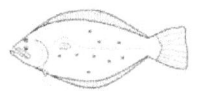

Today recreational black sea bass catches now exceed commercial catches and because of that, restrictive seasons have been applied. The winter band of recreational fishing for sea bass has set up a dilemma in the enforcement of the rule and winter fishing for cod and ling. Since black sea bass move to offshore waters and cod move south and inshore, both are commonly found at the same locations in deep water with structures off the Jersey coast in winter. To say that winter sea bass is a by-catch of cod and pollock is incorrect: cod, ling and pollock is a by-catch of black winter sea bass. When a fish is brought up at such depth the rapid decompression exposes a gas bladder of the fish and death will follow if not returned properly. Rather than returning an injured fish properly many of the sea bass are kept illegally. In 2012, a popular party boat out of Brielle, NJ, was sighted when undercover DEP agents observed this practice. Three dozen fishermen were summonses, facing fines of $3,000 each when the undercover agents confiscated over 800 fish. The Captain was also placed under investigated for permitting this illegal activity.

Black Fish or Tautog
Tautoga *onitis*
The poster picture fish for dental hygiene

If your boat does well in catching Tautog fish give your captain credit for his correct anchoring placement over their hole. These fish congregate in tight groups near reefs, and structures of any kind in depths of 20 to 60 feet. The average size of these fish range between from one to six pounds. Because of the diet of crabs and mollusks they have small blunt teeth inside a small mouth with large lips. The twisted and odd shaped teeth and gums of this fish remind me of the posters pictures for gum disease seen at the dentist office. The rest of the fish has much the same features as black sea bass but that is the only thing they have in common. These fish seem to follow the water temperature of 65 degrees moving in and out of shore depending on the water. These fish can be caught in the winter on the open ocean.

BLUE FISH
Pomatomus *saltatrix*
Definition of a preface game fish: They come in great numbers, multiply rapidly, grow fast, large and are always hungry

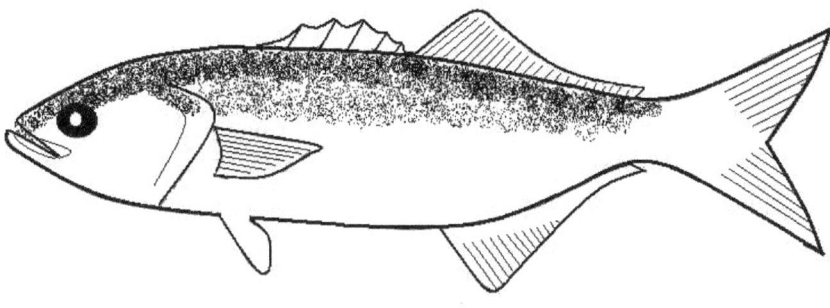

Bluefish

Bluefish Jig

Nicknames like snapper, sea wolf, choppers and slammers are correct indications and comments about this fish. With their razor sharp teeth and an endless hunger it's a good thing for summer swimmer they don't grow bigger than a full size striper. The average Delaware Valley angler may never experience the thrill of a twelve-pound fish on their line until they fish at night on an inshore all night fishing trip. Blue fish can be caught a full six months of the season in inshore waters and the surf of the region. They may not be the best tasting fish in the sea but clearly the easiest when they are in the water and hungry.

Once mature these fish travel up and down the eastern coast of North American with clockwork precision. They spawn in the spring off the coast from the Carolinas to Delmarva, as the water warms, they proceed northward rapidly. By May, they are off the coast of New Jersey and Delaware [3]. The big fish will proceed northward in schools and from experiences, they will hang around the Hudson Bay entrance, south of Long Island and Central New Jersey coast. When the water starts to cools in September they start a slow movement southward, but in the southward journey, they tend to hug the shore. From September to December, you can expect to see reports of catches off the surf for the larger fish when they come close to eat many of the baitfish that have now grown to a more eatables sizes. Schools of blues seem to be uniform in size from a particular age group. The youngest group, snapper blues will range from one to three pounds and found very common on the surf and inlets all summers long. Another size range called choppers are 5 to 8 pound range and will school further out and travel up to the limits of Long Island, and than return tightly along the coast fall. The older ones termed giant slammers by some, range in the 9 to 14 pound range and follow the same route as the choppers (open water in the summer and coastline in the spring and fall).

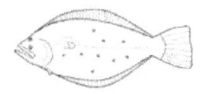

The best, easiest and cheapest way to catch big blues are on the night blue fishing boats that go out in the summer months. They start in mid June and will continue into September if the crowds and fish permit it. Since the fish tend to stop movement off central Jersey, Point Pleasant NJ is the ideal place to go out from. The best month is August when the crowds have started to drop off. A good night is when you can't see the deck from the catch on the return trip back. The fish will eat just about any bait thrown out to feed them. Most boats will use chopped mackerel for bait but just about anything will work. Blue fish can be trolled for with large foot long crank bait lures, diamond jugs, and hard plastic eel lures. Clearly they are not the fickle eaters like striped bass or weak fish. Unfortunately, all night head boats are too crowded to throw and troll lures. On a boat, the preferred method is to anchor up current to a school and chump from the bow. If the fish are shallow in the water column, the captain will order everyone onto one side of the boat with no sinker or a light ½-oz inline sinker and drift through the school. If they are deep, the captain will order sinkers with required sinker sizes. In-line egg sinkers are the preferred sinker arrangement. To be relative tangle free everyone should have the identical set ups and weights. The round egg sinkers can easily be changed without removing the hook, just ask the mate how it's done. A single hook with a wire leader is required. A good rule to follow: when drifting, let out as much line out as possible, and if anchored keep the amount of line out to minimum. When removing the hook from these fish, be very careful the teeth appear to be small and harmless but they are razor sharp and will slice your hand open faster than any filleting knife. It is best to cut the line and come back to the fish later to reclaim the hook later. No need to tell you to hang on to the pole tightly, change the bait regularly and don't play them in.

When going on these trips the boats will rent rods and sell you all of the equipments. Fiberglass bait poles with bait casting reels should be the order of the day or night. People will show up with light duty fresh water rods and spinning reels that will end up broken. Bring a good selection of round egg sinkers and some 1/2 oz split in-line sinkers and plenty of steel leader hooks. A pair of pliers for unhooking the fish and setting the split-inline sinkers is nice to have too. On a good night, it can get messy so a change of clothes or plastic overalls can help with your drive home. Bring an old towel to keep your self clean.

During the summer months, small snapper blues will be in the surf and inlet waters. You can tell they are there by minnow trying to jump out of the water. If you see this, a fresh water rod with a small silver diamond jig is a nice thing to have in such situations. Saltwater fly rods are an excellent chose and used with a saltwater streamer fly with a long hook or short light steel leader. By late September, the bigger fish starts patrolling the surf on a more regular basis. Fall is the time of year you need to patrol the beach looking for bird blitz and small baitfish schools. You will need the rugged rods and lines to handle these strong fish. Bait or lures will both works. When using bait try to keep the bait off the bottom. If fishing from the surf for blues use a rig that has a bobber attached to a steel leader hook. Another trick, to keep the bait off the bottom is to

catch some small bait fish like small spot croakers and use them live. When fishing from bridges attach only a light in-line one ounce sinker and let the cut bait on a steel leader float the bait out from the bridge.

Over the years a market has developed for blue fish which has lead to a decrease in the larger inshore and offshore fish. A result of this can be seen even where catches remain the same but the total weight caught by recreational fishing has dropped. Today many of the boats from south Jersey don't go out at night for blues for that reason.

Sharks

In the early half of the twentieth century the Jersey Shore had a repetition as *the shark infested capital of the world.* The worst cycle of shark attack in United States history happen in Jersey water on 1916 when five reported shark attacked accrued with four facilities in one summer. The death of two boys and an attack on a third in front of onlookers, friends and family in a fresh water creek (Matawan), while trying to save each other shock the nation. Two other separate fatalities on the shore side within 12 days would confirm to the world that the Jersey Shore was not a safe place to bath or swim. These attacks sent the nation into a shark hunting frenzy. The early news media created picnic to the point that people stopped visiting the shore for fear of being attached by a shark. Beaches were closed or paroled by armed guards. Theses rash of killings and fear of water may have inspired Peter Bentley to write Jaws 60 years later. The killings and attacks may not have had anything to do with increasing shark population due to warmer temperatures, a lone great white killer shark or the carnage created from WWI German U-Boats that created an appetite for human flesh among the local sharks; but larger than normal amount of human swimmer that hot summer in 1916. People who could afford to leave the cities did so in larger numbers, not just to escape the higher than normal summer heat, but the fear of Polo and a new flu called the Spanish Influenza. While the hype of the attacks drove people from the beaches the Spanish Influenza would kill tens of millions of people by 1918 with Philadelphia being one of the worse hit cities.

There are hundreds of different types of sharks but only a few are dangerous. Sharks do not have skeletons but flexible cartilage, which adds to its swimmer speed. These fish do not have a swim bladder; they never sleep but must be on the move continually. The most common shark you will catch on the shores is the lonely dogfish

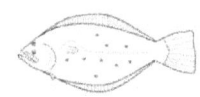

shark. These are long skinny 2 to 4 foot relative harmless fish with a collection of low, flat grinding teeth and several sharp teeth. There are two types of dogfish sharks, the Spiny and the Smooth dogfish. The smooth dogfish is more prevalent here. The spiny dogfish has white dots running down it side and the spiny dorsal fin. Both fish are bottom feeder and are not valued as food. Brown, hammerheads, and sand sharks are common in the bay and inshore waters and can grow up to 150 pounds and average 4 to 6 feet. These sharks have teeth and can inflict damage if bitten but are not noted to be aggressive fish. Bull sharks are not considered common here but have been seen and caught locally. Believe it or not bull sharks may be the most dangerous of the large sharks because they have been known to migrate into fresh water and was most likely the source of the 1916 killings in Matawan Creek. Browns, and sand sharks migrate the coastline and follow the water temperature of 60 to 70 degrees spending most of the time on the bottom. There are several types of hammerhead but they all share one common attribute, the ability to detect living creatures under the sand. Like the MADD detectors tails on the Navy sub-hunters P-3, which pick up the electric and magnetic signature of a submarine, the wide head of the hammerhead does the same for living creatures buried under the sand. Small flounders must be its favorite meal. Hammerhead only average 3 to 4 feet but can grow to 6 feet and are not aggressive "man eaters". They do have a set of sharp teeth and should be handle with care if by chance they find them selves on the deck of your boat. The thresher shark, an excellent fighting fish is another inshore water shark and is distinguished by a long tail. The larger and more famous sharks like great whites, tigers, blue, and makos can be found in the inshore waters but are more prevalent in the off-shore waters [50]. The off-shore Atlantic mako is the fish that will draw the most attention from sportsman. This fish will show its true size, speed and performance when hooked to a wire. It will jump, turn on a dime, dive and come back to attack the boat. This is definitely the shark to go for. They average about 6 to 8 feet with recorded sizes of 12 feet and can weight up to a 1,000 plus pound.

When going out for a fish like a mako or any other larger open ocean sharks the boat should have the room to safely handle these fish along with the equipment and a qualified captain to get it safely aboard. You will be using the same rods, reel and wires, as large offshore fish: 120 pound test line with a 80 pound rods. The captain might be looking for a particular mako but most lightly, they will go for locations where there are plenty of baitfish. On the trip out to the site, they will troll for blue fish to use as live bait and entertainment. Once on station they will set up a chumming slick. To the captains this is the most important part of shark fishing. When setting up a chumming slick, element to consider is the direction of wind, current, and tidal movement. Too much speed in both wind and current will generate a weak but large slick, while light wind and speed will not spread the slick. When there is no wind or current the captain may slowly move the boat to help spread the slick. After the slick is set, the bait is position. Four to five poles are set with bait at different deeps and controlled by balloon floats. The landing rules of safety will be the same as any large offshore fish: listen to what the captain or mate tells you to do, don't wrap any wires around your hand and stay clear of the activity unless asked to do help [49].

DELAWARE BAY SKATES AND RAYS

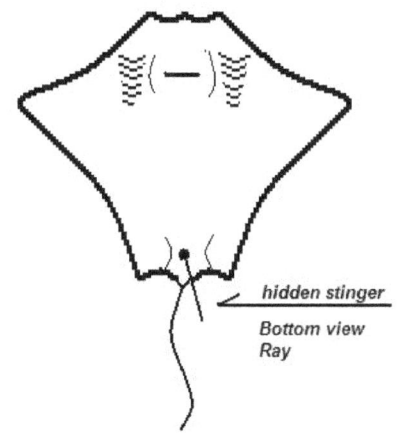

What is the most dangerous fish to bathers and surf fisherman on the local beaches of New Jersey and Delaware? It's the fish you see in the new please touch me tanks at aquariums. According to The American Academy of Family Physicians approximately 1,500 people a year in the United States seek medical treatment from a stingray compared with reported 40 to 80 shark attacks per year worldwide by the International Shark Files. Since stingrays come right up to the edge of the water, waders are more likely to get struck by a ray by stepping on it. The weapon is different for different rays. The Cow nose has a hidden razor sharp spur at the base of the tail on the underside of the fish. The spur can slice through gloves, shoes, wet suits and rib cages. Other rays, like the brunt nose, have a tail with cutting teeth that resembles the teeth on a chain saw. The most serious damage done to the victim my not be the poisonous venom but the cut and following hemorrhage. An account to the severity of an attack by a ray has been recently proven with the death of Steve Irwin (The Crocodile Hunter) who was struck in the chest. Another famous stingray story happened locally. In 1608, the crew of Captain John Smith, began digging his grave after witnessing their Captain's agonizing pain after being hit by one. Legend states that the captain survived the attack and lived to eat the ray that struck him. So sharp is the ray's stinker that it was used by early man not just as a knife and weapon but a surgical tool.

Rays and Skates also pose a threat to the local fishing industry. Chesapeake and Delaware Shell fishermen have accused the increasing ray and large skate populations for damages done to their shell beds. Since rays and skates are not considered game or commercial fish it is hard to verify this statement with any data. However, there are several theories as to why local fishermen believe the populations are increasing. Sharks are the traditional natural enemies of skates and rays. According to surveys, shark populations are decreasing which would permit the rays and skate populations to increase. Another reason for the possible population increase is the newer shrimp netting requirements. These nets were a ray and skate death trap, however new nets require holes for turtles to escape, thus also creating escape routes for rays and skates. A third theory to explain the possible population increase is global warming.

Many people confuse rays and skates, they have some similarities, and including both are members of the shark family and traditional bottom feeders. The biggest

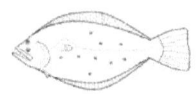

difference is the deadly nature of Rays. A second difference is that rays will swim through the entire water column looking for food from top to bottom. Shakes lay eggs while Rays store eggs in a pocket called a mermaid purse is the main different between the two. A mature skate and ray can easily reach three feet wide and weigh in over 25 pounds. Large rays can quickly de-spool a reel. Once caught or snagged they will move a great distance with surprising strength and speed. When tired both fish type will find a place on the bottom to rest and bury itself in the sand. Once buried in the sand the party with the most patience will win. It best to avoid handling rays, instead, cut the line and release the fish, retrieving your hook or lure is not worth the pain that could follow. If caught while on a kayak cut the line before you are pulled out to sea.

There are many different types of rays but the most commonly seen ray off the local shore are the cow nose rays which come up large schools from the warmer southern waters in the summer and forage for food in the bays of the Northeast. A school can be seen frequently on the surface and at such times become a prime target for archery fishermen. Because their up turned wings resemble a shark's dorsal fin, rays are sometimes confused for sharks when swimming on the surface. Working as a team, a school of rays will swim across the bottom, turning up mud and sand in the search of food. In such a process, they can damage oyster, scallops and grass beds, the home of blue crabs and other small aquatic life. Too many of these fish can disrupted the fragile bottom ecosystem. Because of these problems the Commonwealth of Virginia has tried to develop a commercial market for these fish. Since rays are dangerous many fishermen refuse to handle them.

If struck by one, hot water is said to detoxify the poison. Hot water from a boat engines' cooling system is a good source. Due to the slicing motion of the spur the wound can hemorrhage a large amount of blood. The hemorrhaging must be controlled and the victim should seek medical attention. The mouth of both a ray and skate can crack shells so it's not advisable to place fingers inside them.

Delaware Bay and Inshore Fishing Odds

	January	February	March	April	May	June	July	August	September	October	November	December
Weakfish	P	P	P	G	E	E	E	E	E	E	E	G
Black Drum	P	P	G	E	E	G	F	F	F	F	P	P
Kingfish	P	P	P	F	G	E	E	E	E	G	F	P
Atlantic Croaker	F	F	F	G	G	E	E	E	E	E	G	F
Striped Bass	G	F	E	E	G	F	F	F	G	E	E	E
Bluefish	P	P	P	F	G	E	E	E	E	E	G	F
Flounder	P	P	F	G	E	E	E	E	G	F	P	P
Black Sea Bass	F	F	F	G	G	E	E	E	E	G	F	F
Black Fish	E	G	G	E	E	E	E	E	E	E	E	E

Fishing Odds E=excellent G=good F=fair P=poor
Fishing The Big D

Surf Fishing

Not all beaches are the same. Beaches that are used for bathing and swimming are completely different from natural beaches found in parks. We run tractors that rake the sand for trash in bathing areas. This running of equipment and heavy usage of the beach will compact the sand making it very difficult for sand crabs to live in the tidal limits of the beach. Once a year these bathing areas beaches will undergo further modifications by removing channels and sand bars that can be hazardous to swimmers. The natural beaches will have softer sand for small crabs to bury in. These unprotected beaches will have many sand bars that resemble hooks that baitfish can hide within. The slopes of the natural beaches are steeper than protected bathing beaches giving steep drop offs into nearby channels and within reach of surf rods. These lateral current channels will form right up to the edge of the watermark which is within reach of surface rods. Clearly, natural beaches are better suited for holding and catching fish. In Central New Jersey, Island Beach State Park south of Toms River has 10 miles of unprotected natural beach land. In southern New Jersey, Tucker Island has unprotected beaches just north of the Little Egg Inlet. The Delaware beach at Cape Henlopen has good fishing any time of the year. The many inlets along the shore line are popular place to fish. The mouth of an inlet, has numerous channels and sand bars that act as chock points for the fish. At inlets are bridges that add more than just a structure for the fish to congregate near but at night, many have street lights, which will draw fish. Because of the many channels and changing tides, inlets are always in a state of flex. These changing conditions of inlets and the importance of them for navigation you can expect to find rock bulkheads that were built to control the inlets position which to our advantage will add structure for fish to hid

The Delaware Bay

and feed from. Fishing off these rock walls can be dangerous if the rocks are wet. On the bay side of inlets are sod banks. In some places fishing is not permitted on sod banks. The tide undercuts the lower bank which fish will love to feed and hid at. These under cut will collapse when walked on and one should stay at lease three feet from the edge of them and wear long pant to protect oneself from horse flies.

Successful surf fishing requires travel. In both States of Delaware and New Jersey permits to drive on selected beaches in State Parks can be acquired but have many restrictions. A Delaware beach permit can be bought on line, or at major sporting goods stores or at the park. In New Jersey a separate permit must be purchased from each Town. You must have a four wheel drive vehicle with a seven inch clearance, and stocked with the following equipment: tow rope, jack with a board, low pressure tie gauge and fishing poles with bait. The reason for the fishing pole and bait is that this is for fishing only, not pleasure driving. Always remember to deflate your tires before going out to half the normal pressure, to help with traction. Some of the serious surf fishermen will carry air pumps to re-inflate the tires once back on the road. When you stop, always start slowly, keeping the front wheel pointed forward, so as not to dig your tires deeper into the sand. Many of the truck owners prefer the passenger tires over the off road tires because of the digging affects of knobby off-road tires. Carry a cell phone with good regional reception and extra water, it's easy to get stranded at high tide or stuck in the sand. If you store your poles on front bumper rod holders always remove heavy sinkers and become aware of low tree branches and gasoline station awnings.

- Avoid days with strong surf, like the effects of dredging that adds sediment to the water and drives fish away.
  - Westerly winds tend to flatten the waves less sediment.
  - Northeasterly winds build waves and generate sediment.
- Look for lots of bird activity and bait in the water.
- Early morning and late evening is always best.
- Always fish near rock structures, but for safety reasons not on them.
- Always plan the trip with the tide, weather and season in mind.
- Look for changes in the sand. Gravel indicates nearby channels.
- Study the breakers lines and look for rip-tide channels.
- In the Fall and Spring fishing is always better on the surf.
- Overcast days are better than clear sunny days.

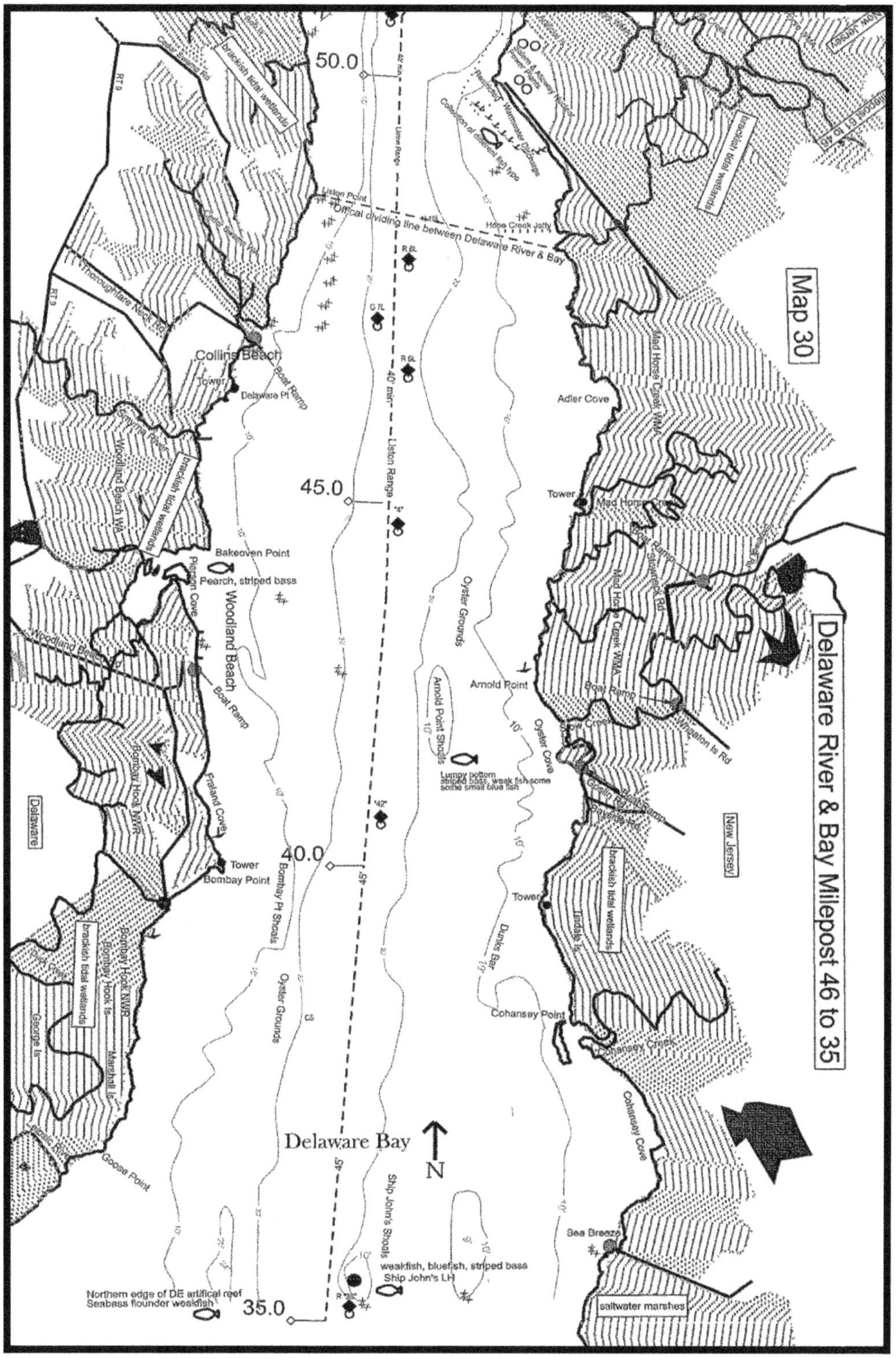

Fishing The Big D

Map 30 — Delaware River & Bay Milepost 46 to 35

The Delaware Bay

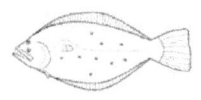

GPS spots Map 31

#	Location	Description	Latitude	Longitude
2	Ben Davis Pt Shoal #34	good weak and flounder spot	N 39 14.80'	W 75 18.92'
3	Gandy Beach Buoy # 6	hilly bottom holds flounders	N 39 15.40'	W 75 15.40'
4	Clubhouse	mix of different fish near creek outlets	N 39 15.10'	W 75 12.70'
5	Buoy # 32 to 34	flounder in deep water	N 39 14.10'	W 75 18.00'
6	Joe Flogger Shoal # R2	stripers in shallow/ flounders in deep	N 39 13.60'	W 75 19.90'
7	Wreak Buoy	fish near old structures	N 39 12.54'	W 75 15.30'
8	False Egg Pt	weakfish near shell beds	N 39 12.21'	W 75 10.90'
9	Cross Ledge Light	stripers in rips	N 39 10.90'	W 75 16.10'
10	Old Flat Top	sea bass and black fish near base	N 39 09.64'	W 75 13.75'
11	Egg Island Pt	good fishing near shell beds	N 39 10.30'	W 75 07.88'
12	Little Egypt Shoal	spring stripers	N 39 09.80'	W 75 06.60'
14	Thompson's Beach	weakfish	N 39 10.30'	W 74 59.50'
16	Shell Beds buoy 4	Mix of drums, stripers, blues	N 39 07.84'	W 75 03.35'
17	Miah Maull LH	all types of fish near rocks	N 39 07.60'	W 57 12.50'
18	Miah Maull Shoal	seasonal mix of blues and stripers	N 39 06.95'	W 75 11.86'
19	Cedar Bush Hole	deep water flounder	N 39 07.07'	W 75 19.20'
21	Lower Shoals GAP	deep water flounders	N 39 02.70'	W 75 18.60'
24	Horseshoe Slough east	fall stripers and blues in channel	N 39 04.05'	W 75 07.56'
26	Punk Grounds	weak fish, croakers & black drums	N 39 05.16'	W 75 04.85'
30	Big Stone Beach	black drums	N 39 02.81'	W 75 18.62'
32	14 Foot Bank LH	good for all fish	N 39 02.90'	W 75 11.00'
41	Cedar Beach	weak fish	N 38 57.50'	W 75 15.80'
70	E Buoy	flounders	N 39 01.20'	W 75 13.75'

Delaware Bay Artificial Reefs

	Size	depth	material	Center of Reef	
AR/1	0.41 sq mile	17-30'	concrete culverts & wreak	N 39 15.60'	W 75 20.90'
	Northwest to Southeast line				
AR/2	0.71 sq mile	16-28'	concrete culverts	N 39 11.20'	W 75 18.15'
	Square				
AR/3	0.68 sq mile	18-28'	concrete culverts	N 39 01.20'	W 75 17.10'
	Northwest to Southeast line				
AR/4	0.63 sq mile	30-38'	concrete culverts	N 39 03.10'	W 75 15.75'
	North South Line				

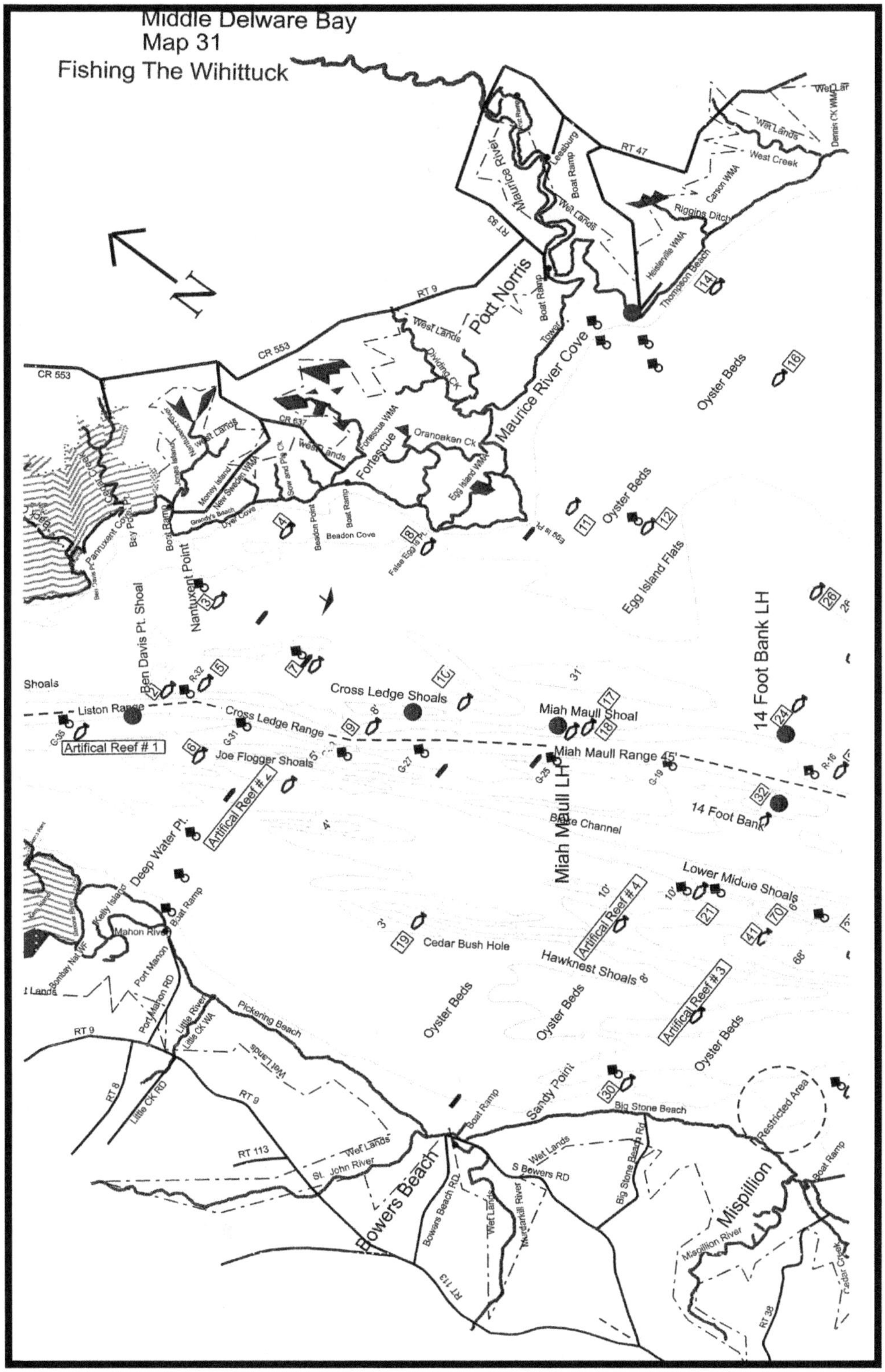

Fishing The Big D

Middle Delware Bay
Map 31
Fishing The Wihittuck

The Delaware Bay

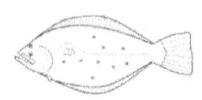

GPS Map 32

#	Name	Description	Latitude	Longitude
20	Coral Beds East	black drums	N 38 53.93'	W 75 14.76'
25	Horseshoe Slough west	fall stripers and blues in channel	N 39 03.82'	W 75 06.51'
27	Deadman Shoal west	spring stripers and fall blues	N 39 05.15'	W 75 00.75'
28	Bug Light	spring stripers and drums	N 39 05.21'	W 74 59.80'
29	20 Foot Slough	weak fish, stripers & blues in channel	N 39 02.91'	W 74 58.89'
32	14 Foot Bank light	weak fish and flounders	N 39 02.88'	W 75 11.06'
33	R 16 Buoy	deep water flounders	N 39 02.15'	W 75 09.20'
34	Pin Top	stripers spring & fall	N 39 01.18'	W 75 07.87'
35	The 60 Foot Slough	spring stripers, fall blues in channel	N 39 00.21'	W 75 02.22'
36	Bay Shore channel N	spring stripers, fall blues in channel	N 39 01.80'	W 74 58.75'
37	Mohawk	wreak fishing	N 39 00.14'	W 75 12.27'
38	F Buoy	deep water flounders	N 38 59.30'	W 75 11.89'
39	Brandywine Shoal LH	all types of fish	N 38 59.20'	W 75 06.79'
40	Bay Shore channel S	spring stripers, fall blues in channel	N 38 59.01'	W 74 59.00'
42	Gary	wreak fishing	N 38 57.04'	W 75 12.20'
44	Flounder Alley	flounders between Art. Reefs	N 38 57.65'	W 75 09.16'
46	Brown Shoals	flounders & fall striped bass	N 38 56.42'	W 75 07.51'
47	wreak near shore	all types of fish	N 38 57.00'	W 74 58.60'
48	Coral Beds West	black drums	N 38 53.85'	W 75 15.75'
50	Golden Eagle/Margaret	wreak fishing	N 38 52.45'	W 75 09.59'
51	Crow shoals	fall stripers in rips	N 38 55.65'	W 74 00.80'
52	Beach Ball	flounders & weak fish	N 38 55.70'	W 75 13.90'
54	Eph Shoal	fall stripers in rips spring blues	N 38 55.35'	W 74 56.40'
55	Prissy Wicks Shoal	fall stripers in strong rips	N 38 54.30'	W 74 57.30'
56	Middle Shoals	fall stripers & blues in rips	N 38 53.74'	W 74 59.36'
57	Somers Shoals	fall stripers in rips	N 38 52.64'	W 74 57.21'
58	The Shears	croaker, weak fish & drums	N 38 50.26'	W 75 08.44'
59	Gypsum Prince	wreak fishing	N 38 48.36'	W 75 04.01'
60	Outer Wall	all type of fish at rocks	N 38 49.95'	W 75 05.91'
61	The Haystacks	stripers near breakers	N 38 50.25'	W 75 06.85'
62	Eights	deep water flounders	N 38 49.45'	W 75 01.60'
63	China	wreak fishing	N 38 49.37'	W 74 54.98'
65	Hen Shoal	fall blues & stripers in shallows	N 38 46.67'	W 75 04.18'
66	King Cobra	wreak fishing	N 38 50.82'	W 74 54.02'
67	McCrie Shoals	wreak fishing	N 38 50.91'	W 74 52.00'
68	Overfalls Shoals	blues & fall stripers in rips	N 38 51.91'	W 74 59.45'
69	Roosevelt Inlet	mixed of small fish at inlet	N 38 47.60'	W 75 09.40'
71	Cape May Lumps	lumps off inlet produces good fishing	N 38 55.17'	W 74 49.74'
72	Wildwood Crest Reef site	wreak fishing	N 38 57.66'	W 74 41.20'

Delaware Bay Artificial Reefs

AR/5	0.65 sq mile	18-24' concrete Northwest to Southeast line	N 38 54.20'	W 75 11.90'
AR/6	0.28 sq mile	20-43' concrete and wreak Northwest to Southeast Line	N 38 57.90'	W 75 09.60'
AR/7	0.41 sq mile	30-40' concrete Square	N 38 56.65'	W 75 08.60'
AR/8	0.96 sq mile	29-72' concrete and wreaks East West Line	N 38 52.10'	W 75 06.40'

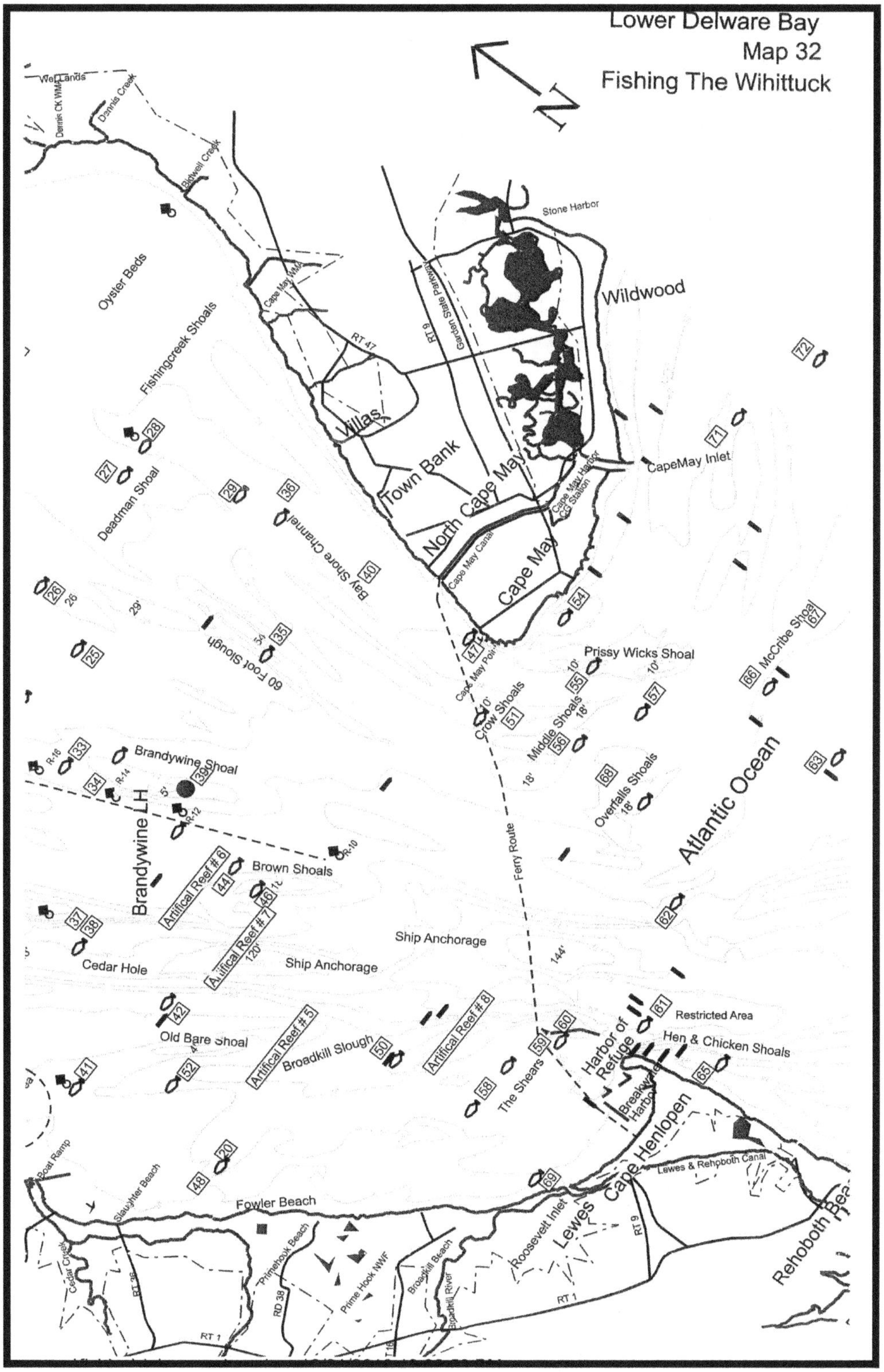

Fishing The Big D

Lower Delware Bay
Map 32
Fishing The Wihittuck

Cape May Coast New Jersey Fishing GPS Location
GPS Map 33

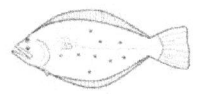

#	Location	Description	Latitude	Longitude
3	Five Fathom Lump E	hilly sandy bottom attracts flounders	N 38 59.45'	W 74 32.22'
4	Five Fathom Bank	shallow water holds bait fish and blues	N 38 57.76'	W 74 38.13'
5	Wildwood Crest Reef site	Bottom Fishing NJ Artificial Reef Site	N 38 57.66'	W 74 41 20'
6	Turtle gut Shoal	shoal attracts weaks, stripers and blues	N 38 75.30'	W 74 48.01'
7	Hereford Inlet	all types of fish	N 39 00.76'	W 74 47.15'
8	Stone Harbor Lumps	striped bass in shallow water	N 39 02.17'	W 74 41.98'
9	Hereford Shoals	hilly sand mounds attracts flounders	N 39 01.64'	W 74 40.75'
10	South Avalon Shoal	blue fish	N 39 02.19'	W 74 34.25'
11	No name wreak	wreak fishing	N 39 04.40'	W 74 39.83'
12	Wayne	wreak fishing	N 39 04.96'	W 74 37.74'
13	Townsend Inlet	produces all fish types	N 39 07.07'	W 74 42.70'
14	Sea Isle Ridge	stripers near bait fish schools	N 39 09.08'	W 74 39.38'
15	The Lump	shoals produces bait fish for stripers and blues	N 39 07.40'	W 74 38.03'
16	Wreak	wreak fishing and nearby flounders	N 39 06.78'	W 74 32.83'
17	Avalon Shoal	flounders near hilly sandy bottom	N 39 05.54'	W 74 33.94'
18	Bell	wreak fishing	N 39 08.77'	W 74 33.20'
19	Corson's Inlet	All types of fish at inlet	N 39 12.27'	W 74 38.41'
20	Corson's Lumps	Sandy hills attracts flounders and stripers	N 39 12.55'	W 74 35.45'
21	Ocean City Reef Site	Bottom Fishing NJ Artificial Reef Site	N 39 10.27'	W 74 33.72'
22	The Great Egg Inlet	All types of fish	N 39 17.65'	W 74 32.00'
23	Ventor Debris field	bottom debris attracts fish	N 39 17.47	W 74 26.49'
24	American Oil	wreak fishing	N 39 14.72'	W 74 22.77'
25	The Great Egg Reef site	Bottom Fishing NJ Artificial Reef Site	N 39 14.50'	W 74 21.50'
26	Darien	wreak fishing	N 39 17.98'	W 74 21.18'
27	Ventor Ridge	stripers and blues	N 39 19.29'	W 74 23.03'
28	Pet	wreak fishing	N 39 19.75'	W 74 17.88'
29	Absecon Shoal	good collection of fish	N 39 20.70'	W 74 23.85'
30	AC Shoals	stripers, blues and weakfish	N 39 20.96'	W 74 21.00'
31	Atlantic City Reef site	Bottom Fishing NJ Artificial Reef Site	N 39 14.70'	W 74 14.10'

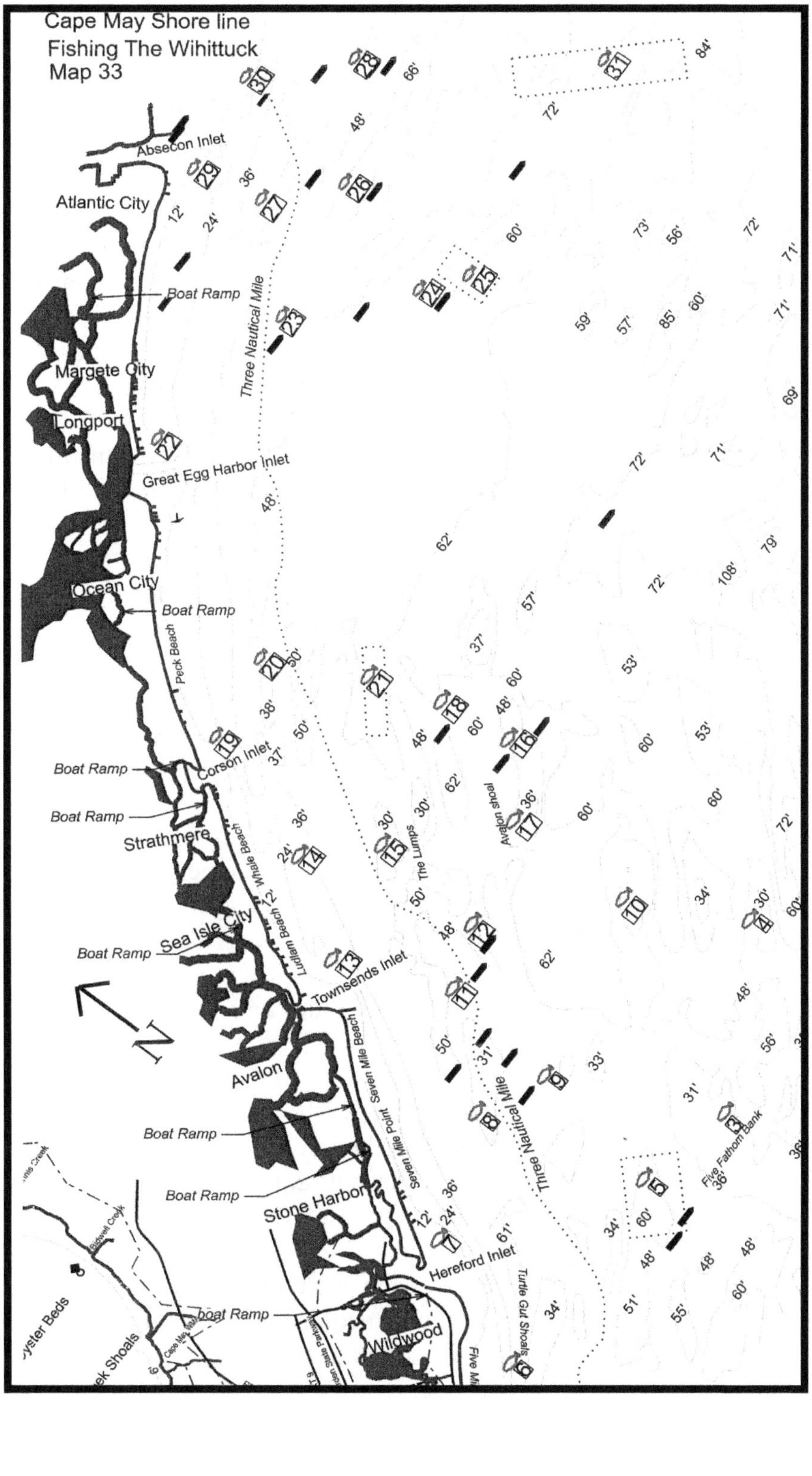
Cape May Shore line
Fishing The Wihittuck
Map 33
Absecon Inlet
Atlantic City
Boat Ramp
Three Nautical Mile
Margete City
Longport
Great Egg Harbor Inlet
Ocean City
Boat Ramp
Peck Beach
Boat Ramp
Corson Inlet
Boat Ramp
Strathmere
Whale Beach
The Lumps
Avalon shoal
Sea Isle City
Boat Ramp
Ludlam Beach
Townsends Inlet
N
Avalon
Seven Mile Beach
Seven Mile Point
Three Nautical Mile
Boat Ramp
Boat Ramp
Stone Harbor
Hereford Inlet
Turtle Gut Shoals
Five Fathom Bank
Oyster Beds
boat Ramp
Wildwood

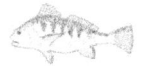

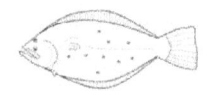

South Jersey inlet list

1   Graveling Point

This is a small sod bank found at the end of Radio Road on Mystic Island. In the month of April the warmer water from the Mullica River excites the striped bass on outgoing tide. Use clams and blood worms here in the spring. Can get crowed on weekend when reports are good.

2   Great Bay Blvd Bridges.

It's unlawful to fish from the bridges but there are many places to fish the channels from the bank. The channels are noted for producing large weakfish at night in May

3   Long Beach Island

This island has two and half miles of natural beaches that can be access by 4 wheel drive trucks with beach permits obtained by Long Beach Township.

4   Brigantine Island

From the island one has access to two good inlets that produce Striped bass, weakfish and blues. The Beaches here are known to produce early catches of blue fish in April. Beach permit fees for vehicles is high on the island

5   Great Egg Harbor Inlet

On the Ocean City side of the inlet is a good spot to catch flounders at slack tide in the summer.

6   Corson Inlet

On the new North Channel Bridge bay side a fishing platform was added. The platform is a hot spot to pack up night time blue fish. A long walk on the North seaside beach should be good for summer flounders. The shallow water make this is a good place for saltwater fly fishing

7   Townsend Inlet

On the northern shore is an excellent spot to pick up summer flounder during low tides. The rock walls on the southern half is great for larger blue fish and striped bass and at low tide one can walk along the foot of the wall.

8   Avalon Wall

A long breakwater wall is noted for producing blues and striped bass during out going tides.

9   Hereford Inlet

Parking is limited and one cannot fish from the 2 bridges but this has great potential to produce striped bass from the sod banks on the bay side. Good summer flounder fishing on the north seaward side of the inlet but requires a long walk. Lots of various fish type can be caught in the back bay.

10 Cape May Harbor and Canal entrance

The Break water walls and some of the beaches are restricted to the public. Military connections are required and permits can be acquired at the main CG station. Reports are good for strong fighting fish at high tide in a deep hole at the end of the wall. It is a long walk to the wall from the north side.

Fishing The Big D

11 West Cape May
The numerous stone breakwaters at the tip are noted for good striped bass in the fall.

12 Cape Henoplen
The long natural beaches here are an ideal place to drive vehicles along the beach in search of bird blitzes and signs of fish.

13 9th Street Causeway Ocean City to Summer Point
A good place to fish for striped bass in the spring from the sod banks within the bay.

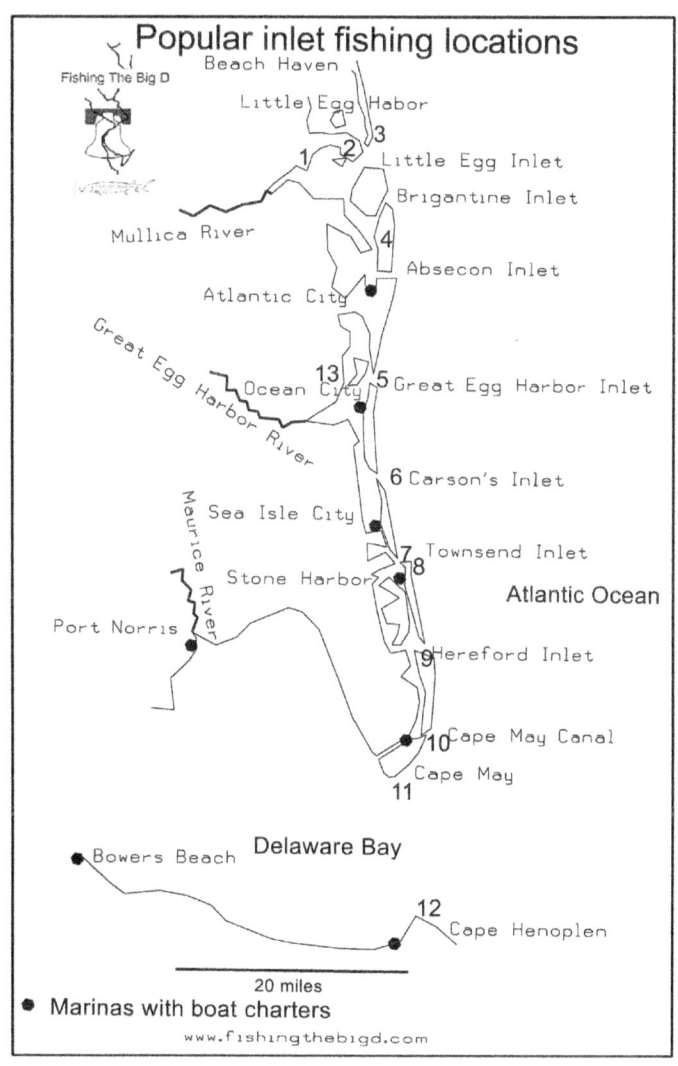

Chapter VI
DELAWARE SALMON

Historically the Delaware was never noted as an Atlantic salmon habitat. Some sources put the lower limit of salmon migration at 40 degrees latitude, the Delaware Bay is 3 degrees below that. The main habitat for Atlantic salmon is north of Cape Cod, far from the mouth of the Delaware and Hudson Rivers. In 1895 and 1896, local newspaper articles told of large strange nine to fifteen pound fish with hook jaws and sharp teeth appearing in the fish markets, nets, dinner plates, and at the point of gigging poles along the entire length of the Delaware River and Bay [163]. The articles went on to tell about lower river fishermen selling the fish as high as a dollar a pound at the market, an unheard of price in those times. Anglers in New York and Pennsylvania reported monster size fish in record numbers crowded into small streams of the upper tributaries as far north as the Beaverkill and West Branch. Many of these reports mistakenly called them super sized trout. The fish were Atlantic salmon in the grilse or spawning stage of life and they brought with them not just eggs and sperm but promises, hopes and dreams of more food and thousands of dollars in recreational fishing. The story was further verified by a report in the Thirty-Seventh Annual American Fisheries Society by Mr. W. E. Meehan in 1908. Was the 1895 to 1906 Salmon runs a result of a reversal of the North Atlantic gyro bring cold Labrador water and fish from the Northwestern Atlantic ? Or was this another nineteen century "bucket biology" experiment done by man.

Attempts to stock the Delaware with salmon began as early as 1871 by Mr. Thaddeus Norris who planted 75,500 young Atlantic salmon fish in the waters in and around Easton, most likely around the Bushkill. According to a report by the New Jersey Game Commission [162], stockings also took place by the state in this same time frame. By 1877, shad fishermen reported catching 15 to 20 adult fish in the grilse stage on the River. The next year no Atlantic Salmon were reported to be caught. In 1890, The Pennsylvania Fish Commission began a much larger stocking program with salmon hatched at its new facility on the Little Lehigh. The first stocking took place as far north as Deposit, NY where 60,000 fish where place in the upper streams of Pennsylvania. The next year, 200,000 more were released with a third and final stocking of the same amount in 1892. Witnesses confirm that these stocking produced Parrs or Juvenile salmon that remained in the water for a season before heading south. Because of the high fishing pressures for parrs, trout and bass, the owners of Blooming Grove Creek were forced to closing all fishing.

In the 1908 Meehan report [166], the returned of the grilse salmon began in 1894 and lasted until 1906. The only comment about quantity of fish came in an 1895 statement that $5,000 of eight to twelve pound fish were caught by shore and gill nets at .25 to .50 cent per pound at the docked. Not a large quantity, but many more may have been caught but not reported because netting salmon would have been illegal. The

Delaware Salmon

Meehan report stated that the last salmon were found dead (24-pound fish) near Bushkill in 1907. These early nineteen century experiments proved that even though the fish survived to the grilse stage the mortality rate still exceed the reproductive rate of Atlantic salmon in the Delaware. The 1908 report of the experiment stated that the success of a Salmon fishery on the Delaware would require the yearly stocking of fish. It was also at this time reported that the river's Biological Oxygen Demand count **BOD** was on the rise as measured in Paulsboro NJ marking the beginning of the pollution block. The last known salmon stocking took place on the Brandywine where Pacific salmon were released by the Commonwealth in 1966. Reports stated that adult salmon were caught at the mouth several years later with no plans to stock again.

The dwindling number of Atlantic salmon this last century has generated further studies and stockings in its native water off of Maine and Canada. Today much concern is placed on escaped farm raised Atlantic salmon which could change the generic make up of the native fish. It was discovered that Pacific salmon did very well in the Great Lakes. In 1980, at Altmar NY, a state fish hatchery was built on the Salmon River to introduce and stock not just Atlantic salmon but various Pacific salmon, steel heads and brown trout into Lake Ontario tributaries. This has turned into a gold mine of success dumping millions of dollars into the local economy which brings in millions of fisherman from all over the east coast. Today, all of the States and Canadian Provinces that boarder the Great Lakes have salmon stocking programs in their local waters.

As for our region, New Jersey has taken the lead to introduce new fish [162]. In 1983, New Jersey hired a research firm, Normandeau Associates, to study the concept of stocking the Delaware with salmon. The firm recommended Pacific salmon and steelheads instead of Atlantic salmon and to be successful it would have to be stocked every year, much as the Great Lake stockings. Later, New Jersey announced that it had plans to stock the Musconetcong and Raritan River with Pacific salmon and steelheads. At the hearing over the Musconetcong stocking, despite over whelming support in signed partitions favoring the stocking, members of the Delaware River Defense Coalition and Trout Unlimited were able to convince the agency not to stock salmon in the Delaware Watershed. The chief reason for cancelling the Delaware stocking was that it would disrupt the local yearly stocked trout in the Musconetcong River. In 1987, New Jersey stocked 1,100 steelheads and 90,000 Pacific salmon in the Raritan River with no plans to stock the Delaware's Musconetcong. Information of the success of the Raritan River stocking seems to be limited but fishermen reported catching large 10 pound rainbow trout up to 2009. There is no information on the success of the salmon.

The main reason for the organized protest against salmon stocking may not be the effect on local trout but the salmon itself and the method of fishing for them [164, 165]. Like shad, the returning salmon do not eat on the way to spawn but will hit small brightly color beads or flies that get in its way. Fishing by-sight for salmon is the most efficient method used where a fly fisherman attempts to floss the mouth of a passing fish with the tidbit and a small fly. Others use a hit or miss technique of drifting nymphs with indicators through narrows channels or behind rocks with the hope that it gets sucked into the mouth of a resting salmon. Either technique is done in close quarters on shallow streams leading to a great deal of casting and crowds. When one thinks of East Coast salmon fishing, pictures come to mind of thousands of anglers all fighting for a spot along a small creek. When the fish die, which they all will, they can leave a strong order along the bank as well. People are concern that thousands of miles of small streams in the Poconos, New Jersey Highland and the Catskills will become like the Salmon River- a waterway flooded with fishermen and dead smelly fish causing stress and pressures on some of the best trout waters in the mid Atlantic. Another common argument is that the migratory salmon will bring back parasites and diseases such as sea lice. The fact is the Lehigh and Schuylkill has dams isolating two thirds of the Delaware basin. The upper Catskills streams all have lakes either New York City's reservoirs or electric and flood control water bodies isolating more water and restricting fish movement. Most of the creeks on the main stem have old dams located right at the mouth. This leaves only a very small percentage of creeks suitable for stocking below any man made dams or natural blockers. Any problems that these new fish bring into the watershed will be isolated to the main stem of Delaware River and a small percentage of the open creeks along the River. The crowds that everyone is concern about would be limited to these creeks where public access is available and in the fall and winter, not in the crowded spring and summer months.

The 1890 salmon runs proved that the Delaware has the capability to support salmon in both the fresh and salt water. Off the coast of New Jersey, a cold counter current is generated by the southern Gulf Stream which must have met at that time the thermal requirements of the fish. The primary food may have been herring which apparently the ocean and bay had plenty. Today the cold thermal flow is still there. The BOD count at Paulsboro is approaching what it was at the end of the 1800s, and decreasing, meaning the river is clean enough. The primary concern and number one argument against stocking salmon is the herring populations have been dropping rapidly since 2008. Increase amount of striped bass, recreational demand, over fishing, and by-catches are all theories for the herring number dropping. For the first time ever there are limits on blue-black and alewife herrings takings on the rivers and inshore waters. Without a healthy bait fish population any increase in praetor fish will further stress the coastal ocean fishery.

WHAT CAN BE DONE TO KEEP THE DELAWARE RIVER AND BAY A GREAT FISHERY
EDUCATION

Ironically it's the fish we see the most in the water that we understand the least. Foremost is keeping the natural herring population healthy. A decline in their numbers is an indicator that something is wrong. Our ignorance of this fish family becomes obvious when we talked about herring and can't seem to define the names in a universal dialog.

Delaware Salmon

What one person calls a minnow, another calls it a shad. Common bunker or menhaden, many times get confused with river herring such as blueback, alewife, juvenile American and hickory shad. Identifying common river fish such as gizzard shad and quillbacks always bring arguments between local fishermen. This obvious dilemma of identifying herring shows our ignorance of the family. We need to investigate and educate ourselves on the fish and what it needs to survive in our environment so we can control its population better. We should educate ourselves on the problems of bucker-biology. It's one thing to stock pikes, flathead catfish, and snakeheads in ponds and lakes, but it becomes another matter when they get into the open waterways of the main stem of rivers. By adding these fish to the rivers, we drop the natural herring populations which will follow to the bays and coastal waters.

We can be proud that our river is cleaner than what it was at the end of the 1800's, but is it? We have become good at getting the BOD and coli counts down, but in order to achieve that, are we poisoning our water with chlorine? This chemical may take the smell out of the water and make us feel safe and secure, but it kills the aquatic insects and plants that start the food chain. Our water treatment plants don't remove the thousand of chemicals we dump down the drain everyday such as petroleum based products, root killer, drain cleaner and phosphates. By flipping over rocks downstream of a treatment plant, one can quickly be convinced that our system needs to be improved, as one observes that no life can be found under the rocks just downstream of these facilities. Clearly, we must educate people that dumping chemicals down any drain is a bad idea.

But our biggest threat for the Delaware may come from our future energy demands. The upper Delaware flows over the eastern half of the Marcellus bedrock a source for natural gas. Will the removal of the gas cause environment problems? The removal and burning of coal clearly has a bigger effect on the environment than fracking and burning natural gas. Today the electric power industry is rapidly converting power generation stations from coal fire to natural gas. Whether its coal or natural gas fire plants we seem to forget the other cost of power generation - water usage. The Delaware Basin Commission warns us that water demands will exceed all other water uses in the future. Our demand to cool reactors and generate steam at first seem harmless to wildlife but once again we are modifying the water they live in. As we try to wean ourselves from fossil fuels and nuclear energy, will we look to hydro electric and end the Delaware River namesake as the longest free flowing river on the east coast?

1	Pennsylvania Fish and Boat Commission http://states.pa.us/PA_Exec/Fish_Boat.htm
2	New York State Department of Environmental http://www.dec.state.ny.us/sebsite/dfwmr/refshl4.h
3	New Jersey Division of Fish and Wildlife http://www.state.nj.us/dep/fgw/digfsh.htm
4	Delaware River Basin Commission, River Facts http://www.state.nj/drbc/drbc/.htm
6	Charles Hardy III, West Chester University, Fish Or Foul
8	Joseph Lee Boyle, Shad Journal, Valley Forge Fish Story
11	Department of Interior, Upper Delaware, Cultural History http://www.nps.gov/upde/historyculture/index.htm
14	US Fish & Wildlife Service, Eels http://www.fws.gov/northeast/ameel/
15	Dennis Scholl, History of Shad on the Lehigh River http://mgfx.com/fishing/assocs/drsfa/history.htm
16	Angler's on Line, Great Rivers, Trout on the Upper Delaware
17	Delaware River Shad Fisherman Association, Delaware Shad
18	Lambertville NJ Web site, Lewis Shad Fishery http://www.newhopepa.com/Lambertville/default.htm
19	US Army Corp of Engineers, Local Lakes Facts http://www.nap.usacee.army.mil/sb/recreation.htm
26	US Army Corp of Engineer, Dredging www.nap.usace.army.mil/cenap-pl/drmc/overview.html
31	Delaware River Basin Commission, mileage system http://www.newjersey.gov/drbc/mileage.htm
32	Jordan and Evermann, 1896-1900, Gulf of Maine Research Institute, http://octopus.gma.org/fogm/Roccus_saxatilis.htm
33	National Park Service, Historic Themes and Resources within New Jersey www.cr.nps.gov/history/online_books/nj2/chap1.hm
34	American Bass Anglers, Inc., rules
36	New Jersey Scuba Diver, fish type Southern New Jersey http://www.njscuba.net/biology/sw_fish_drums_html
37	Bloch and Schneider, Gulf of Main Research Institute, Weak Fish and http://octopus.gma.org/fogm/Cynoscion_regalis.htm
38	US Army Corp of Engineer, Phila. District, Delaware Bay Oysters
39	New Jersey Fish Net, Issue # 1, New Jersey fishing industry http://www.fishingnj.org/njnet1.htm
40	Ralph Knisellhen, Mid-Atlantic Game & Fish, Delaware Bay Weakfish
44	MidAtlantic Fish & Game, "Trout fishing hot spots in the Garden State" http://www.midaltlanticgameandfish.com/fishing/trout-
45	PPL Web site, General Wallenpaupack information
46	Wikipedia, Pepacton Reservoir http://en.wikipedia.org/wiki/Pepacton_Reservoir
48	Gulf of Maine Research Institute, Summer Flounder

Bibliography

	http://octopus.gma.org/fogm/Paralichtys_dentatus.htm
49	Captain Kevin Shea, Sharks Fishing Tips
	http://www.fishingmontauk.com/tips/sharks3.html
50	Beach Net, Life of a Shark, Dogfish, Sand, Mako, Hammerhead
	http://www.fishingmontauk.com/tips/sharks3.html
54	Cannonsville New York (defunct),New York, Hudson Valley Web site,
	http://www//bearsystems.com
62	WHSRN Delaware Bay, Western Hemisphere Shorebird Reserve
	http://www.manomet.org/WHSRN/viewsite.php?id=6
64	Adam Levine, Philly H2O, The History of Philadelphia's Watersheds
66	Lake Wallenpaupack Vacation Home web site, walleyes and lake
	http://www.bgsjusion.com
73	National Park Service, Upper Delaware Scenic and Recreation River, The
	http://www.nps.gov/archive/upde/d&hcanal.htp
75	Wikipedia, Pike County, Facts
	http://en.wikipedia.org/wiki/Pike_County_Pennsylvania
76	Zane Grey's West Society, Zane Grey's Fish records
78	National Wild and Scenic River System, Gov. Web site
	http://www.nps.gov/rivers/about.html
80	Merrill Creek web site, Merrill Creek Reservoir facts
	http://www.merrillcreek.com/home.html
81	Northwest New Jersey Skylands web site, Round Valley Reservoir
	http://www.njskylands.com/index.html
82	Pennsylvania Department of Conservation of Natural Resources web site,
83	Wikipedia, Lehigh River facts
	http://en.wikipedia.org/wiki/Lehigh_River
85	Anthracite and Lehigh Coal & Navigation, Panther Valley Coal
	http://www.oldcompanyslehigh.com/anthra.htm
87	National Canal Museum, Schuylkill Navigation Company
90	Schuylkill River Heritage Web site DCNR, River clean up
	www.schuylkillriver.org/Environmental_Revolution.html
91	Pennsylvania Fish and Boat Commission, PFBC Chronology time line
92	Army Corp of Engineers, History of Easter Rivers, History of anthracite
	www.usace.army.mil/publications/misc/nws83-10/c-2.pdf
93	NJ Division of fish and Wildlife, Time line of NJ fishing and wildlife
	http://www.state.nj.s/dep/fgw/history.htm
94	NYC Water Department, History of New York City Water
	www.nyc.gov/html/dep/watershed/html/history.html
95	Adelaide Hasse, Index of Economic Material for Pennsylvania, pages 865
96	Delaware River Basin Commission, Fish Protection Program
	http://www.state.nj.us/drbc/res-fishries.htm
97	Wallepaupack Watershed Society, History of Wallenpaupack
	http://www.hawleywallenpaupackcc./histroy.htm
98	Keith Sutton, Fishing For Catfish, Creative Publishing 1999, Cat fish
103	Delaware River Port Authority, Responsibilities of DRPA
104	Rod Teehan, Checking The Chain Gang, In-Fisherman, Chain Pickerel
107	Sandy Beuers, Inquirer 10/28/06, limits ruling on flounder
108	Delaware River Basin Commission, Master Plan for DRBC, water flow
	http://www.newjersey.gov/drbc/river_master.htm
109	Delaware Reef Guide 2005, artificial reefs in Bay
	http://www.dnrec.state.de.us/fw/2005reefguide.pdf
110	Delaware Division of Soil and Water Conservation, benthic mapping
111	New Jersey Division of Fish and Wildlife Reef Program, Artificial Reef
	http://www.nj.gov/dp/fgw/pdf/2005reefplan05.pdf
112	Phila Water Department, history of clean water

Bibliography

114	Delaware Indian/Lenni Lenape, Delaware Indians of Pennsylvania http://www.freewebs.com/delawarein/
115	census.gov/population, www/documentation/twps0027.html
121	NY Dept of Environmental Conservation, State of NY, Trout
122	Federal Fish and Wildlife Admin., fish farming status
126	Nat. Park Service, The Landscape Transformation of Coastal New www.nps.gov/history/history/online_books/nj3/chap1.htm
129	New Jersey Department of Fish and Wildlife Population:
131	Bowfin Anglers Group web site bowfins http://www.bowfinangler.com
133	MD. Dept of N. R. Frequently Ask Questions of N. Snakehead
134	Vanessa Washington, Outdoor Life 8/10/2005, Killer Snakehead Fish Returns
135	The New Jersey Angler Dec 2007, Bill Donovan, A Call to Action on Fluke
147	Fishtown and the Shad Fisheries Rich Remer, Historical Society of Pa www.hsp.org
148	Saving Our Sturgeon , Littoral Society www.littoralsocity.org/sosarticale.pdf
149	Philip Simpson & Dewayne Fox ,Delaware State University. www.sdafs.org/sturgeon\presentation.pdf
150	The Founding Fish John McPhee, Spawning and Out-migration pages 87 to 100
151	Ship John Shoal, NJ "Light House Friends www.lighthousefriends.com
152	The Little Pearl , A Brief History of Caviar www.littlepearl.com/articales.html?q11371907932378653
153	Karl Blankenship Shortnose Sturgeon www.fish.state.pa.us/anglerboater/1999/novdec99/shosee.ht
154	Bartram's Garden & Rambo's Rock Wikipedia httn:en.wikipendia.org/wiki/Rambo's's Rock
155	Chesapeake Meteor USGS http://meteor.pwnet.org/impact_even/impact_crater.htm
156	Poultry's Price Peter S. Goodman Washington Post 8/1/1999 www.washingtonpost.com/wp-srv/daily/aug99/chicken1.htm
157	Chesapeake Bay Foundation – Save the Bay- April 20 2009 www.chf/.org/site//New2?abbr+SB
158	United State Department of Ag.2007 Census of Agriculture www.agcensus.usda.gov
159	NOAA Press release October 25, 2006: Observer – guilty www.nmfs.noaa.gov
160	Recreational Fishing Alliance John Depersenaire
161	Damming the Delaware
162	Delaware Rv Anadromous Salmonid NJ Division of Fish and Wildlife December 2005
163	The New York Times: 6/2//1895, 9/4/1896 & The Phila. Ledger. Articles of "Salmon in the Delaware Rv.),
164	The Morning Call: 3/22/1992 Catch a Salmon in the Delaware
165	The Morning Call: 10/4/1992 Delaware River Salmon Program is rejected
166	Transactions of the American Fisheries Society Vol 36-37 page 103
167	Ecological Modeling; Ecopath and Ecosim: MG Fish, TJ Miller, RJ Lator, SJD Martell 2009

Recommended Books about the Delaware

Liquid Assets, History of New York City's Water System, Diane Galusha   Purple Mountain Press 1999
    History of New York City's search for water
Devastation on the Delaware, Mary A. Shafer Word Forge Books 2005
    Story of the 1955 flood
Damming the Delaware: The Raise and Fall of Tocks Island Dam by Richard C. Albert
    Story of the attempt to dam the River.

www.ingramcontent.com/pod-product-compliance
Lightning Source LLC
Chambersburg PA
CBHW081456040426
42446CB00016B/3267